Deconstruction • Derrida

transitions

General Editor: Julian Wolfreys

Published Titles

NEW HISTORICISM AND CULTURAL MATERIALISM John Brannigan
POSTMODERN NARRATIVE THEORY Mark Currie
DECONSTRUCTION • DERRIDA Julian Wolfreys

Forthcoming Titles

MARXIST LITERARY AND CULTURAL THEORY Moyra Haslett
POSTCOLONIAL THEORY Claire Jones
LITERARY FEMINISMS Ruth Robbins
PSYCHOANALYSIS AND LITERATURE Andrew Roberts

Transitions Series
Series Standing Order ISBN 0–333–73684–6
(*outside North America only*)

You can receive future titles in this series as they are published by placing a standing order. Please contact your bookseller or, in case of difficulty, write to us at the address below with your name and address, the title of the series and the ISBN quoted above.

Customer Services Department, Macmillan Distribution Ltd
Houndmills, Basingstoke, Hampshire RG21 6XS, England

transitions

Deconstruction • Derrida

Julian Wolfreys

First Published 1998 by
MACMILLAN PRESS LTD
Houndmills, Basingstoke, Hampshire RG21 6XS
and London
Companies and representatives
throughout the world

ISBN 0–333–68776–0 hardcover
ISBN 0–333–68777–9 paperback

A catalogue record for this book is available
from the British Library.

This book is printed on paper suitable for recycling and
made from fully managed and sustained forest sources

10	9	8	7	6	5	4	3	2	1
07	06	05	04	03	02	01	00	99	98

Printed in Hong Kong

Published in the United States of America 1998 by
ST. MARTIN'S PRESS, INC.,
Scholarly and Reference Division,
175 Fifth Avenue, New York, N.Y. 10010

ISBN 0–312–21392–1 cloth
ISBN 0–312–21393–X paperback

For

Peggy Kamuf

Contents

General Editor's Preface

Transitions: *transition-em*, n. of action. 1. A passing or passage from one condition, action or (rarely) place, to another. 2. Passage in thought, speech, or writing, from one subject to another. 3. a. The passing from one note to another b. The passing from one key to another, modulation. 4. The passage from an earlier to a later stage of development or formation ... change from an earlier style to a later; a style of intermediate or mixed character ... the historical passage of language from one well-defined stage to another.

The aim of *Transitions* is to explore passages and movements in critical thought, and in the development of literary and cultural interpretation. This series also seeks to examine the possibilities for reading, analysis and other critical engagements which the very idea of transition makes possible. The writers in this series unfold the movements and modulations of critical thinking over the last generation, from the first emergences of what is now recognized as literary theory. They examine as well how the transitional nature of theoretical and critical thinking is still very much in operation, guaranteed by the hybridity and heterogeneity of the field of literary studies. The authors in the series share the common understanding that, now more than ever, critical thought is both in a state of transition and can best be defined by developing for the student reader an understanding of this protean quality.

This series desires, then, to enable the reader to transform her/his own reading and writing transactions by comprehending past developments. Each book in the series offers a guide to the poetics and politics of interpretative paradigms, schools and bodies of thought, while transforming these, if not into tools or methodologies, then into conduits for directing and channelling thought. As well as transforming the critical past by interpreting it from the perspective of the present day, each study enacts transitional readings of a number of well-known literary texts, all of which are themselves conceivable as having been transitional texts at the moments of their first appearance. The readings offered in these books seek, through close critical reading and theoretical engagement, to demonstrate certain possibilities in critical thinking to the student reader.

It is hoped that the student will find this series liberating because rigid methodologies are not being put into place. As all the dictionary definitions of the idea of transition above suggest, what is important is the action, the passage: of thought, of analysis, of critical response.

Rather than seeking to help you locate yourself in relation to any particular school or discipline, this series aims to put you into action, as readers and writers, travellers between positions, where the movement between poles comes to be seen as of more importance than the locations themselves.

Julian Wolfreys

Acknowledgements

It is a thankless task thanking people, because the formula, whatever it may be, is inevitably never quite right. Too much effusion, too little gratitude and, all too often and unfortunately, just the right amount of apparent protocol which ends up coming off as insincerity. But despite all these worries, in the words of Jane Austen's Miss Bates, 'It's such a happiness when good friends get together, and they always do' – at least on acknowledgements pages such as this.

First and always, Jim Kincaid, who is always there somewhere, ready to throw a pie in the faces of those who deserve it. Peggy Kamuf helped me begin to come to terms with Derrida, generously, patiently, without hesitation, and I thank her. John Brannigan, Claire Jones, Ruth Robbins, Moyra Haslett, Jane Goldman, Mark Currie, John Abercrombie, Marion Wynne-Davies, Geoff Ward, Jane Stabler, Andrew Roberts, Alison Chapman: all have directly or indirectly influenced whatever is good about this book, as have the rest of my colleagues at Dundee; all have contributed in some manner. Ruth particularly gave me a number of the ideas which helped shaped the chapter on Paul Valéry, as well as inviting me to a conference on the short story at the University of Luton, where I rehearsed some of the material. Also having made contributions – more than I can tell them – are the undergraduates who took part in my Literary Theory tutorials in 1995–96, and students who attended Gender, Sexuality and Feminism and James Joyce seminars and tutorials (1996–97), as well as David Hearn, Malcolm Mann, Brian Niro, Meike Prescher and Leah Wain.

I would also like to thank Nicholas Royle and Martin McQuillan for inviting me to give papers to their Literary Theory graduate seminars, at the Universities of Stirling and Glasgow respectively, where versions of chapters were first tried out. Vassiliki Kolokotroni really knew which questions to ask, and I thank her for that. On another occasion, Stella Swain asked equally pertinent questions concerning a version of the chapter on Iain Sinclair, while Roger Ebbatson also contributed in a most positive and kindly fashion: thank you.

I would finally like to thank Margaret Bartley at Macmillan for having faith in the idea of a series in the first place, and whose untiring efforts and good humour are without equal.

Julian Wolfreys
July 1997

Abbreviations

Full bibliographical details are provided in the Bibliography

Works by Jacques Derrida

A	'Afterw.rds or, At Least, Less Than a Letter About a Letter Less'
A	*Aporias*
Acts	'Acts'
AD	'As *if* I Were Dead: An Interview with Jacques Derrida'
AF	*Archive Fever: A Freudian Impression*
AL	*Acts of Literature*
A*M*	'The Art of *Mémoires*'
ATVM	'At This Very Moment in This Work Here I Am'
BSDF	'Biodegradables: Seven Diary Fragments'
C	'Circumfession'
D	*Dissemination*
DO	'Deconstruction and the Other'
DR	*A Derrida Reader: Between the Blinds*
EO	*The Ear of the Other*
G	*Of Grammatology*
GD	*The Gift of Death*
Gl	*Glas*
GT	*Given Time: I. Counterfeit Money*
I:D	'Introduction: Desistance'
l'ac	*l'autre cap*
LI	*Limited Inc.*
LJF	'Letter to a Japanese Friend'
LOBL	'Living On • Borderlines'
MP	*Margins of Philosophy*
OH	*The Other Heading*

ON	*On the Name*
OS	*Of Spirit: Heidegger and the Question*
P…	*Points …: Interviews 1974–1994*
P	'Psyche: Inventions of the Other'
PC	*The Post Card*
RDP	'Remarks on Deconstruction and Pragmatism'
*R*M	'The *Retrait* of Metaphor'
S	'Spectrographies'
SA	'The Spatial Arts: An Interview with Jacques Derrida'
SM	*Specters of Marx*
SP	*Speech and Phenomena and Other Essays on Husserl's Theory of Signs*
SQ&R	'Some Questions and Responses'
TOJ	'The Time is Out of Joint'
TP	*The Truth in Painting*
TT:P	'The Time of a Thesis: Punctuations'
TWJ	'Two Words for Joyce'
WD	*Writing and Difference*

Other Works

Db	'Derridabase', Geoffrey Bennington
FE	*Flesh Eggs and Scalp Metal*, Iain Sinclair
GE	'The Griffin's Egg', Iain Sinclair and Dave McKean
HD	*Heart of Darkness*, Joseph Conrad
JH	*The Strange Case of Dr Jekyll and Mr Hyde*, Robert Louis Stevenson
LH	*Lud Heat*, Iain Sinclair
LT	*Lights out for the Territory*, Iain Sinclair
RD	*Radon Daughters*, Iain Sinclair
SB	*Suicide Bridge*, Iain Sinclair
WCST	*White Chappell Scarlet Tracings*, Iain Sinclair
YW	*The Yellow Wallpaper*, Charlotte Perkins Gilman

Introduction:
'Deconstruction, if such a
thing exists ...'[1]

... deconstruction bothers people in the university ...

Colin MacCabe

Concerning the institution that is the university put in question by the PC debate, the term 'deconstruction' is most often presumed to refer to a theory, a method, a school, perhaps even a doctrine, in any case, some identifiable or localizable 'thing' that can be positioned – posed and opposed – within that institution, but also that can be excluded from within this defined enclosure.

Peggy Kamuf

Does this mean that so-called 'deconstruction' is what Hegel said art in his time was, 'a thing of the past'? Some people certainly think so or wish that it might be so. To say so has almost become an *idée reçue* ...

J. Hillis Miller

Responses

The three quotations which serve as epigraphs to this introduction all speak of 'deconstruction'. They do so in a number of ways: as something which troubles and disturbs certain members of universities, if not the universities themselves; as something to be defined and subsequently marginalized; and as something which, always supposing its institutional existence to be a fact, has had its day and which subsequently has gone the way of the dodo. There seems to be a lot at stake in this one word. Principally, however, what the three quotations share is a recognition that from a variety of places and positions, polemical, ideological, historical and cultural, there are those who actively search out a meaning and identity for 'deconstruction'.

You might have had people – people within institutions of the kind being alluded to above, people supposedly in positions of authority – tell you that 'deconstruction' existed or exists, and is in fact a method of literary criticism (as indicated in Peggy Kamuf's commentary, above). A variation on this narrative identification might be that 'deconstruction' emerged during the late 1960s and early 1970s, especially in the United States, as a powerful critical force, often taught by particularly charismatic professors. You might come across other narratives insisting on the origins of 'deconstruction', suggesting that 'it's' identity is French. You might be reading this book because you are studying 'literary theory' or 'poststructuralism', or 'literary criticism'; your purpose for studying these subjects might be as part of a course within a university which teaches what J. Hillis Miller above calls 'so-called '"deconstruction"' as (in Kamuf's terms) a 'theory, a method, a school, perhaps even a doctrine'. If you're doing this, stop reading this book. This book will not teach you 'how to deconstruct' literary texts. It will not do so for all the reasons outlined and discussed throughout this book. It will not even pretend to suggest that such a thing is possible.

Instead, this book will discuss the work of Jacques Derrida and, in doing so, it will challenge the idea of a method, theory, school, analytical practice of 'so-called "deconstruction"'. It will then, in the second section of this book, engage with particular textual examples, all the while respecting their singularity as texts to which we must respond, rather than approach with any preconceptions concerning their identities. Each chapter in the second section of *Deconstruction • Derrida* will perform a double gesture, whereby the texts are seen to be encountered in the wake of Derrida, while Derrida comes to be encountered in the wake of the texts and writers which are here our concern. The first chapter, which aims to situate itself as another introduction, and to complicate the idea of the introduction by supplementing this introduction, will look at the question of whether there is some 'thing' called deconstruction, what others have said on this matter, and what Jacques Derrida has had to say on a number of occasions concerning the fortunes of the word 'deconstruction', as well as the assumption of there being a method in his work such as this 'so-called "deconstruction"'. Chapter 2 seeks to follow through the use of various terms in Derrida's writing, terms such as writing, text, hymen, amongst others, in order to see how Derrida's use of these terms changes our understanding of both them and the nature of the literary text.

As we pursue these transformative terms (and Derrida's transformation of them from their more conventional semantic values), we will try to exemplify their function within Derrida's writing by examining particular passages of literary texts. Chapter 3 will pick up on the theme of identity in Derrida's work, which will already have been mentioned in the previous chapters, by looking at the question of the construction of Derrida's own identity in relation to his own engagements with the essays of French poet and essayist Paul Valéry. Chapter 4 offers a 'spectral' or 'hauntological' reading of the trope of the city as a *written, textual* figure or trace in the writing of Iain Sinclair. It will do so, moreover, in relation to the architectural interest in Sinclair's writing. The fifth chapter will offer a reading of Joseph Conrad's *Heart of Darkness* alongside a consideration of a particular reading of that novel by J. Hillis Miller, someone who, it is often claimed, is one of the pre-eminent so-called 'deconstructive' critics. The final, short chapter will discuss in brief the possibility of a politics of Derrida's writing, particularly as that politics is intimately bound up with issues of identity – personal, spiritual, national.

How then might we outline the concerns of this book in the rest of this introduction, that being the conventional function of the introduction in any academic text? What follows in this introduction and in Chapter 1 involves acts of clearing the ground, showing the ground as itself a carefully positioned series of interrelated structures, rather than a basis from which to begin.

Programmed excuses

In this book, *Deconstruction* • *Derrida*, I am concerned with acts and effects of writing and reading. I am concerned also with the identities we construct, for ourselves and others, through the uses and structures of rhetoric. My interest in such things is motivated by my response to various texts, and by my desire to know and reflect upon how and why my response is governed. Consider this book not so much as an attempt to map out a particular territory or to build a particular framework or structure from the ground up and based on allegedly first principles. Rather, comprehend it as a series of responses, responses which are determined in their contours and considerations by the call made by some *other*: some other partly undefinable identity, the other which is at work in any identity, within any text; that, in short, which is alogical within any structure or form and which, when recognized, makes possible our comprehension of the textual structure, the structure or structurality of the structure.

My interest in my response and relationship to the text, or more specifically the idea or identity of the text, is an interest which exceeds the limits of this particular work. Yet, for the purposes of this work, I limit my questions to certain subjects, themes, proper names, and some of the texts which are signed by those proper names. In particular, and to reiterate this point, my concern in this book is with the 'rhetorical analysis of works of literature' and, with that, a certain question of an ethical response through an act of reading.[2]

These concerns are not mine alone. They are certainly not mine originally. In signalling such issues early on in this book I am pointing to that which is indicated and implied in the title of this work: *Deconstruction • Derrida*.[3] You might have already come across these names elsewhere. As we have suggested, the former is conventionally assigned to what is called a theory or method of literary criticism and analysis, while the latter is the surname of a French philosopher who is supposedly, allegedly, the 'originator' of this so-called method or school of critical thought. I want to challenge the idea that there is either a method or school, as part of the breaking up of the critical ground on which such assumptions are built, such identities are constructed. I want also to challenge the notion that Jacques Derrida originates or creates such a so-called school or method. These issues are dealt with extensively in the next chapter, 'Another Introduction / *Entamer*'.[4] This is done so that throughout the rest of this text we might begin to consider the work of Jacques Derrida and what it might possibly have to say to us, what we might learn from it, concerning questions of rhetorical analysis, the question of (the identity of the concept of) identity, notions of writing and text, the concept of literature and literary language, and the possible relation of any or all of these to the question of ethics and the consideration of an ethics of reading.

Thus, as I seek to move through the various issues of this book, as I attempt to consider the work of Jacques Derrida in a very limited and strategic fashion, and as I try to negotiate with the language and rhetoric of particular literary texts in the light of Derrida's writing or what might be learned from that, I will also be situating this work within a series of ongoing debates. I have already done this in fact, in my opening paragraphs. This book is already in the middle of performing, acting out, those very issues which it will attempt to illustrate, recognizing all the while the impossibility of presenting to the reader the entire 'system' of Derrida's thought and the failure built into any such attempt, for all the reasons presented by Geoffrey Bennington in his 'Derridabase' (Bennington 1993, 1, 3–15). In trying to write such an impossible book I am already responding to Derrida's work and to that of others who try to (re)present Derrida's work faithfully (particularly Geoffrey Bennington, in the work just mentioned). I am also responding in this process to others to whom Derrida responds, as well as to the rhetoric of Derrida's responses. In the next chapter I unpack more fully how any act of writing, reading and thinking is always in some sense a response. In Chapter 1 I discuss further how we are already in the middle of a range of debates, concerning responses, as people respond to Derrida in their efforts to construct for his writing a particular identity (so-called 'deconstruction').

For the moment, however, I merely want to make you aware that any apparent starting point, beginning or origin is never simply that. This 'introduction' is merely a series of 'programmed excuses', a strategic 'point of departure', a 'strategic justification' (Bennington 1993, 8, 15).[5] The identity of the introduction is not self-contained, not fully self-sufficient or present to itself. Its identity is always constructed from other places. This is the 'first' thing with which we need to come to terms, to comprehend.

This suggests that, from a certain 'Derridean' perspective, the problem of 'introducing' Derrida or deconstruction is troubled by the very act of 'introduction' itself, and the assumptions behind the idea of an 'introduction'. This is the case whether the 'introduction' is understood as the first chapter to a book, a chapter without a number and therefore somehow partially separable, never quite of the 'book-proper'; it is the 'first' chapter before the first chapter, neither inside nor outside the book, a kind of passport or *passe-partout*. The assumptions concerning the identity of the very idea of the introduction are also troubled when and if the entire text of the book is (mis-) taken as a form of 'introduction'. Derrida discusses such problems and (im)possibilities in the first part of *Dissemination*. A preface, suggests Derrida, would presume to present what will happen in the book as though that book or group of ideas were somehow reducible to a comprehensible and seemingly finite range of thoughts or theories. As he puts it, a

> *preface* would retrace and presage here a *general* theory and practice of deconstruction, that strategy without which the possibility of a critique could exist only in fragmentary, empiricist surges.... The preface would announce in the future tense ('this is what you are going to read') the conceptual content or significance ... of what will *already* have been written. (*D* 7)

He continues:

> Prefaces, along with forewords, introductions, preludes, preliminaries, preambles, prologues and prolegomena, have always been written, it seems, in view of their own self-effacement. (*D* 9)

So you read this 'introduction' entitled *Deconstruction • Derrida*, the whole purpose of which is to get you to a point where you can then put it behind you, even as you have already put behind you that which is in the 'introduction', that section of the book you are now reading. However, even though you put it behind you, leaving it alone, it leaves on your thinking a certain trait, trace or mark, a partially erased, yet partially indelible writing. As Derrida suggests, what remains are the marks of that erasure which serve to suggest a certain contradiction. The contradiction, in part, is that we are assuming we cannot tell you what 'deconstruction' is, while at the same time pointing to what others might have to say about it; and while attempting all the time to erase all the marks of the possible ground from which a methodology might emerge, yet necessarily reinscribing some of those very traces which we seek to efface.

Thus this 'introduction' enacts the condition of all introductions: coming after all the work already done, it must assume, however problematically, that it can present itself in some manner as having come before all the other material, while simultaneously avoiding what the introduction or preface usually does, which is to offer a general theory or totalizable history of a reading practice. And of course, these are the chances we have to take as part of our response and responsibility, which are inescapable. In order to be faithful to Derrida we have to move beyond the conventional identity (of the introduction, of deconstruction), and the limits which that imposes, on the reader, in order that we might be able to talk about the subject.

Once again, this raises the question of identity. What, for example, is the 'proper' identity of the introduction? The whole question of 'deconstruction' might be said to be one concerning identity. Is this a question of a particular identity? Does that identity exist? Is that identity discernible? Or, as the subtitle of Chapter 1 puts it, is there such a *thing* as deconstruction? I've just cited myself, ahead of the event, so to speak, and you'll notice that the title of this introduction is partly a quotation. 'Deconstruction, if such a thing exists ...', responds Jacques Derrida in an interview. If Derrida, who is always accused of being the progenitor of so-called 'deconstruction', calls into question and casts doubt on its existence or identity, then, clearly, as readers of Derrida, we have a duty to respond carefully, responsibly to what we read (not only in Derrida's texts but, by inference, in all that we read).

As I have already indicated, for the rest of this book, I am going to challenge the identity of deconstruction when conceived as either a method of interpretation or a school of literary criticism or theory. This is a false identity imposed on both the term 'deconstruction' and Derrida, by critics, institutions, newspapers, journals, historians and theorists of literature for the purposes of pinning down what they perceive to be occurring, to have occurred at certain times, principally in departments of English, but also elsewhere. The principle behind this is: give something a firm identity, insist that it is some *thing* (so-called 'deconstruction'), give it a label, and it is easier to make house-trained, to keep under control.

Yet, as Derrida can teach us, any definition of any identity is only ever possible because of that which is not that identity, because of that which is different from it. Identity is constituted and only possible by difference. It is not simply a question of the difference at the heart of any single identity. It is not merely a question of my saying that I know who I am through recognizing that you are not me, that my 'I' is constituted differently from the 'I' you call yourself. Even the very concept of identity, what Derrida calls the 'identity of the principle of identity', is marked by difference. Identity as a concept is only articulable because of a field of other concepts, principles, ideas which serve in its articulation. Difference between identities is precisely what makes possible the meaning or value of an identity:

> The identity of the principle of identity itself is ... constituted by difference ... the principle of identity implies difference.... Difference is indispensable for the principle of identity itself. (SQ&R 258)

The rhetorical movement of Derrida's statement is interesting. Beginning with the principle of identity and difference as its subordinate and secondary term, Derrida inverts this order as he responds to the question concerning the nature of identity, until difference becomes the primary term, that which makes identity possible. This rhetorical gesture is often taken to be the method or technique of so-called 'deconstruction' (as we will discuss below). It is this movement which at a certain moment in the history of literary criticism was constructed, not by Derrida but by others, as the methodological ground of Derrida's so-called method of reading. Those who present such a view, those who would try to define 'deconstruction' as a method or school along such lines, do so only by ignoring those aspects of the critical writings of Jacques Derrida, Paul de Man,[6] J. Hillis Miller (to give only those names most immediately associated with deconstruction as a movement or method) which are different from any perceived identity of 'deconstruction'. Also being ignored in such a gesture is the singularity of Derrida's work, the idiomatic quality of his, or Miller's, or de Man's writing. This is a singularity which marks and is marked by the difference between the writing of these men, or the difference between, say, Derrida and Phillipe Lacoue-Labarthe, Derrida and Jean-Luc Nancy, Derrida and Peggy Kamuf, Nicholas Royle, or Geoffrey Bennington (or any combination of these names, any permutation you may care to imagine).

Derrida has commented on the question of singularity, relationship and difference, with respect to his work and that of Lacoue-Labarthe and Nancy: 'What I share with Lacoue-Labarthe, we also share, though differently, with Jean-Luc Nancy'.

> But I hasten immediately to reiterate that despite so many common paths and so much work done in common, between the two of them and between the three of us, the work of each remains, in its singular proximity, absolutely different; and this, despite its fatal impurity, is the secret of the idiom.... The most urgent thing ... would be to break with the family atmosphere, to avoid genealogical temptations, projections, assimilations, or identifications ... (I:D 6–7)[7]

Any definition of 'deconstruction' as a method or school is one which relies on the 'family atmosphere' for the possibility of suppressing and denying difference and singularity, and as part of its identificatory, assimilatory project. It is precisely such gestures that Derrida's work mediates against, and against which he cautions us above. The singularity of any text, whether 'theoretical', 'philosophical' or 'literary' (such terms are problematic in that they make assumptions about family while ignoring difference), must always be respected. Any act of reading, which is also, always a response to the textual other, must aim to respect and respond to that singularity and difference. This is to respond ethically to a text, not imposing upon it some ready-made identity, some family likeness, which domesticates and calms down its play. Those who insist on deconstruction as a method of analysis are already imposing an identity on a heterogeneous range of texts and signatures.

Once more, we will challenge such notions further in the next chapter and at other places in subsequent chapters. For now, however, for the remainder of the introduction, I want to suggest to you, as a continuation of the strategic gestures in which this introduction partakes, what 'deconstruction' might be, if it is not a method, not a theory, not a school or movement, and as if such a suggestion were so easily expressed. This is, at least, a provisional introduction.

Good reading as such

Deconstruction, if such a thing exists, 'is nothing more or less than good reading as such'. These are the words of J. Hillis Miller, whose critical work has had a significant effect on literary criticism in the twentieth century, and whose name is and has been associated with the idea of deconstruction since the 1970s. Miller's statement might well outrage those who find so-called 'deconstruction' to be a game of endless word-play, reliant on jargon and puns. That at least is, we imagine, what someone who finds Derrida's work distasteful might say, while, ironically, allying him/herself on the side of 'good reading'. Before looking more closely at this statement of Miller's, however, along with other comments of his concerning 'deconstruction', I want to place Miller 'historically' in relation to so-called 'deconstruction' while, at the same time, mentioning briefly the so-called Yale School, to which Miller was supposed to have belonged, in order to explain why there is no discussion of this 'school' in a book apparently concerned with 'deconstruction'. This moment is another of those necessary yet strategic gestures, as a means of opening onto the subjects of this book, while also undermining the ground on which books such as this are supposedly constructed.

Miller taught at Yale University in the 1970s and in the first half of the subsequent decade. In any conventional discussion of so-called 'deconstruction', his name is usually associated with that of Paul de Man, the other critic whose name is most often linked with decon-struction-as-methodology in the United States, along with Geoffrey Hartman and Harold Bloom, both of whom were at Yale, as was Jacques Derrida who was a Visiting Professor at Yale during this period. Although the work of all these men differs widely and a close reading would show that they can hardly be said, with any justice at least, to share a methodology, nonetheless they have been referred to consistently (and erroneously) as the Yale School of literary criticism or the Yale School of deconstruction. This identity is never one the colleagues in question ever sought or deliberately promoted. Yet despite this, both within the academy and outside, in the media, the constructed and homogeneous identity still persists, even until as recently (as I write) as the spring of 1997, in an article in *PMLA* (the journal of the Modern Languages Association) (Shumway 1997, 85–100). The article, which ostensibly seeks to focus on and question the 'celebrity' or 'star' status of certain professors in departments of English, concentrates significantly on images of Hartman, Bloom, Miller and Derrida, first presented in an article, entitled 'The Tyranny of the Yale Critics', in *New York Times Magazine*. By doing so, it once again constructs the 'family atmosphere' spoken of by Derrida, and gives credence to the idea of the existence, now past, of a Yale School, as a definitive, bonding identity for a group of disparate critics.   -

Despite the fact that he writes of 'deconstructionist criticism' as though there were a methodology at work, Geoffrey Hartman says of himself and Harold Bloom that not only are they 'barely deconstruc-tionists [but they] even write against it on occasion' (1987, ix). He also points out that de Man, Miller and Derrida all 'enjoy' their own style (ix). This assessment is supported if we take a remark of Miller's who suggests that de Man and Derrida do not offer a 'method' but provide us instead with '"exemplary acts of reading"'; as he goes on to suggest, 'you can learn quite a bit, to speak in litotes, about how to read by reading Derrida and de Man' (Miller 1995a, 80). Following from this, all I can say is that in this book I try to read Derrida in order to suggest to you that you also read Derrida (having read me reading Derrida) in order to see what you can learn about how to read. Were I to include a chapter on the so-called 'Yale School', assuming for the writers mentioned a common goal, a common theory, a common practice or programme of reading, this would be to miss both Miller's and Hartman's points. I can say nothing more on this matter, other than to urge the careful reader to read each critic as practising 'exemplary acts of reading', and as showing us 'good reading as such'. I would merely point to the effect that pinning labels on groups of people can have. The effect of naming and identifying deconstruction as a discernible practice ensconced institutionally and recognized as such in English departments is one of what Peggy Kamuf terms closure, which, she suggests, is an 'institutional effect ... that works to dispel uncertainty' (Kamuf 1997, 140–1). Kamuf offers an admirably lucid and cogent argument concerning the history of deconstruction's identification in US universities (1997, 141–5). As she puts it so pithily, in tracing the arguments of those who fear what they perceive as the threat of deconstruction, there are those who believe that 'deconstruction is the name of something that *has no place* in the university' (1997, 143).

Yet why fear acts of 'good reading'? Why feel so troubled by 'good reading as such' that you have to give it a specific identity? Why pin down the act of reading rigorously and responsibly under the title 'deconstruction', if only to excoriate it and desire its exorcism? Let's return to Miller's statement concerning 'deconstruction' which, let us remind ourselves, 'is nothing more or less than good reading as such'. It is also Miller who was cited earlier in this introduction who describes deconstruction as the rhetorical analysis of works of literature. Good reading. Rhetorical analysis. Aren't these qualities which we would expect a Yale School of literary criticism to teach? Would we not in fact demand this of so prestigious a department in so prestigious a university? And aren't these qualities which most critics, arguably, would wish to aspire to in their own writing, regardless of their theoretical, methodological or philosophical orientation (presumably, a number might even desire that their students were encouraged to adopt such qualities as standards for their own writing and reading)? What then is Miller describing, precisely? Nothing, more or less, than acts of reading, interpretation, analysis and writing which are 'deconstruction' only inasmuch as they are carefully, rigorously pursued. Such a statement would seem to qualify heavily what deconstruction might be said to be, if not actually cancelling out any specific approach to the act of literary criticism which claimed to be deconstruction, unless it could show itself to be done well and to be engaged in rhetorical analysis. In this sense, which is Miller's, deconstruction has no prior theoretical being; it is only ever made manifest in those exemplary acts of reading. This is typical of the rhetorical slide constantly in performance in Miller's writing. My recourse to Miller in this introduction is precisely in order to trouble any certainty you may feel you have concerning your perception of the possible identities of 'deconstruction' ('so-called' or otherwise). Whenever you feel like you have a handle on so-called deconstruction, having read, for example, Terry Eagleton, Frank Lentricchia, Richard Rorty, Christopher Norris, or anyone else making claims for a school or method, it is salutary to read Miller's statements. On the one hand they all seem to say one thing, while on the other, read carefully, they perform in quite another manner. Let's look at some of these remarks on the subject of deconstruction. I am going to stitch together a series of four quotations, taken from a number of different essays and lectures, written over a number of years, on different occasions, in differing contexts (all, with one exception, are to be found in Miller's collection, *Theory Now and Then*[8]).

Thinking that because Paul de Man is one name all his work must be of a piece or that because 'deconstruction' is a single and singular name 'deconstruction' must be one single, univocal, homogeneous thing is one example of mystified thinking. So-called 'deconstruction' has itself, if there is such a thing, shown, among other things, the fallacy of letting the singularity of proper or generic names do your thinking for you. By a principle that has no exceptions, sentences that take the form 'deconstruction *is* so and so' are nonsense. So if deconstruction has no now, there is no deconstruction as such either. On the other hand the fact that so-

Deconstruction as a mode of interpretation works by a careful and circumspect entering of each textual labyrinth. The critic feels his way from figure to figure, from concept to concept, from mythical motif to mythical motif, in a repetition which is in no sense a parody. It employs nevertheless, the subversive power present in even the most exact and ironical doubling. The deconstructive critic seeks to find, by this process of retracing, the element in the system studied which is alogical, the thread in the text in question which will unravel it all, or the loose stone which will pull down the whole building. The deconstruction, rather, annihilates the

called 'deconstruction' is not inherently fascist does not mean that it is something neutral, able to be appropriated by the right or the left for any political purposes. No, 'deconstruction', if there is such a thing, whatever it is, is inherently untotalizable, anti-totalitarian, even, I should say, inherently democratic, if we define democratic justice not as something already accomplished somewhere, say in the United States, but as a promise, as something that belongs to the future, as something that is to come, perhaps. (Miller 1992b, 9–10)

ground on which the building stands *by showing that the text has already annihilated that ground,* knowingly and unknowingly. Deconstruction is not a dismantling of the structure of the text but a demonstration that it has already dismantled itself. Its apparently solid ground is no rock but thin air.

The uncanny moment in Derrida's criticism, the vacant place around which all his work is organized, is the formulation and reformulation of this non-existence of the ground out of which the whole textual structure seems to rise ... (Miller 1991, 126; emphasis added)

Sentences of the form 'Deconstruction is so and so' are a contradiction in terms. Deconstruction cannot by definition be defined, since it presupposes the indefinability or, more properly, 'undecidability' of all conceptual or generalizing terms. Deconstruction, like any method of interpretation, can only be exemplified, and the examples will of course all differ. (Miller 1991, 231)

As opposed to the deconstructive work of Jacques Derrida, with which de Man's work is of course often paired, de Man has a tendency, in spite of the fact that each of his essays is the 'reading' of a particular text, to move to levels of absolute generality and to say, for example, that *all* texts narrate the impossibility of reading. Derrida on the other hand, seems more interested in what is irreducibly idiomatic ... (Miller 1991, 351)

The citations are aligned with one another in order that you can compare them more effectively. This structure also helps get you away from a linear string of comments running down the page, the layout of which might be read as indicating a progression. Reading each of these passages against each other, it is to be noticed that Miller speaks of what deconstruction can and might do, while simultaneously demonstrating that it cannot be made into a form of analysis. None of his statements allows you to decide on deconstruction's identity. We see from these four passages the following points:

- deconstruction is not the same every time; each reading differs from the ones already gone and those to follow
- the work of one critic is not like that of another; therefore there can be no deconstructive method, much less a school of deconstruction; de Man reads towards generalization, Derrida reads the singular and idiomatic
- deconstruction transforms the text by imitating its every move, its every contour, doing so in such a fashion that, through the closeness of the reading, the alogical is unveiled
- deconstruction does not do anything; it only performs what is already done by and in the text being read; it does not take things apart, it is not an operation, it only reveals how things are put together
- what is performed is the absence of any ground, origin or centre, an absence which is not imposed by deconstructive reading but which is revealed as at the heart of the text through good reading
- one can never say what deconstruction is because deconstruction does not allow for such statements
- all conceptual, abstract or universal terms are self-contradicting because they have elements within their conceptualization which make their final meaning or value undecidable

None of the points made here could be transformed into a methodology or practice, even though each of these points has to be made with regard to whatever misconceptions there are concerning 'deconstruction'. What we must understand from Miller's writing is that the slipperiness of his prose is absolutely, rhetorically necessary to his ability to make statements which respond to queries concerning deconstruction. The remarks cited, and others like them throughout Miller's work, are all readable as responses, and as marked by a responsibility to avoid the type of mystification which accompanies the 'deconstruction is X' formula. Miller only ever responds; he never defines. Certainly, none of the statements above could be defined as a definition of deconstruction.

It is of course in the nature of language, conventionally conceived, that meanings are sought, definitions desired. This is because we use language in the vast number of instances without respect for the singular or the idiomatic. Instead we ignore language's figurality in favour of a single figural model whereby all language is in the service of representation. Conventionally language functions mimetically, or, at least, it is assumed to have this ability, to become a copy, to assume a likeness, of that which is not present, that which we seek to describe. Hence the mystificatory nature of phrases such as 'deconstruction is ...' All such phrases all too readily and blithely assume that 'deconstruction' names some thing; what that thing is can then be represented, the reader provided with a copy, providing we can just imitate its identity with an expression of the formulaic order.

J. Hillis Miller, however, shows how this is not the case. He does so moreover in a performative manner, whereby his own statements enact or perform their own rhetorical evasiveness, even as they appear to be discussing that very subject for which a definition, an identity, is desired. As we have already suggested, to say that deconstruction is good reading or rhetorical analysis is, effectively, to obscure 'deconstruction' as a privileged term, and, along with that, the technological fervour which accompanies the deployment of a term as a noun which provides a short-hand for a so-called practice. All of which belongs to Miller's 'ethics of reading':

> By 'the ethics of reading' ... I mean that aspect of the act of reading in which there is a response to the text that is both necessitated, in the sense that it is a response to an irresistible demand, and free, in the sense that I must take responsibility for my responsibility and for the further effects ... of my acts of reading. (Miller 1987, 43)

Deconstruction may be nothing more or less than the response necessitated by the text; it may be nothing, more or less, than taking responsibility for the act of reading, rather than seeking to avoid that responsibility in the name of some institutionally approved method of interpretation. In either case, 'it' is not something we can lay out like the components of some engine in order to assemble a 'deconstruction machine' which churns out reading after reading in exactly the same manner. We need to avoid precisely such a temptation. About J. Hillis Miller's work we may suggest, perhaps, that Miller avoids avoidance, and this is an important lesson to learn, concerning our acts of reading. We have to encounter each text on its own terms. If this is learnt from Miller it is learnt equally from Paul de Man and Jacques Derrida, despite the numerous differences in 'how' they read. If deconstruction is good reading as such, good reading may be said to be that which never avoids its responsibility, and which never falls into reading by numbers.

It is not enough, though, merely to make such recommendations, even though such gestures might begin to displace, in their own small way, 'so-called "deconstruction"' in favour of an undecidable space of debate. It is important to understand how and why the mystification and misapprehension concerning deconstruction arises, even while we acknowledge, along with Gayatri Chakravorty Spivak, that we 'cannot get a grip on deconstruction' (Spivak 1995, 244). Not 'getting a grip' on deconstruction may well be an important act of letting go the desire to pin something down. Not 'getting a grip' is in a certain way synonymous with 'good reading, as such', because our concern is with the abandonment of a particular desire for mastery over the text. We might well take heart over our inability to 'get a grip' from a passage concerning reading from Derrida's *Glas*. In this passage, Derrida offers us an interesting metaphor for his attempts to 'read' Jean Genet:

> I am seeking here the good metaphor for the operation I pursue here. I would like to describe my gesture, the posture of my body behind this machine.
> [...]
> So I am seeking the good movement. Have I constructed something like the matrix, the womb of his text? On the basis of which one could read it, that is, reproduce it?
> No, I see rather (but it may still be a matrix or a grammar) a sort of dredging machine. From the dissimulated, small, closed, glassed-in cabin of a crane, I manipulate some levers and, from afar, I saw that (*ça*) done at Saintes-Maries-de-la-Mer at Eastertime, I plunge a mouth of steel in the water. And I scrape {*racle*} the bottom, hook onto stones and algae there that I lift up in order to set them down on the ground while the water quickly falls back from the mouth.
> And I begin again to scrape {*racler*}, to scratch, to dredge the bottom of the sea, the mother {*mer*}.
> I barely hear the noise of the water from the little room.
> The toothed matrix {*matrice dentée*} only withdraws what it can, some algae, some stones. Some bits {*morceaux*}, since it bites {*mord*}. Detached. But the remain(s) passes between its teeth, between its lips. You do not catch the sea. She always reforms herself. (*Gl* 204–5b[9])

As the good reader J. Hillis Miller imagines, Jacques Derrida seeks, appropriately, the good metaphor, the most appropriate metaphor, which best describes the process of trying to read Jean Genet's text. The metaphor of the dredging machine might seem a curious choice initially for describing how one reads, but the power of its operation is not to be denied. The force of the image is such that the effect is perhaps best described not as metaphorical but as an example of catachresis, whereby the exchange of images is so forceful as to estrange, defamiliarize, denaturalize, the assumed relationship. To imagine reading as dredging is to offer a wholly unfamiliar figure for a particular activity. This in itself forces us to consider the image as presented specifically through the workings of language, rather than assuming there to be some more or less mimetic correspondence. Derrida follows through his image in describing how, as the teeth scrape the sea-bed, so, while random particles are picked up, something is dropped, something remains, and something cannot be scooped up in the first place. This suggests that no act of reading can ever attain mastery over the object of its inquiry. It cannot do so for at least two reasons: (i) what reading 'picks up' cannot be wholly determined ahead of the event of the textual encounter, and (ii) whatever the reading does gather up, there is always that which remains, which is the remains of reading, the excess or supplement beyond the act of reading. This is acknowledged through the performance of Derrida's writing, indicated above where French words appear in parentheses. Each of the words carries within it a supplement to itself, another possible meaning in its sound and/or inscription, which the act of reading cannot wholly gather up, but which falls back into the play of language.

Furthermore, Derrida leaves us with that image of the sea-text reforming itself, as though untouched by the act of reading, of dredging. The good reader must acknowledge all this as part of the responsibility of *being the good reader*. No theory of literature can ever account for the totality of the text. Derrida has taught us this. In addition, and amongst so many things, Derrida has taught us that the nature of the text is such that all the 'boundaries and divisions' which we assign a text are always already overrun by textuality itself. Being the good reader means, amongst other things, that we acknowledge in response to textuality that what Derrida calls the 'accredited concept, the dominant notion of a "text"' has to be extended and expanded (LOBL 83–4). This is so because, as we will see in responding to

Derrida's texts, a text is always 'a differential network, a fabric of traces referring endlessly to something other than itself, to other differential traces' (LOBL 84). Responding to Derrida responsibly means that we must begin by revising our most fundamental notions concerning 'texts', 'writing', 'literature' and other concepts related in our thought.

Let's begin again then, by asking: is there some *thing* called 'deconstruction'?

Part I

The Make-Believe of a Beginning

1 Another Introduction / *Entamer: In Medias Res* or, Is There Some *Thing* Called Deconstruction?

> I have nothing left to begin with.... But we can begin without a beginning, can't we?...
> [...]
> I am commissioned with something to say, and I dare say I shall say it wrong, but I won't if I can help it ...
> [...]
> This is what it is
>
> Bella Wilfer, *Our Mutual Friend*

> We know that the name 'deconstruction,' which quickly took off both in the United States and in France – but without Derrida's ever assuming it as the name of a method or even of a theory ... – to name 'what Derrida does,' is in part a translation of Heidegger's *Destruktion.*
>
> Geoffrey Bennington (Db)

First bite

In discussing the self-generating and self-perpetuating discursive structures, forms and functions of English institutions such as the Law, Parliament and, specifically, parliamentary committees, along with the philosophical concepts which underpin such structures, Charles Dickens stages a hypothetical series of minutes, in the form of question-and-answer:

> 'Question (number five hundred and seventeen thousand eight hundred and sixty-nine). If I understand you, these forms of practice

> indisputably occasion delay? Answer. Yes, some delay. Question. And
> great expense? Answer. Most assuredly they cannot be gone through
> for nothing. Question. And unspeakable vexation? Answer. I am not
> prepared to say that. They have never given *me* any vexation; quite
> the contrary. Question. But you think that their abolition would
> damage a class of practitioners? Answer. I have no doubt of it.
> Question. Can you instance any type of that class? Answer. Yes. I
> would unhesitatingly mention Mr Vholes. He would be ruined.
> Question. Mr Vholes is considered, in the profession, a respectable
> man? Answer'. – which proved fatal to the inquiry for ten years – 'Mr
> Vholes is considered, in the profession, a *most* respectable man'.
> (Dickens 1996, 622)

Dickens's imagined minutes perform their argumentative procedures,
replicating not only the vexation but also the perpetuation of a system
based on such questions, a system where all is worked out beforehand, where the protocols of question and answer are known ahead
of the game. You'll notice no doubt that the number of questions
already asked is given, such precision marking a potentially endless
sequentiality as a condition of the structure. As the rhetoric performs
its own structure, thereby collapsing any distinction between the discussion of the subject and the subject's own performance, it also inadvertently shows us both its blindness to its own functioning and the
critical reading made available as a condition of that form's myopia.

As Dickens shows us, the answer is inevitable, it is the guarantee of
the system's continuance. At the same time as the 'ineluctable modality'[1] of the politico-discursive structure is unveiled, unfolded, so too is
there unfolded a critique of that structure's movements, traced in the
very writing of the system. Also unfolded or applied is an understanding of the condition of all systems, all institutional structures being, in
some manner, a form of writing (in a broad sense, which we will
discuss below). Dickens thus illustrates the fact that, given a particular epistemological, discursive, politico-institutional system, and the
rules which govern that system, no one ever asks a question, however
rhetorically positioned, without supposing that an answer will come.
Even if the person asking the question supposes the question to be
unanswerable, then the unanswerability of that question is itself a
form of answer predicated in the act of raising the question.[2]

Where the answer comes from, supposing that it arrives at all, is
usually supposed to be somewhere other than the place from which

the question has issued. More generally, the very idea of the question, and the very idea of the positing or positioning of a question *qua* question presupposes a response, a reaction, a gesture, whether from the one being questioned or, less often, from the one who questions (even) or from somewhere within the interrogator. The question cannot exist as question unless there is the promise of a response in some form, even in the form of ignorance ('I don't know', 'I can't tell', 'I'm not sure') or another question ('what do you mean?', 'can you clarify?'). The truth of the question, its being proved to be or shown as a question, is guaranteed only on the premise of some enunciation or articulation, some demonstration, which is not part of itself, outside of, extrinsic and alien to itself, and yet which nevertheless it is reliant on for its self-understanding. The question is thus only guaranteed once the answer arrives; coming as it does, whether from within or without, yet always from somewhere *other*, some place which, being so totally *other*, is never absolutely identifiable as a locatable place, the answer answers the question of whether the question can be put, ahead of any specific question being formed.

It is thus the idea of the answer, rather than any specific answer itself, which generates the structure of questioning *as a structure* with the possibility of completion and of wholeness, and with that possibility the idea of the formation of a whole, self-sufficient identity. As we see in the passage from *Bleak House*, the structure of question-and-answer, when pursued within pre-agreed, politically determined limits, provides the self-fulfilling promise of the very idea of a unified identity.

You might say that all of this is obvious in a certain manner. So obvious, in fact, that none of it needs stating. Yet, let's put that another way, turn it around a little, so as to see it somewhat more obliquely, seeing in the process what such an oblique perspective reveals.

Whatever seems obvious, whatever appears as 'natural' or 'common-sensical', relies often on an immense body of knowledge and ways of thinking, which are in their broadest sense philosophical or conceptual, regardless of whether the subject ostensibly belongs to the field of philosophy or to some other field, discourse or discipline. Different bodies, different knowledges, different disciplines, epistemologies, philosophical frameworks, concepts, discourses: all rely on grounding ideas, conceptual constants, such as the (assumed and acknowledged) respectability of Mr Vholes, as in the passage above, or what Jacques Derrida describes as *philosophemes*.[3] What we assume to be obvious or, for that matter, common sense, or perhaps even natural, rely for their truth on a number of assumptions about other truths.

The assumption about such truths often lies with the idea that somewhere behind or beyond all the questioning and debate, all the discursive and textual movement, there is a guaranteed, solid, unchanging absolute, a value at the heart or centre (supposing such a location to exist is the work of certain kinds of thought and discourse, the purpose of their questions being to offer signposts to the imagined centre). This assumption imagines that the heart or centre around which questions are permitted to proliferate is self-sufficient, fully formed, and not open to questioning itself, with regard to the ideas, concepts, discourses which serve to structure it. Within the immense body, so immense we mistake its immensity for infinity, there are boundaries, limits, provisionally finite contours which serve to map out some aspect of knowledge regarding the subject in question. We assume that the idea or belief which has a truth value and which is absolute, beyond question, lies like a quiet centre in the eye of a storm of words and discourses.

Such a truth or value – let's call it Truth, Beauty, Logic, Reason, Good – holds fast and does not get questioned, as I've just suggested. It is not available, within the system of belief or ideas in which it holds a so-called centre, to questioning, except to those forms of questioning which that truth by its internal logic and economy authorizes beforehand, which it is seen to deem proper to the reassertion of its truth in order to prove its purpose as a centre or originating location. The questions which can be asked – say, for argument's sake, within a particular academic discipline, to narrow the discussion for a moment – are only ever those which re-centre the truth-value as unquestionably true; beyond all discourse and questioning, the truth-value occupies in our thoughts a nebulous quasi-position,[4] a metaphysical position. The really clever and adaptable, flexible truth-value is that which appears to hold true in the face of a number of different types of questions. Yet still the questions are to a certain extent preconditioned, preprogrammed or preordained. They are understood to be 'proper' to the subject, in a double sense: of being fitting or appropriate, and of belonging to that truth-value, of being, if you will, its *property*.

The truth-value, that which is obvious – as in the circular structure of the first words of the American Declaration of Independence, 'we hold these truths to be self-evident' – appears then not only to have the quality of a response (which means that it's not really a pre-positioned centre but a reaction from somewhere other than the invisible centre) to questions; importantly, it also seems to fulfill the definition of a question as discussed above: the truth-value, in order to be shown to be absolutely true, to be the organizing central location, functions only by being able to ask a question or set of questions of itself, centring the propriety of the question ahead of its being asked: 'Am I true?', 'Can I prove myself'?, 'Am I up to questioning?'. So the idea of a centre, a central truth, is paradoxical and relies upon the suspension of the very logic which that centre supposedly proves. We have to accept the answer but still ask questions while, all the while, having an idea of what the answer might be. And we must never ask a question which somehow shakes the whole system on which such truths are predicated. Such a question is considered illogical, improper, sometimes even indecent. Thus, academically and culturally, we are trained or conditioned to raise questions which are always mapped for us and ahead of us, within the parameters of a particular discipline or field of thought. It is – or it used to be – supposedly improper to ask questions concerning the nature of Being (in the sense given that term by Martin Heidegger) in relation to the texts of Jane Austen. (But why?)

Second bite

This secondary, supplemental introduction introduces itself with a question which has already been put in play in the previous introduction: is there some *thing* called deconstruction? This is a crude question, crudely asked, and I have already certain answers in mind, which it is the purpose of this book to spell out along the way, as part of what is to come in the latter part of the book. We might ask the question in other ways. For instance: is there a practice called deconstruction, is there a form of critical interpretation known as deconstruction, or is there a literary theory defined as deconstruction? Some people might answer yes to all of the above, as I've already indicated. Some of those who will read this book might think they already know the answers to such questions. Thus this text in asking such a question as 'is there some *thing* called deconstruction?' might arguably be seen as inserting itself into the middle of a question-and-answer session which has been going on for some time between a more or less shadowy and variable group of interlocutors, of which and whom more in a moment. In asking the very question which partly entitles this introduction, I might seem to be suggesting that there is an answer or several answers already in place and that, in asking the question, I am positioning this book in relation to what interests me, what I find myself in the middle of, to use that phrase once again. The question thus comes after some answers which have apparently been articulated already, while placing itself before what is to come after it, as a question, in this book. The question, like this entire text, is therefore *in medias res*, placed in the middle, within ongoing *inter-ests*.

The Latin tag which serves as the other part of this introduction and which was just now repeated means 'in the middle of', 'being in the middle of', while, at the end of the previous paragraph, the word 'interest' was italicized and split by a hyphen. This was done to emphasize its etymology, and its more literal meanings, which are, amongst others, 'to be in the middle of', or the 'difference between', a 'being among' or 'present', a 'taking a part in'. All these phrases and others relating to them are spelled out as the possible meanings of 'interest' and 'interesse' in the *Oxford English Dictionary*, and are entirely relevant to the concerns of the title of this introduction, the concerns of the text as a whole, and the rhetorical positioning which this introduction has already undertaken. By beginning with the question of the question, and by alerting the reader in a brief and, admittedly, highly telegraphed fashion to this question, I have sought to indicate what the interests of this volume are, what interests this study, and where – in the space between certain ongoing questions and answers – this discussion and the following chapters may be read as being situated. I am not pretending to begin here.

I am not pretending that either this is or what precedes this in the book constitutes an original introduction. Nor am I supposing that such a thing is possible. There are already a fairly large number of 'introductions', all with competing claims for your attention, all with various merits or faults, and some of which I shall refer to below, both in this/these introduction/s, and elsewhere in *Deconstruction* • *Derrida*. What I do intend to convey is that in talking of 'deconstruction' we are already in the middle of a discussion which has been underway for some time now. It is this discussion which *interests* me for precisely the reasons to do with *interest* discussed by Jacques Derrida:

When I write 'what interests me,' I am designating not only an *object* of interest, but the place that *I am in the middle of* and precisely the place that I cannot exceed or that seems to me to supply even the movement by which to go beyond that place or outside of it. [...]

This value of 'interest' is thus no longer an object for demonstration like any other.... Once it envelops or exceeds (within the contextual opening we are considering here) our whole 'history,' 'language,' 'practice,' 'desire,' and so forth, the modes of demonstration should no longer be prescribed or coded by anything that belongs simply within these borders. (*P...* 67–8)

Here Derrida points to the way in which what is of interest to us should not (nor indeed can) be limited – prescribed or coded, as he puts it – to forms of questioning which are contained and defined by the parameters of a subject, or otherwise defined by those who teach it according to what is considered appropriate or proper. If I quote Derrida at this point, in a book which, in its conventional pedagogical senses, is supposed to be an introduction in part to the work of Jacques Derrida, as well as an introduction to what is called deconstruction within, for example and merely to limit the problematic issue for the moment, departments of English; if Derrida is taken out of context in order to make a certain point, this is only to show how nothing I can say here, of Derrida, on Derrida, about Derrida's concerns or interests, is something which Derrida has not already interested himself in or concerned himself with, throughout the length of his publishing and writing career at least. What Derrida forces us to admit to is that, in being interested, we can no longer pretend to stand outside, or in a somewhat disinterested relationship with the subject. This quotation above is saying something, albeit obliquely, concerning what has already been said in this introduction. I can say nothing original on the subject in which I am interested.

I am not even saying something which other commentators on Derrida have not already said before me, commentators such as Geoffrey Bennington in his brilliant (I will not say 'original'; Bennington, like Bella Wilfer and George Eliot, has given up the make-believe of both originality and beginning[5]) 'Derridabase' (from *Jacques Derrida*). As Bennington himself points out, the difficulty

hangs on the fact that *all* the questions to which this type of book

> must habitually presuppose replies, around for example the practice
> of quotation … the relationship between commentary and interpre-
> tation, … the identification and delimitation of a corpus or a work, …
> the respect … owed to the singularity … or the event … of a work in
> its idiom, … its signature, … its date … and its context, … without
> simply making them into examples or cases … are *already* put to us
> by the texts.… Our little problems of reading-protocol cannot there-
> fore remain enclosed in the space of a preface; they are *already* [*déjà*]
> the whole problem. This *déjà*, in which we might be tempted to
> recognize the signature we are trying to respect, is of course also
> interrogated by Derrida, as what precedes every interrogation and
> makes it possible.… The remark we wanted to make before beginning
> turns out to be already in some sense a quotation and an anticipation
> of our most intractable problems. (Db 9–10)

I could go on quoting Bennington here, but I won't. Otherwise, I
might well find myself typing out his entire text, a text which, as he
admits, is in some sense already (*déjà*) written across the texts that are
signed in the name of Jacques Derrida.[6] It is enough to note for now
exactly those issues and problems which Bennington notes, and
which Bennington notes Derrida has already noted. The ellipses in
the quotation above are the places where Bennington has had
recourse to referring to a number of Derrida's texts without quoting
them. The quotations to which Bennington alludes (but which he
abstemiously and rigorously avoids bastardizing) themselves raise the
issues mentioned by Bennington in each phrase which precedes each
ellipsis.

Given that Geoffrey Bennington problematizes the question of
quotation sufficiently, not in an original manner but in a fashion
which directs the reader to the ways in which Derrida has already
questioned and troubled the act of quotation,[7] I am left only to follow
on in the wake of both Bennington and Derrida, breaking faith with
both them in this book, by quoting Derrida out of context, as well as
other writers whose work comes under the heading of 'deconstruction' (with which we have not yet done). And yet this is done with the
awareness of the problems of which Bennington writes, above.
Another Derridean critic has written of imagining the possibility of
Derrida one day passing into the language in such a way that it will no
longer be necessary either to quote him or refer to those texts that are
signed in his name, so that what we are left with is a kind of 'fictional,
theoretical' writing (Royle 1995, 170). This is, of course, problematic,

inasmuch as it points to a certain 'normalized' or 'domesticated Derrida' (as much as does the idea of a 'practice of deconstruction' as a method for textual interpretation), whereby Derrida becomes a spectre at the feast of writing, a ghostwriter in the machinery of our discourse whose ideas surface from time to time in a seemingly normal, yet spectral manner. In this way, Derrida and everything that his name signs might become common-sensical in a wholly predictable fashion. This is of course a risk we run with any textuality in our efforts to comprehend it.

There are then a range of problems in attempting to write a book such as this, one which claims, rightly or wrongly, to be an introduction to a particular signature – that of Jacques Derrida – and to a supposedly delimitable corpus or body of thought, sometimes called 'deconstruction'. Bennington's commentary above concerning the recognition of those 'little problems of reading-protocol' which cannot remain 'enclosed in the space of a preface ... [because] they are *already* [*déjà*] the whole problem' is indeed one possible version, a commentary and interpretation, on and of the preceding quotation from Derrida himself, on the subject of what interests him.

Third bite

I have thus set up this introductory supplement in such a manner so far that it may be read as behaving internally in a self-referential and reflexive manner, a manner which wishes to acknowledge the problems of being faithful to Derrida's texts, and yet which can only be faithful by being unfaithful in a somewhat knowing fashion. I know that what will follow will be troubled by the problems of reading-protocol while also being aware that Derrida himself has troubled such protocol, as well as suggesting that we who write 'after Derrida', to use a phrase and title of another of Derrida's commentators, Nicholas Royle (Royle 1995), also concern ourselves in these problems, without necessarily merely imitating Derrida. Geoffrey Bennington's 'Derridabase' never once quotes Derrida's texts in any conventional sense. Yet as he says, there *is* a sense in which everything he writes may be taken as a form of extended quotation. Whether we quote directly or not, we always run the risk of misunderstanding, mistranslating.

This is, quite categorically, fundamental to any act of reading, and to the protocols of interpretation. Nicholas Royle argues that no matter how faithful a reading or interpretation may be, it 'necessarily differs from that which it expounds. Any exposition of a text is necessarily a transposition, a translation and transformation inseparable from invention' (Royle 1995, 4). This of course – and I feel sure that Nicholas Royle would agree – is to say nothing which, in some way, Derrida has not already said, *in other words*, and which he does every time he involves himself in what he calls 'writing transactions' or 'writing performances' between himself and the texts or subjects on which he writes (*AL* 61). Royle's exposition of Derrida is a translation itself, as well as being both a transaction and a performance, as is Bennington's, and as is mine: none are readings in the conventional sense, even though they are all responses (even as Derrida has said his acts of writing are not readings but responses to the texts of others [*AL* 62]). Yet all our translations are necessarily different from one another, marked in part by a difference of what interests us, what places us as writers responding to Derrida between various texts.

All of which suggests an enormous debt to Jacques Derrida, a debt which can never be repaid but which is acknowledged in Bennington's *déjà*, in Royle's *after*. Already after Derrida? I've a feeling that we've not yet begun to catch up with him, and it is with this sense that Derrida's thought remains a horizon always receding before us that I've 'begun' to discuss by trying to situate myself in such a way which hopefully indicates to you some of the issues at stake in acts, if not of reading exactly, then of writing, and, in doing so, responding.

But there is still that question: is there some *thing* called deconstruction? At this risk of repeating myself, it is now well known that 'deconstruction' is a term associated (1) with the work of Jacques Derrida and (2) with a certain institutional practice of reading, involving a range of protocols which determine, once acquired, how we read, how we comment, how we interpret, and how we write on what we read. It is certainly true that the word 'deconstruction' is used by Jacques Derrida, as it is equally true that for a time, particularly in the 1970s and early 1980s, there were those who claimed to practice a form of critique or exegetical methodology known as 'deconstruction'. There are still some who claim to practice deconstruction, while there are others who claim that there is an approach to interpretation known as 'deconstruction'. In fact, you can find 'deconstruction' taught in most English departments as a subject on courses in Literary Theory. 'Deconstruction' is not as widely expounded as it was a few years ago, at least in the United States, and this, it is claimed (largely by detractors), is because 'deconstruction' is no longer fashionable; it is passé, it is dying, it is dead. But for something to be dead, it had once to have been alive, it had to have existed in some form. So perhaps, once – still? even as a corpse – there was some *thing* called deconstruction. You might think so, and indeed, the way in which many people talked and wrote, from lecturers and professors of English to members of the media in both the United States of America and Great Britain (refer, for instance to back issues of either the *New York Times Review of Books* or the *Guardian*, the *Los Angeles Times*, the *Chronicle of Higher Education* or the *Times Higher Education Supplement*),[8] it could be argued that there was deconstruction, and the vestiges of its presence still remain. I want to turn now to some of these commentaries, especially those which claim to be introductory or expository.

Fourth bite

> A message, if there is one, never stays intact. Why should philosophy be reserved for professional philosophers?
>
> Jacques Derrida

This section looks at some of those texts which address 'deconstruction' in a limited, introductory fashion as one 'movement' among many under the more general rubric of 'literary theory'. There are a number of other 'introductions' which focus specifically on 'deconstructive theory' and Jacques Derrida; these, we'll turn to further on in this study. We may as well begin, for now though, with a dictionary-like introduction to 'Jacques Derrida', provided by John Lechte in his *Fifty Key Contemporary Thinkers: From Structuralism to Postmodernity* (1994, 105–10).

Lechte describes deconstruction as a 'process' which 'investigates the fundamentals of Western thought' (1994, 107). He goes on to suggest that 'one way or another, the whole of Derrida's *oeuvre* is an exploration of the nature of writing in the broadest sense as *différance*. To the extent that writing always includes pictographic, ideographic and phonetic elements, it is not identical with itself. Writing, then, is always impure and, as such, challenges the notion of identity, and ultimately the notion of the origin as "simple".' Writing is 'what makes production possible' (1994, 108). Given the limited space of a dictionary entry, Lechte's definition is, despite brevity, perhaps one of the least flawed of definitions. It remains true to Derrida's insistence on writing and *différance* to a degree, even though, on the evidence of this example, Lechte retains the idea of writing in its narrow, conventionally understood sense, rather than in the broader sense given to it by Derrida.

The choice of the term 'process' is an attempt to avoid some of the problems of comprehension around the status of the term 'deconstruction'. For, in so far as 'process' describes an activity which may or may not be 'internal' to the act of writing in the narrow sense of that which one inscribes, and to the logic which accompanies, for argument's sake, the writing of a sentence, deconstruction may indeed be said to be a process which inhabits, infests or contaminates the structure of the conceptual or philosophical logic at work behind that act of writing. If one talks, however, of an active 'investigation' of Western thought, its premises, major statements, founding arguments, and so on, such a gesture is to mobilize the process as a consciously controlled activity. Placed as a means of investigation, a method put to work in a regular pre-determined and programmable way, as part of a perceived investigative procedure, deconstruction is, in such a statement, no longer merely the internal necessity of a structural logic, but something supposedly separable from application, rendered as a theory, and then available for re-application. Indeed, Lechte admits as much when, in talking of American literary critics who profess to 'practice' deconstruction as a so-called methodology, he argues that 'one may indeed wonder about the extent to which such a strategy [with reference to 'deconstruction'] *can* be under the (conscious) control of the critic' (1994, 108).

Lechte's point is that, if we attempt to read Derrida carefully enough, we might begin to doubt the possibility of transforming deconstruction into a methodology or reading practice, because of all that Derrida has to say about the workings and movements of 'deconstruction' as one of many elements in the condition of writing, or as another term for 'writing' in its broad sense. In the United States particularly, within academic institutions and departments of English, the 'technical and methodological "metaphor" that seems necessarily attached to the very word "deconstruction" has been able to seduce or lead astray' (*DR* 273).

We can observe such seduction at work in another encyclopaedic entry, not on Derrida this time but, significantly, on 'deconstruction', from the *Encyclopedia of Contemporary Literary Theory: Approaches, Scholars, Terms* (Adamson 1993, 25–31). The article on 'deconstruction' states, quite confidently, that deconstruction is 'a *school* of philosophy that originated in France in the late 1960s, [and] has had an enormous impact on Anglo-American criticism. Largely the creation of its chief proponent Jacques Derrida, deconstruction upends the Western metaphysical tradition' (1993, 25; emphasis added). The very idea that there is a school implies, obviously, that there were a group of thinkers, historically and culturally identifiable, who began to deconstruct as a conscious (in this case philosophical) activity having to do with philosophy as a discourse and as a field of institutionally approved enquiry. The article continues in a similar vein, with phrases such as 'Deconstruction seeks ...' or 'deconstruction celebrates limitless interpretation and an unrestricted semantic play' (1993, 25).

Aside from whatever criticisms we might have or could wish to make of the veracity – or otherwise – of such statements, it is clear that 'deconstruction' is conceived in certain quarters as, first of all, an active verb signifying a practice presumably operable or capable of being put in place by some guiding consciousness who has learned 'how to deconstruct', some mental presence itself actively manipulating the workings of the deconstructive machinery. Here we see how the 'technical and methodological "metaphor"' has been so seductive as to shape the entire thesis of the encyclopaedia entry. Whether we like it or not, deconstruction has been translated, becoming in the process a semantic, interpretive crowbar and, at the same time, an institutional practice or operation which has the potential of transforming texts into perpetual motion machinery, behind all of which stands a god-like authority capable of deconstructing. It is always tempting to assume, as do the statements so far quoted, that there is a traceable origin, a point of genesis, or locatable (though hidden or obscured) presence behind 'deconstruction'. In the case of this article, the genesis of deconstruction lies in Parisian thinking of the late 1960s, the originator of which is Jacques Derrida. Derrida is tired of countering such false statements and errors of perception. In 1996 he said on the subject of the falsity of such assumptions '... we know this, it is totally exhausted, I won't insist on that, you know the answers' (*AD* 218).

However, as he then went on to point out in the same interview, deconstruction is not a new word, but a very old French word, the fortunes of which underwent particular sea-changes when arriving in the English-speaking world. Deconstruction became transformed in – in retrospect – a wholly predictable fashion beginning with 'the institutionalisation of this word in academic circles in the Western world … especially in the United States' (AD 218). What we see then, in the light of this statement, and turning our attention to the Encyclopaedia once more, is a process of transference and erasure or, at least, elision: definitions of 'deconstruction' as a technology of reading, an exegetical practice given institutional authority or treated with institutional distrust, emerge from North America, from the place where deconstruction was first translated in this manner.

Yet, in an effort to hide the act of translation, as though it were an act of bad faith on the part of Derrida's Anglophone readers, other readers from the same locations, the same institutions, direct attention away from the acts of misconception in the home, by pointing to, and creating a narrative out of, a supposed foreign origin, even in some cases an identifiable source of foreign monstrosity which has infected 'native' acts of reading and critical thinking. This speaks to a certain politics of the institution,[9] already advertised in Peggy Kamuf's epigraph to the (first) introduction, but which we will have to abandon for the moment, although we should call it to mind throughout this book. We will return briefly to this subject in the conclusion of *Deconstruction • Derrida*.

What we can say for now though is that the assumption of an origin, the identification of a source, is ultimately reassuring, if only in the sense that we know what the target is, we know where the threat lies. It means that, if we can only pin down the source of a term and thereby provide it with a context in which the term has a supposedly determinate meaning (contexts are already being provided by terms such as 'school', 'movement', and so on), we can also imagine or invent a single figure who generates this way of thinking.

In fairness, the article does say that 'deconstruction as practised by Derrida should be carefully separated from the work of his American counterparts' (26). Whether or not we wish to argue with that 'as practised by Derrida' as though deconstruction were an active practice (which we do), this arbitrary separation and division (one which is echoed, amongst other places, in Frank Lentricchia's assessment of the post-war critical scene in America [Lentricchia 1980, 164–88]) is important, and one which this book reproduces in part. However, the problem is still that idea of the possibility of a conscious practice. Deconstruction may well have been transformed into a metaphor or proper name for a practice, if not a practice itself, especially in the United States, inasmuch as those who claim to practice it have ignored, forgotten or mistranslated what Derrida has said. In talking of Derrida's texts, Geoffrey Bennington has commented that

> All of Derrida's texts are already applications, so there is no separate 'Derrida' in the form of theory who might *then* be applied to something else. Insofar as 'Deconstruction' tends to become a method or a school, we might say that it has forgotten this, and has begun at least to make Derrida into a theory which it wants to put into practice. (1996a, 17)

This immediately serves to cast a somewhat harsh, but necessary light on the statement above concerning the idea that deconstruction is a separable school of practice in France (Adamson 1993, 29), revealing that idea, that statement as being in error. Thus seduction and the technological metaphor.

So, with regard to 'deconstruction' in the United States at least, it may well be the case, as the encyclopaedia puts it, that '*the approach* has largely become a method for reading texts as allegories of deconstruction itself.... What began as *a critique* of methods and systems of reading can be legitimately accused of having succumbed to the normative methodization *it criticized*' (1993, 30; emphases added). The reification and institutionalized domestication of 'deconstruction' may well have been inevitable in retrospect. In a culture where use-value is tantamount to a shared psychic drive and where the active voice in writing is so privileged it could hardly have been otherwise; giving some *thing* which is not a thing a voice and a value provides it with a determined presence of sorts. With regard to the American dimension of the above-cited article, the commentary's critique is somewhat accurate. But the chief problem lies in those emphasized phrases, to which I have alerted the reader. Once more, we see in the writing the misunderstanding that 'deconstruction' can be got to grips with, grappled consciously, wrestled to the ground and then put to work, *technicized*, turned into a prosthesis of critical consciousness, whether at the individual or institutional level. This is the project of the entire encyclopaedia entry, a project which the entry both re-presents as a retroactive teleological gesture (moving back to that 'school' in France in the 1960s) and which it also typifies in its rhetorical mapping of discernible 'approaches' and 'critiques'. This article is thus a symptom of a broader process of interpretation. There is still a problem, though, which the very act of separation runs the risk of. This problem of separating 'what Derrida does' from a supposedly perceivable American institutionally authorized – and, sometimes, excoriated – practice of a sometimes fashionable, sometimes unfashionable, methodology named 'deconstruction' is that it relies on the very possibility of 'what Derrida does' being transformed into a methodology, once it has been separated. Separating Derrida, while laudable, still remains a dangerous activity. There is a double danger here: first, there lies behind this separation the idea that what Derrida does, he does, and always did do, before anyone else. Derrida thus serves as the name of a beginning, an origin which, while not 'deconstruction', is nonetheless locatable. In this equation, Derrida *is* deconstruction. This points us to the second problem: citing Derrida as the source, the origin, or *even* the father of deconstruction (or as some have put it in a gesture which expresses a desire to locate both criminality *and* metaphysics, the *god*father of deconstruction) makes possible the violent chance to turn Derrida's writing into a theory, however distinguished from 'deconstruction', which can then be applied as though it were deconstruction-with-a-difference. Derrida may thus be reduced, through the argument that his activity follows certain discernible rules, protocols or programmes, into a practice of critical interpretation, constraints and regulations.

A number of critics and philosophers have already attempted this. Geoffrey Bennington's article 'Deconstruction and the Philosophers (The Very Idea)' wittily and quite ruthlessly explores and exposes the effort on the part particularly of Irene Harvey and Rodolphe Gasché to delegitimate and debunk literary critics' uses of Derrida (1994, 11–60). According to Bennington, the philosophers claim that mere literary critics (such as myself) are either not properly trained or otherwise unversed in reading philosophy (as an institutional discipline); therefore, we just don't know how to read Derrida *properly*. One of Bennington's primary targets in the essay, Rodolphe Gasché, has subsequently written more on the subject of the 'improper use' of Derrida, in his *Inventions of Difference: On Jacques Derrida* (1994; see, particularly, Chapter 1, 'Deconstruction and Criticism', 22–57).[10] In this, Gasché adopts a tone of philosophical *hauteur*, claiming that literary criticism conceived fashionably as 'theory' has turned its attention to the 'ridiculous *application* of the *results* of philosophical debate to the literary field' (1994, 23). Examples of this misappropriation on the part of the lawless literary critic are cited later by Gasché when he rescues Derrida's 'Ulysses Gramophone' as an almost *exclusively* philosophical text (1994, 231; Gasché is forced to admit that Derrida's essay does have '"literary" features').[11]

This essay, which focuses on aspects of James Joyce's *Ulysses*, might, argues Gasché, 'easily be construed as an irresponsible spinning out of private fantasies, wild jokes, and totally arbitrary associations – in other words, as a text of so-called deconstructive criticism where everything goes' (1994, 231). It is nice to know we're in the presence of an expert here, who provides us, *in other words*, with a definition of 'deconstructive criticism' (you see, there is some *thing* called deconstruction!). However, we only construe Derrida's text in this fashion – that is to say if we believe in the first place, however misguidedly, that there, *there!* is deconstructive criticism at work with its little triangular road signs all spread out before us – if we cannot see or refuse to acknowledge with Gasché that 'this text belongs to philosophy' (1994, 231). Never mind the fact that Gasché is forced by the very procedure of Derrida's text into saying that the piece has '"literary" features' in that it 'performs what it establishes through its argumentative procedures' (231; as though this were a definition of the literary feature). Still we can see, following Gasché, that 'this text belongs to philosophy'. Got that clear? Good.

Except that there is a slight problem with Gasché's assumptions. Regardless of the fact that he suggests the literary features of 'Ulysses Gramophone' are definable as a self-enacting rhetorical movement, what is assumed in the passage is that such a performative in its so-called 'literariness' is that ill-named thing, 'deconstructive criticism'. The falsity of the assumption lies not so much in its pinning 'literariness' to a performative act of writing and textual exchange as in the idea – the horror, the horror – that Derrida's act with its '"literary" features' is one which might be mistaken as deconstruction (almost as though Gasché were chiding Derrida for not being vigilant or *philosophical* enough). Arguably, most if not all of Derrida's writing is marked by its tendency to perform what it establishes through its argumentative procedures. But this is still not to say that there is a methodology to Derrida's writing engagements which can be effortlessly reproduced by literary critics. Let's take a comment of Derrida's at this stage, a remark made as an effort to provide a history of what he does. The commentary sheds considerable light on Derrida's own understanding of his work and is worth quoting extensively:

> During the years that followed, from about 1963 to 1968, I tried to work out – in particular in the three works published in 1967 [*La Voix et le phénomène, De la grammatologie, L'Écriture et la différence*; trans. as *Speech and Phenomena and Other Essays on Husserl's Theory of Signs, Of Grammatology, Writing and Difference*] – *what was in no way meant to be a system* but rather a sort of strategic device, opening onto its own abyss, an enclosed, unenclosable, *not wholly formalizable* ensemble of rules for reading, interpretation and writing. This type of device may have enabled me to detect not only in the history of philosophy and in the related socio-historical totality, but also in what are alleged to be sciences and in so-called post-philosophical discourses that figure among the most modern ... to detect in these an evaluation of writing, or, to tell the truth, rather a devaluation of writing whose insistent, repetitive, even obscurely compulsive, character was the sign of a whole set of long-standing constraints.... I proposed to analyse the non-closed and fissured system of these constraints under the name of logocentrism in the form that it takes in Western philosophy and under that of phonocentrism as it appears in the widest scope of its dominion. Of course, I was able to develop this device and this interpretation only by according a privileged role to the guideline or analyser going under the names of writing, text and trace, and only by proposing a reconstruction and a generalization of these concepts: writing, the text, the trace as the play and work of *différance*, whose role is at one and the same time both of constitution and of deconstitution. This strategy may have appeared to be an abusive deformation ... of the current notions of writing, text or trace, and have seemed to those who continued to cling to these old self-interested representations to give rise to all sorts of misunderstandings. But I have untiringly striven to justify this unbounded generalization, and I believe that every conceptual breakthrough amounts to transforming, that is to deforming, an accredited, authorized relationship between a word and a concept, between a trope and what one had every interest to consider to be an unshiftable primary sense, a proper, literal or current usage. (TT:P 40–1; emphases added)

As it is possible to see, there is no intention to provide a system, programme or methodology. Nor is there a sense in which what Derrida has to say about the investigation of graphic systems is in any way reducible to a series of rules. As he puts it of his own work, his interest in the concepts of writing, text and trace are not formalizable into a reading practice. By Derrida's own admission, then, he seems to be admitting to an interest in the very language which Gasché would excuse or otherwise outlaw. Instead, and *pace* Gasché, we see a Derrida emerging from this retrospective self-assessment who fits the bill of Hillis Miller's good reader, that is someone whose interest is in the rhetorical analysis of written language for the purpose of demonstrating the illusory ground of conceptual structures which are employed to prop up the conventional functions of Western thought.

All we can say is that Derrida's writing traces the various contours of the text, or phrase, being considered (as J. Hillis Miller has argued the good reader should do). Derrida's writing does indeed perform, as well as its own argument, those points it draws from rhetorical structures, out of a sense of responsibility Derrida feels to the other of the text – and the other *that is* the text – to which he is responding. What James Joyce may be said to represent for Derrida is a certain optimum mobilization of equivocacy and undecidability, which Derrida acknowledges in 'Two Words for Joyce' (TWJ 149). Derrida's turn to Joyce, his literary turn in Joyce's wake, is dictated by the fact that, for Derrida, *Finnegans Wake* speaks 'several languages' (TWJ 149). Here, Derrida is not only referring to the plethora of different languages (English, French, German, and all the rest) which are to be discovered in the *Wake*, even though language and translatability are Derrida's provisional starting points. For Derrida, 'several languages' can also be taken to refer to the various languages – literary, philosophical, political, ideological, theological – which can be read as speaking in any text equivocally. That Gasché finds the disturbing trace of the literary in Derrida's writing is no surprise then, except perhaps to Gasché, for whom, I would suggest, the discovery of the trace is in itself so disturbing that he needs to assert 'Ulysses Gramophone' as being stamped immediately 'property of philosophy' in a somewhat peremptory fashion.

It seems as though Gasché is one of a small number who maintain the separation of 'deconstruction/Derrida' in a certain fashion, and who have taken it as their role to justify the ways of Derrida to man [sic.], to recall John Milton's representation of God. Despite such good intentions to put us literary critics right, however, Gasché will insist throughout his writing on thinking of deconstruction as an analytical or methodological practice, albeit shamefully sloppy. Such

Podsnappery (or Gradgrindery) is daunting, but we should proceed nonetheless.

Christopher Norris (of whom more below), another of Derrida's rescuers in the face of sloppy practice, has shown more caution in discussing the thorny issue of whether there is a discernible methodology to be named deconstruction. Also, he alerts the reader to some of those statements of Derrida's concerning why 'deconstruction' cannot be reduced to a methodological procedure (Norris 1987, 18–22). Indeed, Norris is keen to assert that we should not merely write off Derrida's American commentators and associates as being guilty of 'wilful misappropriation' (1987, 20). Norris does issue a *caveat*, however, which is that those who do construct a simple reading practice out of Derrida's writing do so by taking his writing at face value in terms of the emphasis on 'limitless interpretative license' (1987, 20). To do so is to ignore the 'rigorous *work* of deconstruction'. Norris is wary of making hard and fast distinctions such as those made by Gasché between 'rigorous ("philosophical") and non-rigorous ("literary") forms of deconstructive activity' (1987, 21). His reason for being wary is that, in making such distinctions, we run the risk of entrenching ourselves in the kind of blind positions belonging to the falsely polarized debate over 'philosophy vs. literature', which Derrida has been at pains to open to questioning, from another place: hence, Derrida's interest in the 'literary' within the philosophical text or the trace of the philosopheme in literature.

Like Norris, Frank Lentricchia is similarly careful in his own critique/commentary on Derrida's writing (Lentricchia 1980, 164–88). Throughout his discussion he strives to avoid referring to deconstruction as a methodology. Instead, he prefers the term 'Derridean', using the proper name as a means of identifying a type of critical practice. (This is still problematic, in that the assumption is that the proper name provides a unified identity for what might then be understood as a methodology.) The chief criticism Lentricchia makes of 'Derridean criticism', following comments of Edward Said's, and paralleling remarks made by Terry Eagleton (of whom more in a moment), is that Derrida's contentions concerning Western metaphysics are so broad, however 'utterly persuasive' (as Lentricchia puts it), that they deny a specificity for a particular text in historical terms (1980, 176).[12] This leads Lentricchia to assume that 'Derrida's deconstructive project is formalist through and through' (177), a quality which he admits is Derrida's skill and strength. In this light, Derrida can be said to have failed Lentricchia's Marxist-influenced criteria concerning the function of criticism. We might respond to this, however, by suggesting that Lentricchia's is a system of questioning or methodology which is unable to question its own critical criteria, and which can only conceive of the 'historical' in a particular form and as a particular system, which Derrida's thinking might question from another place so as to show the workings and limits of that system.

Like Frank Lentricchia, Terry Eagleton also finds Derrida's so-called formalism lacking in historicist specificity or contextualization, in his *Literary Theory: An Introduction* (1983). His 'introduction' to the subject of literary theory is, again like Lentricchia's, polemically positioned, with an eye to what interests the politically committed critic (that is to say, politically committed in some obviously doctrinal or systematic manner) in other areas of critical thinking. Eagleton contends that:

> 'deconstruction' is the name given to the critical operation by which ... [binary] oppositions can be partly undermined, or by which they can be shown partly to undermine each other in the process of textual meaning. (1983, 132)

This is a more or less reasonable comment as far as it goes but it hardly goes far enough, even for an introduction. It points us to the seductiveness of the metaphor in being able to lead astray, while demonstrating how necessary it is in certain areas of thinking to think through a *technics* of reading, in order to be able to say what supposedly happens in a form of interpretation. Once this is achieved, saying what is lacking or what is at fault in such a reading becomes easy (supposedly) to identify.

Eagleton's comment reduces Derrida's thought to a game of 'deconstruction-by-numbers', an operation whereby deconstruction is the hunt for the binary opposition – such as man/woman or good/evil – and the subsequent inversion of that binarism for the purpose of showing how a particular text is undermined in its logic according to its reliance on such paired oppositions, both of which suppose a truth-value allegedly peculiar to themselves, but which truth-value is dependent for its meaning on the operation of the opposite term. Inverting the pair of terms reveals mutual dependency in the structural relationship by demonstrating how meaning is context-dependent and the product of a structure rather than a discrete unit, and rather than there being any full meaning inherent in any one term. By Eagleton's definition, this activity of 'hunt the binarism' is what deconstruction is. Certainly, there was a point in the recent history of the term when, in some quarters, the act of 'deconstructing a text' was understood as following such a procedure as described above. If deconstruction was ever a method, then this was it. Apparently.

But this is to reduce all of Derrida's work to a momentary discussion in one particular text within a highly specified context. Derrida has repeatedly denied that this was in fact a method or programme for reading, but merely one commentary among many, none of which could or should be generalized in such a manner as to provide a tool kit for 'deconstructive analysis'. Eagleton's 'introduction' thus opts for the mechanic's approach to reading; at least he can claim that his is 'only' an introduction, thereby excusing reductiveness. He does however make some other interesting comments worth addressing. Soon after the passage just quoted, he suggests that 'deconstruction ... has grasped the point that the binary oppositions with which classical structuralism tends to work represent a way of seeing typical of ideologies' (1983, 133). In understanding deconstruction as a methodology based on the critique and exposure of the hierarchically distorted power relations which binary oppositions signify as they are deployed in Western thought and culture, Eagleton sees such a 'method', belonging to what the Anglo-American critical and academic institution has termed 'poststructuralism', as having a political potential.

This point is followed through later on in Eagleton's introductory study, and we see precisely why, and for what reasons connected to Eagleton's own politico-critical agenda. He argues that 'in the Anglo-American world' deconstruction has taken on an apparently radical stance with regard to everyone's statements except its own. Of Paul de Man and J. Hillis Miller Eagleton has said that, in their view, 'literature does not need to be deconstructed by the critic: it can be shown to deconstruct itself' (1983, 145). Identifying a supposedly 'doctrinal obsession with "undecidability"' (1983, 146) in Anglo-American 'deconstruction' and seeing this as a form of 'liberal scepticism' (1983, 147), Eagleton inadvertently asserts a quasi-truth about 'deconstruction': that it is a textual quality or structural element and not a practice. Even though Eagleton writes about what Anglo-American 'deconstruction' 'does' in terms of texts, his statement concerning de Man and Miller, although written with the intent of being a part of an indictment of 'deconstruction's' lack of political commitment, is nothing more than the admission that deconstruction is not a methodology. The problem for Eagleton is that, keen as he is to see the idea of the text deconstructing itself as a kind of liberal evasion of political responsibility, he cannot see that he needs deconstruction to be a critical practice – as do so many critics – in order for him to criticize it. Eagleton's discourse therefore invents the deconstructive methodology which becomes a target for his commentary, which he can find at fault, and which he can blame for its political shortcomings.

Of course Eagleton is not the first to set 'deconstruction' up in such a fashion, in order to knock it down again, even in a partial and hesitant manner. The making of deconstruction into some *thing* is usually the first part of an all too common critical gesture of definition for the purpose of attack. All too frequently 'deconstruction' is a word latched onto by critics in order to find a way to criticize and even attack Derrida for being nihilist, irrationalist, a hopeless pun-smith without sufficient respect for the institution of critical thinking in general and philosophy in particular. Yet about 'deconstruction' Derrida has stated that he has 'often said I do not need to use this word ... deconstruction is always a highly unstable and almost empty motif' (RDP 85). It seems that those who write introductions, whether in the form of critical books or articles for encyclopaedias and other forms of reference book, are cursed by the very act of what they do. The very idea of the introduction relies for its cogency on setting out a series of questions supposedly appropriate to a subject which has arisen prior to the raising of questions and which thus dictates the very form of those questions, all of which then aim to stabilize that which is most unstable.

There is thus the question of the question, that point with which we had apparently begun, but which we were using as a way of entering into a debate already in progress, and of pointing to the problems attending non-recognition of the instability of an 'almost empty motif'. Derrida has addressed the nature of the accusations made against deconstruction, and the attendant misunderstandings surrounding that 'subject' in relation to the question of the (critical) question(ing) at the institutional level: '... I think that the accusations that are often made against deconstruction derive from the fact that its raising the stakes of argumentation is not taken into account. The fact that it is always a question of reconsidering the protocols and the contexts of argumentation, the questions of competence, the language of discussion, etc' (RDP 78). The problem some seem to have with 'deconstruction' is that 'it' – if 'it' is an 'it' at all – does not behave within supposedly defined, determined and pre-agreed parameters. Instead, the question of deconstruction is a question of questioning the structuring of the parameters within which argumentation, critical thinking, analysis, interpretation all take place. Not only this, but there is also the question of how fit one is to ask a question in the first place (you'll recall the brief discussion of Rodolphe Gasché) and the terms in which the question is couched. It would have been a step forward not to have to mention the word 'deconstruction' at all in this book (but you cannot have everything).

To conclude this section, we will take a brief look at one more 'introduction' to 'deconstruction', this time written by Richard Rorty, a philosopher who has frequently engaged with Derrida's work, in a critical yet mostly positive manner. The article comes from *The Cambridge History of Literary Criticism: From Formalism to Poststructuralism, Volume 8* (1995, 166–96). Rorty begins promisingly enough with the phrase 'the movement known as "deconstruction"' (1995, 166). This phrase signals an initial wariness about assuming uncritically that deconstruction is in fact a movement, while Rorty's use of quotation marks is admirably cautious. He soon abandons caution, however. By the next page we encounter the '"deconstructionist movement"' (167). We still have the quotation marks, but the movement is assumed, however equivocally, and Rorty proceeds from this to look at the broad and narrow features of such a movement. The term 'deconstructionist' is ungainly and awkward, but signals a significant change in thinking; we've gone from 'deconstruction' as a concept which may have been violently translated and transformed into a methodology and the name for that methodology; and we've arrived at a term which clumsily apportions an *a priori* verifiable practice to critical thinking as a whole. Never mind whether we want to pursue the debate over the applicability – or otherwise – of a word of a not particularly useful kind to a form of analysis or a school of critics. Now we're already in the land of the 'deconstructionist', and we'd better just get on with things as they are: (for Rorty at least) there is some *thing* called, if not deconstruction, then deconstructionism *and the sooner we figure out what's going on out there the better.*

For this purpose, Rorty stakes out his territory in a mercifully clear way. He sees the 'deconstructionist movement' as part of an effort to politicize the function of English literature departments, *pace* Eagleton and Lentricchia (1995, 168). Furthermore, Rorty states quite clearly that:

> [T]his chapter will be concerned with the deconstructionist move-ment narrowly construed as a school of literary criticism. Despite this focus ... it will be necessary to spend a good half of the available space on deconstructionist philosophizing. This is because decon-structionism is perhaps the most theory-oriented, the most specifi-cally philosophical, movement in the history of literary criticism. The catchwords which pepper its readings of literary texts ... are unintelli-gible to those who lack a philosophical background. (1995, 168)

In the light of comments such as Rodolphe Gasché's, such a bold statement seems almost foolhardy and reckless. But that's pragma-tism for you (or Rorty's brand, at least). The comment on the philo-sophicality of deconstruction(ism) seems to ignore a certain history of critical thinking which would include at the very least Matthew Arnold and Samuel Taylor Coleridge, but we'll let that go. There is, however, that sop to philosophy at the end of the extract and we find a kind of quasi-Gasché being snuck in behind literary criticism's back. The very idea that 'deconstruction-ism' has catchwords points to a will-to-methodologize on Rorty's part. Having catchwords means, in other words, a technical language or discourse specific jargon. At a very simple level if we (mis)take certain passing *bons mots* for catch-words, if we allow Derrida's *en passant* coinages, neologisms and strategic resurrections of old terms to become set in stone and subse-quently monumentalized, we're well on our way to having the frame-work of a pseudo-theoretical apparatus which we can apply in countless reading acts.

These are just some of the implicit assumptions behind Rorty's rhetoric. What is somewhat troublesome is that Rorty appears to be accepting that all this has happened quite unproblematically. Also quite unproblematic is the assumption on Rorty's part that the mater-ial in question can be divided into 'deconstructionist theory' (168–84) and 'deconstructionist criticism' (184–94). Rorty takes a somewhat cavalier approach to making such distinctions, arbitrarily quoting Derrida, Hillis Miller and Paul de Man in the first half when he sees them talking about what literary texts do, as opposed to what texts say, as though this were the qualification for theory as distinct from criticism. Roughly speaking, Rorty sets out to introduce first those philosophers he considers as antecedents to 'deconstructionist theory', followed by commentary on what the 'deconstructionists' themselves have to say about the nature of texts. This is then followed by the much shorter 'practical section' which follows 'how deconstructors read texts' (1995, 184). Rorty's textual sleight of hand is so structured as to make the division of texts between those which are taught in departments of philosophy and those which are taught in departments of English clear and irrefutable. In doing so, he uses cognate statements on the 'nature of the literary text' as a series of links between philosophy and literary criticism, between theory and practice, as though statements about the literary text were of a different order than those on the content of the text itself.

'Deconstructionist theory' thus emerges as the bastard offspring of its philosophical parents which, because of its interests in rhetoric and language, can then be abstracted from in its various commentaries, disciplined in the most literal sense of being made to conform to an institutionally recognized methodology, which in turn can be utilized for the purpose of textual interpretation. However, let us not forget that radical politics of which Rorty insists we be aware. Moving on to 'deconstructivist criticism', he concludes his overview by arguing that, seen from the point of view of looking at 'what it does with texts', deconstruction is 'a gesture in the direction of a groundswell of suspicion and impatience with the status quo among the intellectuals' who are part of 'an amorphous movement' (1995, 196). This is a well-intentioned idealizing gesture on Rorty's part. Notice though how that phrase 'gesture in the direction of a groundswell' aids in the disenfranchisement of the very connection he would have us comprehend as being part and parcel of 'deconstructionist criticism' whereby the supposed radicalism of an alleged movement becomes a somewhat effete ripple in a much larger, somewhat stagnant pond. After all, suspicion and impatience are hardly the rallying or clarion calls of any radicalism, however theoretically conceived. We find ourselves, I would argue, with a sense of liberal scepticism, as so called by Eagleton, but seen from another side.

Whatever the case, 'deconstruction' viewed as a movement, school or method appears to attract critics and thinkers whose own frustrated ideological desires and goals come to be transferred onto 'deconstruction', once it is identified as being out there and in motion. The introductions to which we have briefly turned monumentalize deconstruction as a movement either in order to make the questions they have to ask easier to answer, or otherwise so as to find in that monument cracks in an edifice which has never been built by those who are accused of being the structure's prime architects. It would seem that if deconstruction did not exist, someone would have had to invent it, if only so as to have a convenient whipping boy. This is not to say, still, that there necessarily is some *thing* called deconstruction, except for those who need it to exist.

Fifth bite

In the face of such a history of critical commentary, it would clearly be foolhardy to pretend that deconstruction in whatever form has never existed. However, whether or not what is called deconstruction is analogous with or similar to the reading or writing practices of Jacques Derrida, is another matter. What I want to argue in this book is that deconstruction, as a practice of literary interpretation, may well have come about as a result of commentary on and interpretation of the texts of Jacques Derrida, but that Derrida himself has never practised deconstruction. Indeed, I want to argue, through quoting Derrida, in commenting on Derrida and in translating Derrida, that deconstruction cannot be practised because there is not an aspect of Derrida's work which, when translated, can be turned into a theory which then can, in turn, be put into practice as a method for reading, *pace* Eagleton, Lentricchia, Rorty, and a host of lesser commentators. This will be the concern of the final section of this chapter. If there is deconstruction-as-method, then its form is not recognizable as being 'what Derrida does' except in the most reductive and even crude form, and it is neither the intent nor the purpose to discuss such a method.

However, because the purpose of this book is largely – supposedly didactic, pedagogical and expository (these are the determining parameters of its having been commissioned), because it is supposed to serve the function of an introduction to both deconstruction and Jacques Derrida, I am still obliged to provide a certain overview of practices of reading in the context of literary interpretation as a whole. The title of this volume gives this away: *Deconstruction* •

Derrida. These are my subjects, these are the terms into which I attempt to insert this discourse as an extrapolation or translation of what interests me. You'll notice that I've kept the terms separated, the one from the (its) other. There's deconstruction. And there, *there* is Derrida. The bullet point – • – divides graphically without giving the indication of connection or hierarchical subordination, as a colon would. The bullet point is silent but serves to articulate in its own mute, inescapably inscribed, rather than voiced, fashion, the uneasy, disjointed yet undeniable relationship between the two. Given that Derrida has suggested that deconstruction is disjointing (TOJ 25) – a spatio-temporal dis-articulation which makes the structure all the more visible – the bullet point appears to point *in writing* to the problematic textual concerns of this book. The bullet point thus serves a particular function which the colon or another normalized mark would not. Were I to have written *Deconstruction: Derrida,* you might reasonably have expected that Derrida would be the subject of deconstruction, the subject even to have been deconstructed, were such an activity possible.

On the other hand, I could have offered as the title *Deconstruction and Derrida.* 'And' is a little too cosy, a little too familiar. Its use in titles implies a domesticity if not a relationship which we are forced into assuming through that one word. 'Deconstruction *and* Derrida': it's like salt and pepper, bread and butter, milk and sugar. Or in the words of a song: 'love and marriage, love and marriage, they go together like a horse and carriage ... you can't have one without the other' (except that you can; *and* only makes you believe that there's no alternative). From particular, limited perspectives or philosophical ways of thinking this may be true, but the logic of the dualism is forced upon you not by either of the terms so much as that *and.* It creates a little interpretive tyranny all of its own; it's relentless in its function, and it makes you interpret pairs of otherwise disparate, heterogeneous terms according to its own peculiar powers, which drain both words of their singularity and, to paraphrase Geoffrey Bennington from above, the respect we owe to them in their singularity. Thus, as a partial resistance in writing: *Deconstruction* • *Derrida.*

Sixth bite

> What deconstruction is not? everything of course!
> What is deconstruction? nothing of course!
>
> Jacques Derrida, 'Letter to a Japanese Friend'

This still leaves us, though, with the question concerning deconstruction; whether there is a methodology to it, whether we can assert that there is an 'it' for which we can assume a methodology, is still open to question. If there is a methodology, is it one which Jacques Derrida would necessarily recognize or acknowledge, except as a way of distancing himself from the transformation of the word? Everything I have suggested so far in an effort to complicate the picture which this chapter attempts to sketch is that 'deconstruction' may have been constructed to inhabit a certain Anglophone-institutional space, but its relationship to Jacques Derrida is problematized, both by the assumptions of many critics who presume to treat deconstruction as though it were a methodology, more or less, and by the ways in which Derrida has responded to 'deconstruction's' institutionalization or its being placed in what he has called the 'family atmosphere'.

In the conclusion to this chapter, I want to turn to Derrida's own comments on 'deconstruction' as he responds to those who claim there is such a *thing*. Derrida has insisted on a number of occasions that there is no such *thing* as deconstruction, that it is not formalizable, that it cannot be transformed into a programme or model for the purposes of analysis and interpretation. Where Derrida has made comments on what 'deconstruction' might be, these acts of resistance on Derrida's part have emerged as specific, strategically located resistances to the idea of a deconstructive methodology. He has issued such statements from a number of varying perspectives and contexts, though specifically and for the most part in interviews and other situations where he has been called on to speak, rather than write. It is instructive to follow Derrida in these arguments.

Consider for example the following statement, one of a number of similar comments on Derrida's part:

> ... deconstruction doesn't consist in a set of theorems, axioms, tools, rules, techniques, methods.... There is no deconstruction, deconstruction has no specific object ... (*AD* 218)

Clearly, if we are to follow such a statement, if we are to acknowledge as our duty[13] our attempt to be faithful to what Derrida has said on the subject of deconstruction, then it has to be said, after such a comment, that there is no programme to 'deconstruction' which I could pretend to demonstrate to you. There is no programme, model or code which I could define which would provide you with the tools for 'deconstruction' as a theory to be applied to literature. Nor, after such a statement as the one immediately above, could I pretend to offer you a model of 'deconstructive criticism', a phrase which can be read as saying 'forget the theory, let's assume we know the method and let's just get on with the criticism, let's just talk about texts', or to put it another way, in a particularly American idiom of an insistent nature, 'let's get with the program'.

In response to such a call, Derrida has made it quite clear that the desire for a programme often comes from those who seek to pin something on Derrida, on what he does. As he says, this is 'symptomatic of certain political and institutional interests' (DO 124). In response to the question being asked directly, whether 'deconstruction can serve as a method of literary criticism', Derrida has answered:

> I am not sure that deconstruction can function as a literary *method* as such. I am wary of the idea of methods of reading. The laws of reading are determined by that particular text that is being read. This does not mean that we should simply abandon ourselves to the text, or represent and repeat it in a purely passive manner. It means that we must remain faithful, even if it implies a certain violence, to the injunctions of the text. These injunctions will differ from one text to the next so that one cannot prescribe one general method of reading. In this sense deconstruction is not a method. (DO 124)

Being faithful to a text, to any text, means resisting the temptation to impose a single *method* of reading onto all texts. If deconstruction can be said to *do* anything – and I offer this in the most tentative fashion, with an awareness of gathering together and recalling all the warnings made so far in this introduction about not imposing a method, approach or programme – it might be said to suggest that we examine, and *ask questions of,* the protocols of reading which we employ. Of key importance in the passage is Derrida's insistence on remaining faithful to the particular text being read. We cannot bring an idea of reading to a text ahead of its being read. The particularity of the text precludes the possibility of a theory or method of reading. For reasons such as this, the 'deconstructive' is that which escapes and exceeds the programme and which questions the very idea of the programme. In response to the demand to 'get with the program', deconstruction might be said to respond, 'why'? Again, if deconstruction can be said to do something, for Derrida it

> can also serve to question the presumption of certain university and cultural institutions to act as the sole or privileged transmitters of meaning. In short, deconstruction not only teaches us to read litera-ture more thoroughly by attending to it *as language*, as the produc-tion of meaning through *différance* and dissemination, through a complex play of signifying traces; it also enables us to interrogate the covert philosophical and political presuppositions of institutional-ized critical methods which generally govern our reading of a text.... It is not a question of calling for the destruction of such institutions, but rather of making us aware of what we are in fact doing when we are subscribing to this or that institutional way of reading. (DO 125)

The necessity of reading, perhaps as that which the singularity of any text can teach us, is the very idea of a resistance to the programme, to programmaticity in general; deconstruction might then be said to be that resistance which affirms the textual. At the same time as resisting the programme, however, I am going to attempt to introduce you to a small amount of the thought and work of Jacques Derrida as a way of suggesting what reading and writing imposes on us, rather than exploring what we can impose upon reading. Even as I am borrowing these statements of Derrida's to help illuminate the resistance to methodology, so I shall be borrowing elsewhere to illustrate Derrida writing on particular topics, and in order to try to imagine how we might read and write after Derrida.

The statement above which insists on resistance, and resists getting on with the programme by suggesting that there is no programme – at least with regard to 'deconstruction' – to get on with in the first place is only a more recent reiteration of similar comments. As Derrida has insisted, what has been called 'deconstruction' is 'neither an *analysis* nor a *critique*'.

> All the same, and in spite of appearances, deconstruction is neither an *analysis* nor a *critique*.... It is not an analysis in particular because

the dismantling of a structure is not a regression toward a *simple element,* toward an *indissoluble origin.* These values, like that of analysis, are themselves philosophemes subject to deconstruction. No more is it a critique, in a general sense or in a Kantian sense....   I would say the same about *method.* Deconstruction is not a method and cannot be transformed into one.... It is true that in certain circles (university or cultural, especially in the United States) the technical and methodological 'metaphor' that seems necessarily attached to the very word 'deconstruction' has been able to seduce or lead astray. Hence the debate that has developed in these circles: Can deconstruction become a methodology for reading and for interpretation? Can it thus let itself be reappropriated and domesticated by academic institutions?

[...]

It must also be made clear that deconstruction is not even an *act* or an *operation.* Not only because there would be something 'passive' about it.... Not only because it does not return to an individual or collective *subject* who would take the initiative and apply it to an object, a text, a theme, etc. Deconstruction takes place, it is an event that does not await the deliberation, consciousness, or organization of a subject ...

[...]

The word 'deconstruction,' like all other words, acquires its value from its inscription in a chain of possible substitutions, in what is too blithely called a 'context.' ... the word has interest only within a certain context, where it replaces and lets itself be determined by such other words as 'écriture,' 'trace,' 'différance,' 'supplement,' 'hymen,' 'pharmakon,' 'marge,' 'entame,' 'parergon,' etc. (LJF 273–5)

Although this passage is taken from a very short piece, a letter on the subject of translation (what might be called one of several key topics in Derrida's writing) in general and the translation of the term 'deconstruction' in particular, it is, nonetheless, perhaps one of Derrida's most important statements on what deconstruction is or is not. This statement is important because, like the previous comment, it forms a critique of and challenge to what passes as 'deconstruction' or deconstructive criticism (or the even cruder terms, 'deconstructionism' and 'deconstructivism'). It even challenges those who would teach 'deconstruction' as a method or theory of criticism. In doing so, it argues for an understanding of the highly provisional and interchangeable nature of the word. The word is interchangeable in a range of contexts and as part of larger statements because it, like the other words Derrida mentions, has the possibility of positioning within a statement a certain semantic ambiguity which makes a single meaning undecidable. None of the terms are reducible to definitions of an either/or variety. And also, equally importantly, none of the words await the arrival of a consciousness to put their ambiguity into operation; they are all traced by the possibility of their own disarticulation.

This precondition of the term deconstruction as one possible term among many, makes it impossible to hijack the term for a particular purpose. As Derrida goes on in the same piece, '[a]ll sentences of the type "deconstruction is X" or "deconstruction is not X" *a priori* miss the point, which is to say that they are at least false' (LJF 275). This is precisely because the word carries within it its own 'deconstruction', its own possible semantic contradiction. Given this condition, it is hard to imagine the ways in which such a term can be roughly handled so as to transform it into a technical metaphor for reading. The very idea of methodology is difficult to conceive, if one pays close enough attention both to Derrida's own statements and to the nuances of terms such as 'deconstruction'. We can see from the extended quotation above – and I would refer you to all of 'Letter to a Japanese Friend' as a possible starting point for reading Derrida carefully – that the very idea of 'reading deconstructively' is an impossibility as a proposal for a general act of reading, or as an example of the application of a theory called 'deconstruction'.

Derrida has never claimed to have 'proposed a general reading of' some of the various literary texts on which he has commented (*AL* 62). He has explored certain words, phrases, grammatical constructs and tropes (among many other things). But he has never offered a commentary on an entire text which could then be abstracted and rendered as a theory for reading in general. This is why there is no discernible method in Derrida's work, despite the claims for deconstruction. In talking of his essays on Maurice Blanchot, Paul Celan and James Joyce, Derrida describes his act of writing on a text as a response or transaction (as already mentioned above) to some particular textual moment which forces itself on his attention (*AL* 62). However, he goes on to say that if his transactions should 'provoke other *singular readings*, I should be delighted' (*AL* 62; emphases added). Derrida is here not ruling out the possibility of an act of reading inspired by his own efforts; but it is important to acknowledge the idea of the singular reading, of singularity in reading. The purpose of this book is to introduce the reader to a certain Jacques Derrida, and certain writings signed by the name 'Jacques Derrida', which, it is to be hoped, will provoke other singular readings.

For Derrida, each act of reading should be in its approaches and mode of comprehension absolutely singular and therefore not reducible to an economy of reading which could then be practised on any number of texts in the same predictable manner. This has already emerged above, but given the misunderstandings which have abounded around 'deconstruction' in the past, you can't be too careful. Indeed, you can't be careful enough. When we write on a text, about some aspect of a text, we should be guided by the contours of that text, and by what the text dictates to us, as Derrida has already been quoted as saying. The idea of a 'theory' of reading precludes such a possibility, and dictates to us a programme of interpretation wherein the questions we ask of any text are already determined ahead of the game.

Derrida has further distanced himself from the very idea of generalizable readings, when talking on the subject of 'deconstruction' in America. In a conference keynote address entitled 'The Time is Out of Joint', Derrida has made a number of important distinguishing comments with regard to his relationship to 'deconstruction'. He begins by calling into question the relationship assumed by others to exist between 'Jacques Derrida' and the institutional practice called 'deconstruction':

> I have never claimed to identify myself with what may be designated by this name [deconstruction]. It has always seemed strange to me, it has always left me cold. Moreover, I have never stopped having doubts about the very identity of what is referred to by such a nickname. (TOJ 15)

Derrida not only places himself at a remove from what is called 'deconstruction'; he also calls into question that which calls itself and gets called from other places (such as, for example, media representations or critical works which supposedly address 'literary theory' either positively or negatively).

Further on in his address, Derrida has occasion to address the possibly hesitant definition of 'deconstruction' in contradistinction to those very definitions which seek to assume for deconstruction the identity of a discernible field, practice, discipline, methodology or programme:

> I have often had occasion to define deconstruction as that which is – far from a theory, a school, a method, even a discourse, *still less a technique that can be appropriated* – at bottom *what happens or comes to pass* [ce qui arrive]. (TOJ 17; first emphasis added)

Nothing can be clearer perhaps than this denial of all which some have claimed deconstruction to be. For Derrida, deconstruction can only be defined as a chance occurrence. Yet there is still the sense, *pace* Derrida, that for some 'deconstruction' is some *thing*. Derrida defines this as an act of translation: 'Deconstruction, as we know it, will have been first of all a translation or a transference between French and American' (TOJ 27).

Thus deconstruction becomes some *thing* only in not being, but in being made other than what it may have been, always translated, transformed or deformed into some *thing*, some other identity. Yet it is precisely because of this possibility of its 'translativity', Derrida suggests, which 'destines deconstruction to erring and voyage' (TOJ 28). All of which leaves Derrida to ask questions and make suppositions concerning the fortunes of this very old French word:

> Is there an irreplaceable place and a proper history for this thing, deconstruction? Is there anything else in it but transference in all the senses this word assumes in more than one language and first of all in the sense of transference among languages?
> [...]
> Perhaps deconstruction has never done anything but ... interpret interpretation. (TOJ 28, 29)

Derrida resists the technicizing impulse which has so plagued the fortunes of 'deconstruction' in its translation from French into American-English of a particular, institutional, academic variety. In this talk, he claims an activity for deconstruction, but one which is installed in language, across languages, rather than one which can be extracted at some theoretical level and then imposed elsewhere. This installation, this chance – the very chance, arguably, which the word 'deconstruction' has undergone in having been transformed into a concept or general principle – is within language itself as the necessity which makes language open to comprehension but also, inevitably, open to mistranslation.

What then might deconstruction be said to be, if anything? Derrida imagines, in a tentative expression, that

> ... perhaps deconstruction would consist, if at least it did consist, in ... deconstructing, dislocating, displacing, disarticulating, disjointing, putting 'out of joint' the authority of the 'is'. (TOJ 25)

Deconstruction, were it to exist, would not be some *thing*, but, assuming its possibility, would be that which consisted in the possibility of undermining the confidence behind that which makes possible the assertion of some *thing*. Derrida cites the word 'is'. In any statement 'is' implies and authorizes a self-sufficient identity for the reader. It is a word which commands and directs the attention of the reader, while diverting attention away from itself. It acts as a sign of definition, determination, equation and the elision of difference. It is a sign of the impossible: the full translation without loss or residue. 'Is' is the sign that covers over the movement in writing of writing or, to use Derrida's term, *différance*. (This is discussed further in Chapter 2.) As an example of the operation of 'is' and the authority it attempts to convey, consider the following example, a comment on what deconstruction 'is' from an essay by Christopher Norris (you'll also no doubt recall J. Hillis Miller's commentary on statements such as 'deconstruction is ...'):

> To 'deconstruct' a text *is* to draw out conflicting logics of sense and implication, with the object of showing that the text never exactly means what it says or says what it means. (Norris 1988, 7; emphasis added)

Look at and read the way in which 'is' is the keystone or linchpin in the statement, a typical definition of deconstruction as a critical practice (*pace* Norris's own statements to which we referred earlier). 'Is' works in a number of ways. It implies an equivalence between the two statements on either side of it. One side apparently says the same thing, more or less, as though 'is' were, in this case, either a mirror offering a reflection, or a conduit whereby the meaning of 'To "deconstruct"' is passed through 'is' so that the reader understands what it is, to deconstruct a text. This suggests that, somehow, the first statement is inadequate, partially untranslatable; it requires a certain critical activity implied by the 'is' to make the statement function. In this way, all that follows 'is' slides over the first phrase, partially erasing it but allowing enough of it to show through, so that we always assume elision to equal equivalence.

However, if we return to Derrida's highly provisional and wary statement concerning what deconstruction could be – not what it *is* – as the movement of disjointing, as that which is within the structure which refuses or resists the authority of 'is', we see how Norris's statement is itself not itself, but disarticulated in the very attempt to articulate the definition, and so control the meaning of deconstruction. Norris's definition finds itself undone. The second, post–'is' part of the sentence translates and amplifies the first part, so that deconstruction is forced to become 'deconstruction is'. Deconstruction is thus pinned down, made orderly and proper, transformed into a proper name for some activity which it is the work of the second part of the sentence to state plainly. Yet this plain statement, in its effort to articulate 'deconstruction' from its logic of equivalence, and making that which is different and in other words seem the same, misunderstands deconstruction. In so doing, it renders deconstruction as a practice determined in its activities by that consciousness which 'draws out' the inequivalence between saying what we mean and meaning what we say. Yet, the sentence is marked by the very nonequivalence which the authority of 'is' seeks to eradicate.

Thus Norris's commentary is marked internally by the movement of deconstruction precisely at that point where it can be read as attempting to calm down the deconstructive. To make this point more clearly, if this is possible, I, as a critic and reader, am not practising a deconstruction of the statement which begins Christopher Norris's essay, even though some might suggest that this is *exactly* what I am doing. Instead, I am observing the dislocating of which Derrida has spoken; the dislocation of a desired meaning by the very event of trying to articulate that meaning. This dislocation is what Derrida has termed on occasion 'deconstruction' (one among many other terms which are not his and which he has not coined or invented). But this is not to reduce what I have just said to the statement: 'dislocation is deconstruction'. The only way I could write such a statement would be to place the 'is' *sous rature*, or under erasure, a practice adopted by Derrida in *Of Grammatology* from Martin Heidegger. Placing the word under erasure would mean writing the word and then placing a cross over it, while keeping the word visible, so: dislocation)✕(deconstruction. The purpose in so doing is to signal that the function of the term placed under erasure is exhausted, it can no longer be taken to function as it should. This, however, is only a momentary strategic gesture and not one to be assumed as part of a Derridean practice in any general sense. Were we to do so, we would be elevating the gesture to the level of a principle, beginning to turn Derrida into a methodology, the very activity against which I have argued throughout this introduction. The X which erases and leaves visible the 'is' marks the resistance to methodology, and we should not mistake it for methodology itself. Saying 'dislocation)✕(deconstruction' and imitating for the moment the gesture of *sous rature* (an unacknowledged and improper quotation, if you will) in the middle of the statement, is nothing other than writing: dislocation.

Dislocation thus dislocates, disarticulates the very possibility of statements which begin with 'deconstruction is'. In doing so, dislocation stresses that 'deconstruction cannot be "theoretical", beginning with its very principle. It is not limited to concepts, to thought content, or to discourses' (*P*... 28). Or, as Derrida has pointed out, parenthetically (almost *en passant*, as it were, as if not to have to insist on what is already exhausted):

> ... (but deconstruction is not a critical operation; it takes critique as its object; deconstruction, at one moment or another, always aims at the trust confided in the critical, critico-theoretical agency, that is the deciding agency, the ultimate possibility of the decidable; deconstruction is a deconstruction of critical dogmatics). (*P*... 54)

In giving us to understand such issues, Derrida complicates in advance any effort to read in a particularly delimited or systematic fashion. This is because deconstruction may be seen as a process of radical questioning which occurs as the possible articulation of any language, prior to, and without the necessity of a subject. Questions which we can ask as subjects of language, as subject to the workings of language and concepts, such questions are always predicated on the functioning of a system which relies on the opening of the system through the question and the closing of the system through the answer. Opening the system by questioning we have already, as the condition of this *incipit*, closed the system. However, deconstruction, as a radical questioning, allows for 'a reflection on the system, on the closure and opening of the system' (*P*... 212).

Thus the question which it asks is not predicated on an answer. Such predication, such spacing and movement between question *and* answer, is the opening and closing of systematicity itself, which deconstruction makes available for questioning. Rather, the question asked, its answer is affirmed in itself as not-itself. Deconstruction, if such a thing exists, imagines, makes possible the imagination of, not the unanswerable question, but the question as answer, as that movement which '*inscribes* contradictions' (*D* 6 n.8), and which 'disorganizes "historically," "practically," textually, the opposition or the difference (the static distinction) between opposing terms' (*D* 7). And that answer is the response we are obliged to make to the other. Derrida has done nothing other than seek ways in which to respond to the other, and to prepare for the arrival of the other in so many unexpected ways; for this reason, if for no other, Jacques Derrida's writing is not reducible to a methodology or a programme of reading. Instead he raises the stakes for the reader. As Derrida can teach us, we cannot be prepared to read, we can only hope to read in as singular and unprepared a way as it is possible to imagine.

2 Preparatory to Anything Else: Derrida's Interests

> ... the possibility of this repetition is the very thing that interests me ... and I should like slowly to move closer ... slowly to bring myself closer to this, namely that I can no longer formalize, since the event ... will have precisely defied within language ... this power of formalization.
>
> Jacques Derrida (ATVM 12)

The writing of identities • identities of writing

This chapter sets out to explore in a very limited fashion a number of interests in Derrida's writing, interests such as writing, the proper name, the signature, the gift, the hymen. In considering these interests, and in beginning to unfold and trace Derrida's thinking on the subjects in question, we will have recourse to a series of returns, so that the chapter will fold back on itself, reiterating ideas, concerns and themes.

One of the most insistent interests in Derrida's writings is the subject of identity.[1] Derrida repeatedly asks questions concerning identity and the (written) structures which inform and perform an identity, whether these are the structures of what we too hastily describe as a literary text or the human subject. Derrida interests himself repeatedly, and in a range of varying broadly philosophical contexts and discursive-political-cultural structures, with the nature of how identities come to be formed, how the illusion of unity or univocity is constructed and projected from a particular structure in writing, whether that writing is the immediate script on the page or, otherwise, is understood in a broader sense (as we will discuss in this section). This structure draws on concepts and philosophemes, which are themselves articulated and structured, while hiding their structurality. As Derrida points out, 'every concept ... belongs to a systematic chain and constitutes itself a system of predicates' (*LI* 21). Yet he never raises the issue of identity to the level of a concept itself, if only because identity is always being formed in countless ways, dependant on what is blithely called 'context'. Identity is never known until perceived in a particular form (see Derrida's essay 'Khōra'). There can be no concept of identity which we can put in place ahead of our encounter with a specific identity. Identity is then never identical with itself. What is interesting to note is that, whether the issue of identity is one related in Derrida's texts either more ostensibly to the literary or to the subject of Being in its more overtly philosophical milieu (and as we shall go on to show, the literary and the philosophical are themselves not discrete identities, but complexly contaminated by one another), the question of identity is always shown to be fraught with paradoxes, contradictions and other disjointing movements which make the unity of identity impossible. That which is named deconstruction within a field of forces is the location of the paradoxical or contradictory, and provides the 'means of *intervening* in the field of oppositions' (*LI* 21) by showing the articulation concealed within the supposed unified presence. We come to understand that identity, in whatever form, is always already doubled, within its own constitution, and as a necessity of its own performance.

Think, for the moment, of the identity you as readers construct from these words. You may come to find these words here – *where?* – on the page. Wherever this is or will be is, in all likelihood, where I am not present. After my death, these words will remain, will be a trace of what remains of me in my absence. Yet they will still be potentially readable. As Derrida suggests, the 'possibility of the sign is this relationship with death' (*SP* 54). Words, signs, graphic marks or traces are always readable in my absence. The possibility of their being read and repeated is already installed in them *as graphic marks*, and this possibility is not a condition of the presence of either an author or an audience. As such, they are open to interpretation, translation, analysis and questioning in ways which I can neither foresee nor limit; ways in which I cannot control or predict. Thus my identity, an identity constructed not only by myself but also partly by my reader, will come to be formed in my absence, in ways which are unpredictable. This is understandable in the figure of a written signature, that sign which is supposedly unique to me and which apparently signals me as its signified in some equally supposedly stable signifier/signified binarism. Yet, '[b]y definition', writes Derrida, 'a written signature implies the actual or empirical nonpresence of the signer' (*LI* 20). Whether I am present or not, alive or not, there is always the possibility of my signature being read, being repeated, independently of me. Indeed, despite its supposed uniqueness, in order for the signature to function at all, it must be repeatable: 'In order to function, that is to be readable, a signature must have a repeatable, iterable, imitatable form; it must be able to be detached from the present and singular intention of its production' (*LI* 20).

The signature operates then in a manner particular to all forms of writing (this operation erasing its singularity), all acts of signification. We will return to the question of the signature and the proper name further on; but for now, we can suggest that writing determines and unveils the structure of what I call my identity, and figures my identity as always already written and in a certain relationship to the trace, even ahead of 'my' death, what I call 'my death', which is inscribed in these very words in a certain manner. These remarks (and the ideas which make them possible), in which you find yourselves immersed, are undergoing a process of articulation, iteration, even as I write 'of' those self-same ideas. They are rearticulated and translated in your acts of reading and writing. My ideas are coming from some other place which is not reducible – either by myself or by you – to a single source or origin; or even knowable location. Even what I call my discourse is being read by you, which places 'me' in the position of the other. 'I' is placed in a position I do not know. My identity is thus doubled already, anticipated and performed in the act of writing which always acknowledges my absence, my otherness, and my eventual disappearance. It acknowledges a structural relationship which dismantles the notions of unity and presence through the possibility of repetition, which is itself the figure of structure and articulation. Such repetition leaves open the potential for translation and interpretation. Far from communicating, writing, suggests Derrida, 'is not the means of transference of meaning, the exchange of intentions and meanings…. [Writing exceeds or splits] the semantic horizon that habitually governs the notion of communication…. [Writing is] a *dissemination* irreducible to *polysemy*. Writing is read; it is not the site "in the last instance" of … the decoding of a meaning or truth' (*LI*

20–1). Writing is not the place where truth lies, that place from which a final meaning is generated. Because of the very structural and graphic nature of writing, there can never be a simple, unproblematized 'communication' (as we shall see in Chapter 5, in the reading of Joseph Conrad's *Heart of Darkness*). Indeed, it is in the act of reiteration that the 'semantic horizon' becomes destabilized.

Here, though, is situated a problem which has haunted Derrida's writing from its earliest translation, even as it is the problem which demonstrates the points made by Derrida concerning the possible functioning of writing. In challenging the possibility of writing's unequivocal communicative potential, Derrida has been taken, particularly in the United States in the 1970s and early 1980s, as having suggested that, once one acknowledged the disseminative nature of writing, one was free to interpret the text as one wished. The text was open to complete freeplay and undecidability, and to endless readings. In *Limited Inc.* Derrida responds to such accusations concerning the perceived work of deconstruction: 'I never spoke of "complete freeplay or undecidability" … Greatly overestimated in my texts in the United States, this notion of "freeplay" is an inadequate translation of the lexical network connected to the word *jeu*' (*LI* 115–16). The meanings of *jeu* are numerous. There is, obviously, play, in several senses, such as performance, game, acting, the opposite to work, although in the translation and, more importantly, the reading of Derrida (especially amongst detractors), 'play' only ever has seemed to signify 'freeplay' and the notion that one can read how and as one wishes, that words can mean anything you want them to mean. Such a translation no doubt calms down the disjointing of the identity of 'play' which, in French, is installed within the very inscription of the word every time it is written or read, repeated or reiterated; this is the chance the word, and by extension Derrida's work, undergoes in its translation and subsequent domestication within the Anglophone academic world.

Yet *jeu* also signifies gambling or gambit, a stake, certain strategic gestures or risks. Moreover, *jeu* also suggests the English 'torque', already used in this book, signifying articulation, the 'play' within a system or structure which makes the structure as structure possible. In particular contexts, within certain phrases, *jeu* can be taken to signify 'hand', as in *montrer son jeu*, to show one's hand. There are numerous other uses of the term, which we haven't the time to go into here, except to suggest that, in a certain way, *jeu* is a deconstructive term *par excellence*, playing as it does in itself, disjointing, disarticulating its own identity within its very inscription. Play, we might say, plays with play, playfully. Play plays its own gambit in staking everything on articulation and the possibility of its being remarked. Play plays with its own identity in its inscription, raising the stakes. That Derrida's use of the word has been in many ways overlooked, while in other ways overestimated, suggests a lack of give and take, a lack of play on the part of certain commentators as they seek desperately for meaning, for truth, for identity, mistaking the 'play' in writing, of writing, for its semantic horizon. This is not to suggest of course, and following Derrida's comment above, that there is endless play. This is certainly not the case. As the example of French can show us, the play of 'play' is always limited, determined. The reading of writing's play is always subject to a field of forces or oppositions which are not merely part of the writer or reader, but subject to a certain torque between positions, between identities, dependent on what we call historical, cultural, institutional, political, ideological, philosophical, contexts. But this has been ignored in certain cases.

... writing ...

'Writing' is clearly an important figure in Derrida's thinking (Db 42–64), and it is worth bearing in mind what Derrida means by the term. As we've already begun to explore in the introduction to this chapter, he has a far broader definition of the term in mind than the conventional interpretation, meaning the script produced by the hand on paper or some other similar substance. For Derrida, 'writing' is a metaphor, a figure which names, in the words of Gayatri Spivak, 'an entire structure of investigation, not merely ... "writing in the narrow sense," graphic notation on tangible material' (Spivak, 'Translator's Preface' in *Of Grammatology* [G ix–lxxxix]). Spivak, in providing a summary of Derrida's argument in *Of Grammatology*, points out that Derrida is not merely opposing writing to speech, in the process of reversing a binary opposition (Speech/Writing), so as to give precedence to a term which is traditionally considered in our thought to have a secondary role, while speech is then relegated from its important role to a secondary position.[2] This requires a brief explanation involving a provisional definition of what is taken to be 'deconstruction' (as a technique or methodology) and why this is a misrecognition of Derrida's processes of reading.

In Derrida's earlier writings, there was discerned a process of identifying binary oppositions (figures such as Good/Bad, Day/Night, Man/Woman, Speech/Writing, Reason/Madness, Truth/Falsehood, and so on) which are important conceptual pairings in the history of Western philosophy or that branch of philosophy which is identified as metaphysics (this belongs also, more or less directly, to Derrida's critique of linguist Ferdinand de Saussure in his course on structural linguistics). For Derrida, the reason for identifying such apparent oppositions is to show how, despite the fact that the terms are supposed to be equal pairs, in our thought, the first, or left-hand term, is always given greater value or priority than the second term, which, concomitantly, is assumed inferior. Furthermore, in the history of our thought, all the prior terms are used as substitutes for one another in the proof of some absolute Truth. This privileging and substitution Derrida terms logocentrism.[3] In observing this reiterated structure in Western thought, and in observing how the value of the terms was uneven and hierarchical, Derrida also noticed that the first term was always in some manner related to the natural, the organic, the seminal, and other senses of centre, origin, essence, source and so on; all such terms hide the fact that they are structured by other thoughts, ideas, concepts, *structures*. There is no original term or concept which is not in turn constructed by other ideas, as I have already said; there is no original term which does not in fact operate as a metaphor for, or which can be substituted, supplemented for, other similar terms. Further, the oppositional values or terms are only apparently oppositional; one term always informs and serves to determine the other, each term being contaminated by the imminence of the other within its identity. As Derrida says in an interview, 'it is impossible to reduce the couple outside/inside as a simple structure of opposition. This couple is an effect of *différance*...' (*P*... 33; for further discussion of the term *différance* see below). All concepts perform as writing, as writing effects or structures, their meanings articulated on the basis of their difference from other terms and concepts. Once we recognize these ideas, we can then see how all terms are part of structures, and how all terms prove the structure (or structurality) of structure.

One of Derrida's suggestions was that the reader might invert the binary opposition, placing the secondary term in the place of the primary term, and vice versa, and, in so doing, see how such an initial inversion or displacement revealed structure and relationship, showing how the meaning of any term is only produced by its difference from other terms (that is to say how meaning is not inherent in the term); and how there was no absolute centre which was not also, already, a supplement itself. It is this process, of first identifying binary oppositions and then inverting them in order to reveal how a text is structured through the privileging of certain metaphors over others, which has come to be known as 'deconstruction'. What is in fact merely a passing strategy at a certain time in Derrida's acts of reading has become the basis for a certain methodology which, at the extreme, has been used to suggest how, because meaning is not fixed, all textuality is infinitely interpretable, and all texts are composed of an endless freeplay of meanings (already discussed in relation to the term *jeu*/play).[4]

As Spivak points out, 'writing' is a key figure in Derrida's writing (certainly his earlier texts), but as a figure which announces structure, and not merely as the opposition to speech. Writing once again, says Spivak, is a 'broader concept than the empirical concept of writing' (*G* xxxix). Writing becomes a term for Derrida (and for which he owes Freud, amongst others, an enormous debt, which he has always acknowledged) which announces both the structured ('written') condition of all forms of text, including human identity, and also the idea that all such writings are never completely logically coherent or homogeneous, but are in some way marked or traced by what we term alterity or otherness: moments which subvert, contradict the logic, figures, traces, conceptualizations for which we cannot account, which our reading cannot make fit in with the overall structure, and which, because of their heterogeneous nature, announce the structure they inhabit *as* structure. But once more, it is important to insist that the term 'writing' not be given a central importance, any more than the term 'deconstruction', or, indeed, any other term which we will refer to as having been used by Derrida. As Spivak cautions us, Derrida 'does not hold on to a single conceptual master-word very long ... such important words ... do not remain consistently important conceptual master-words in subsequent texts' (lxxi). Such words are not 'congealed', to use Spivak's term, but remain constantly on the move, their definition being altered by their subsequent use in various, different contexts. And it is for this reason, if for no other (although there are others too numerous to go into here, each requiring a rigorous analysis in their own right), that we should not accord 'deconstruction' a privileged place. This refusal of privilege on Derrida's part is actually a performance, as well as a demonstration of how writing is structural, and how meaning is not fixed but is always provisional, always a condition of *différance*.

This is another term, worth referring to at this point, itself related to 'writing' and 'deconstruction', and used by Derrida in his early writings. This is another neologism, this time in French. Clearly this term bears a resemblance to the English word 'difference' and the French 'différence'. (It is already a question of a certain 'play' that we read both French and English in a 'single' phrase.) But you will notice that Derrida's neologism is spelt with an 'a'. However, this is silent, and, in French at least, 'différance' sounds no different from 'différence'. Derrida coined the term for several reasons, amongst these being a critique of structuralism and Saussurean linguistics, which had always privileged voice over writing in the study of the structural production of meaning. The silence of the written 'a' and its phonic 'in-difference' to its conventional counterpart are, for Derrida, a demonstration of the alterity that always inhabits and haunts writing. But this is no mere pun or word-play for Derrida, for his neologism combines the possible writing of two concepts, these being deferment and differentiation, both of which are implied in Derrida's term, and performed for him in the silent 'a'. The first implies a temporal displacement, while the second announces a spatialization; which two ideas, temporality and spacing, are key in Derrida's understanding of writing as a notion incorporating a recognition of structurality, and the differences which articulate it.

But what to do once we recognize structures? How do we dismantle them? Spivak, in illuminating the difference between Derrida's approach to reading and traditional methods, states that '[t]raditional textual interpretation founds itself on ... [the] understanding of metaphor [as] a detour [or path] to truth' (lxxiv). Derrida's performances dismantle 'metaphysical and rhetorical structures which are at work, not in order to reject or discard them, but to reinscribe them in another way' (Derrida cit. Spivak, *G* lxxv). Words, metaphors, Spivak points out, operate not as keys which unlock the way to truth (yet another reason why we should not trust a single term such as 'deconstruction'), but as levers which, in being jiggled, loosen up the text enough to show it not harbouring the absolute truth at all, but being merely a structure which in various ways produces various meanings which we mistake for the truth. As Spivak suggests, if words or metaphors in texts seem to harbour unresolvable contradictions or suppress implications, we should grab hold of those words and metaphors, following their workings in order to 'see the text come undone as a structure of concealment' (lxxv).

What the textual structure of concealment conceals is its structurality, the possibility of its reiteration and the 'play' (in all its senses) of *différance*, which is a condition of writing. Thus we return to the question of the 'primordial structure of repetition' already mentioned earlier (*SP* 57). In considering this, Derrida expands the notion of writing to include the writing, the written-ness, of the subject's identity. He says:

> ... the primordial structure of repetition ... must govern all acts of signification. The subject cannot speak without giving himself a representation of his speaking.... we can no more imagine effective speech without there being self-representation than we can imagine a representation of speech without there being effective speech.... speech represents itself; it *is* its representation. Even better, speech is the representation of itself. (*SP* 57)

I understand myself to exist and to be present when I speak. Speech creates the illusion of presence and plenitude, while the graphic mark of writing is suggestive of absence, delay, deferral, by the fact that its mark is both iterable and not the sign of presence. I hear myself speak, whether in my thoughts, or when speaking to others. I therefore believe my presence to be self-signifying in the act of speech, which is, I assume, an act of presentation. My speech is an act, though, not of presentation, but of *re*presentation: I *re*present myself to myself through articulation and enunciation, both of which are marked – or, rather, *re*marked – spatially and temporally. Precisely because the speaking subject – I – does represent itself to itself, because the fundamental or 'primordial' structure behind *re*presentation lies in that emphasized prefix, identity is always marked, not by unity or presence, homogeneity or plenitude (which are the illusions fostered by the idea of full speech), but by the spacing and deferral which are the conditions of all writing. *Re*presentation, *re*iteration, *re*petition. These movements or structures are what make possible all acts of signification. Speech is therefore a writing, it operates precisely as the written act does. 'I' am therefore written. Being is a writing. For there to be the possibility of signification, there must be the movement of difference – or *différance*, as that mute 'a' articulates – and, as Derrida informs us, 'language is properly the medium for this play of presence and absence' (*SP* 10). My identity is only comprehensible in its self-difference, in its being marked by difference from and within itself. The presentation of the self to the self – and to others – is always that representation marked by the movement of difference. The truth or presence of the subject is not revealed at all. What comes to be revealed is the writing which marks and is traced in textuality, speech, the subject. The notions of presence, truth or meaning rely on structures of concealment and the concealing of their *written* structures. As Derrida suggests in *Writing and Difference*, 'writing will never be simple "voice-painting" (Voltaire). It creates meaning by enregistering it, by entrusting it to an engraving, a groove, a relief, to a surface whose essential characteristic is to be infinitely transmissible' (*WD* 12). Meaning or value are therefore never intrinsic or imminent in the written sign; they only become possible by the chance of their repres>entation. Inscription precedes meaning.

At the same time there is also involved in the written spacing and remarking a certain issue of performativity, which serves to confuse the discernment of discrete identities. As Derrida says above, 'speech is *the* representation of itself'. We can read this in a sentence from Joyce's *Ulysses*, in the first clause of the opening sentence from 'Eumaeus', the sixteenth episode of the book. The sentence reads:

> Preparatory to anything else, Mr Bloom brushed off the greater bulk of the shavings and handed Stephen the hat and ashplant and bucked him up generally in orthodox Samaritan fashion, which he very badly needed. (Joyce 1993, 569)[5]

The opening clause collapses the distinction between constative and performative utterance. In doing so, it addresses the ways in which language is supposed to work and the ways in which the written-ness of all language is open to semantic 'play'. As the first sentence of an episode, the sentence is 'preparatory to anything else'. Its place at the head of the episode marks it as a beginning of sorts, but also just one more narrative ploy with which to begin. Like all beginnings it begins and signifies the necessity of the 'make-believe of a beginning', to borrow once again George Eliot's words from *Daniel Deronda*.[6] Yet, if the opening sentence – any opening sentence – does this, if it *is* preparatory to anything else, why the need for that opening clause, which is itself preparatory to anything else, in the sentence, in the episode? In this case, the opening phrase, '[p]reparatory to anything else', breaks the illusion of unity by immediately doubling itself at the levels of both content and form. Not only this but, in doubling itself, it partially erases the semantic levels at which it is supposed to operate. It is supposed to act as an analytical comment on the details of the narrative (this is the way all third-person narrative functions); apparently, conventionally, it is meant to frame the actions of the characters and give us, as readers, a certain position from which to view the events of the narrative. The statement is supposed to be a reading. Yet a reading can only happen after the event, its condition is that it can only occur after actions have taken place. So, despite the claim that it is 'preparatory to anything else', and despite the structural placement at the beginning of the sentence, what we read is that the events have been read and the possibility of the narrative reiteration of those events is based in the self-displacing, disjointing and redoubling activity of that preparatory statement. Its 'preparatoriness' is in fact a *secondarity*. Derrida clarifies the experience of the collapse between supposedly discernible positions (or identities of writing) in *Writing and Difference* when he asks:

> … is not the experience of *secondarity* tied to the strange redoubling by means of which constituted – written – meaning presents itself as prerequisitely and simultaneously *read*: and does not meaning present itself as such at the point at which the other is found, the other who maintains both the vigil and the back-and-forth motion, the work that comes between writing and reading, making this work irreducible? Meaning is neither before nor after the act. (*WD* 11)

There is no simple identity for Joyce's opening clause as it performs its own 'back and forth' movement, its play between self and other (the give and take as the articulation of both self *and* other), its movement between analysis and performance, form and content, writing and reading, saying and said. The rhythm of Joyce's clause is a performative display of the deconstruction of a range of conceptual pairings or binary operations. The clause functions as it does precisely because *in writing* it shows how the 'conceptual order' (*LI* 21) is only operable because of the articulation of, and contamination between, supposedly separable and hierarchically orderable terms. The clause gives us to understand that the very possibility of meaning is always at risk because of the destabilizing effect at work in writing. There is no single meaning or meaning-effect, meaning-position, which we could ascribe to the clause (or, by implication, the sentence, the episode, the book, writing in general).[7] In its position, the phrase in question locates at/as the origin (while placing the concept of simple origin under erasure), secondariness, supplementarity, 'duplication, original repetition, auto-affection and *différance*' (*WD* 197); and, as Joyce's sentence economically articulates, to 'say that *différance* is originary is simultaneously to erase the myth of a present origin' (*WD* 203).

To take this point further: the operation of Joyce's sentence is exemplary in this particular instance, as its articulation banishes either simple, full meaning or presence, or that reading which would see the signifiers of writing as merely indicators of some form of presence. Because of the structural, semantic work of the clause (a work which is at work in all writing as the condition of its transmittability, its reiteration), the text can never be taken as signalling anything other than the 'weave of pure traces' (*WD* 211). 'Preparatory to anything else', writing consists of those traces which are '*always already* transcriptions', signifiers of signifiers: 'Everything begins with reproduction. Always already: repositories of a meaning which was never present' (*WD* 211). Joyce's '[p]reparatory to anything else' reproduces itself, reading itself as never quite simply present to itself as an unequivocal moment of meaning. Meaning is, then,

> already, and thoroughly, constituted by a tissue of differences, in that there is already a *text*, a network of textual referrals to *other* texts, a textual transformation in which each allegedly 'simple term' is marked by the trace of another term, the presumed interiority of meaning is already worked upon by its own exteriority.... It already differs (from itself) before any act of expression. And only on this condition can it constitute a syntagm or text. Only on this condition can it 'signify' ... there is no signification unless there is synthesis, syntagm, *différance* and text. (P 33–4)

Of course, in the history of Western thought, the condition of writing has been repeatedly repressed, according to Derrida in his readings of Plato, Rousseau and Lévi-Strauss, amongst others. This gesture has occurred repeatedly as part of the effort to locate centres or origins, figures which imply or affirm presence. Yet the signified can never be present as such; it is always spaced from the signifier (the vocalized sound and the graphic mark are never the things to which we assume they refer) (*G* 18). Writing troubles the search for origins because it is always already at a double remove from whatever is being signified: '... writing is the supplement par excellence since it marks the point where the supplement proposes itself as supplement of supplement, sign of sign' (*G* 281). The production of meaning and the concomitant production of an identity is, therefore, contingent on writing's ability to produce paradoxical effects in the act of being read. Identity is that which can only ever be produced through *différance* and the articulate movement of signification as primordial, reduplication, reiteration and representation. The *a* in *différance* announces this, even though, when heard, its doubling and disjointing remain indifferent. Yet the identity which is read as having been produced by the very structure of writing is perceived (mistakenly) as singular, unified, and sovereign. This is the same effect whether we assume that 'identity' to be (a) the particular 'meaning' we conventionally assume to be 'in' the text as its subject; or (b) the identity of a particular character who is the subject of narration; or (c) the identity of the author who, though 'extrinsic' to the text, is assumed, nonetheless, to be its subject.

We see the paradox effectively unveiled in Robert Louis Stevenson's *The Strange Case of Dr Jekyll and Mr Hyde*, where writing is shown as effecting the 'erasure of selfhood, of one's own presence' (*WD* 230). As Derrida suggests, 'we are written only as we write.... The subject of writing is a *system* of relations between strata' (*WD* 226–7). In his reading of *Jekyll and Hyde*, Stephen Arata states that the novel 'takes as its explicit theme the possibility that the self is not unique and inviolable' (Arata 1996, 51). He goes on, in the same paragraph, to reiterate a point made by a number of critics, that Stevenson is not 'sufficiently "present" in his own writings' (51), and that *Jekyll and Hyde* 'enacts the modernist "disappearance of the author"' (51). Following this, Arata offers us a brief reading concerned with demonstrating the 'dissociation of writing from selfhood' in Henry Jekyll's 'autobiographical narrative'. This is also part of the allegedly covert enactment of a 'crisis in realist writing alongside [the novel's] more overt thematizing of a crisis in bourgeois subjectivity' (52). The double-crisis (if crisis can be said to be the right word) is therefore aesthetically contextualized by Arata, who places Stevenson's text as an act of writing which performs certain gestures of modernist writing while simultaneously interpreting or reading a perceived epistemological crisis concerning subjectivity at the close of the nineteenth century. For the critic the text is readable as moving between the dualism of inside/outside, covert/overt, and it is this movement which locates the identity of the text historically. This historical-philosophical framework which the critic constructs is further re-enforced by the reference to other critical assessments of Stevenson's style by his contemporaries and near contemporaries, William Archer, George Moore and Virginia Woolf.

The construction of the frame by the critic within which to locate what Stevenson does (Stevenson's writing is a synecdoche for Stevenson in Arata's reading, another gesture connecting and reproducing the inside/outside binarism) is interesting to us inasmuch as, while Arata steps swiftly around issues of writing and identity, around the apparent identity of Stevenson's writing (or lack thereof), he resolutely avoids writing as/of identities. Indeed, as already quoted, the critic claims to observe the 'dissociation of writing from selfhood', as apparently unfolded by the text.

In response to this, we may suggest in passing that, if anything, writing is not dissociated from selfhood at all in *The Strange Case of Dr Jekyll and Mr Hyde*. Rather, selfhood is understood as a production *of* and *in* writing, in both the narrow and broad senses of that term. The title even implies a type of writing, with its self-acknowledgement of legal documentation. It claims a certain truth for itself even though, ironically, the 'evidence' of the text does nothing to produce a stable meaning or account of events. The text is comprised of several statements by different witnesses. It also offers a number of letters to the reader, which are either referred to indirectly or reproduced in the text as parts of the various narratives (the letters may be said to arrive to disrupt the stability of the narratives in which they are found). The subject of the text – which is, of course, a double subject brought together, though not unified, by the various acts of writing – is therefore unmistakably and inextricably a subject produced and performed by writing. Even 'Henry Jekyll's Full Statement of the Case' is a written statement. This is made plain in the final sentence:

> Here then, as I lay down the pen and proceed to seal up my confession, I bring the life of that unhappy Henry Jekyll to an end. (*JH*, 76)

Letting go the pen enacts both the end of the act of writing and the end of the subject. The reference to 'that unhappy Henry Jekyll' marks a certain spacing between the subject who writes and the other of the subject whose identity is expressed only through and by writing. As Steven Arata points out, 'I', the trace of the subject in writing, is particularly and strikingly unstable throughout Henry Jekyll's statement, to the extent that one cannot be sure whether 'I' means either Jekyll or Hyde. This can, of course, be read 'simply' as the duality in Jekyll's personality (or Hyde's, for that matter). This supposition would still rely, however, on notions of a stable, unique and originary identity, a centre or location which is constant. What Jekyll/Hyde's narrative (the one he/they write/s) can show us is that writing the subject involves the articulation of the other within the same and the necessary movement of difference as the possibility of any articulation and representation of both. *Jekyll and Hyde* can be read as being in the act of performing the very contingency of selfhood as an effect of *différance*, of writing. To go back to that earlier remark of Derrida's, Henry Jekyll's statement demonstrates that we are 'written only as we write.... The subject of writing is a *system* of relations between strata.'

Taking a view of *The Strange Case of Dr Jekyll and Mr Hyde* as a collection of disparate texts, we may comprehend how this is the case: the subject of the text is only performed as a result of and from the various narrative acts, as the work which goes on, ceaselessly, between the strata of writing which comprise this text in so foregrounded a fashion. No one statement or narrative assumes a central importance or greater meaning than any other. Each text constantly supplements every other, supplementarity being the very order of the text's signification. Regardless of any split personality, Henry Jekyll is always already produced as the subject of a number of competing texts, all of which focus on him as the subject of their analysis. Jekyll is thus an effect of supplementarity as the text repeatedly supplements itself (which movement serves to destabilize and disjoint any possible identity). In so doing, the text may be read as showing how each trace, each narrative is already a transcription or reading (as the term 'case' suggests). The text's movement is marked by a 'network of textual referrals to *other* texts' which no narration can stabilize. There can be no Henry Jekyll (or Edward Hyde) except as the product of conflicting forces. The subject cannot be produced unless as an effect of signification on the part of the text which works to dispel the illusion of a single presence. As the final sentence shows us, the subject is never present as such. *That* Henry Jekyll has always already disappeared into the writing which performs him and reiterates his identities.

Indeed, in the play between the various, competing texts, all of which signify each other as traces, Henry Jekyll is only ever understandable as a trace. Henry Jekyll is performed, and performs himself as double, always decentred, already other. When he writes 'He, I say – I cannot say, I' (73), he is not merely confirming that this is a narrative concerned with the crisis of the divided self. Instead, his writing performs the spacing, the remarking of the subject in writing as the subject *of* writing, that which writing produces, and that which is written. Writing one's own statement reduplicates the writing of identity, and the last sentence of the text, already quoted, is the death sentence, addressing as it does not only the question of identity's spacing but also the temporal movement of writing. In reading the supposedly present tense, 'Here then, as I lay down the pen ...', we read that there is no present, no presence. The sentence paces and temporalizes itself, inscribing in its movement the double time of anticipation of an end and, simultaneously, the reading of that end already having passed. The fact that this is readable at all points to the present of the sentence as an effect in writing rather than some exterior truth carried as the meaning of the statement. That this sentence is repeatable, that it anticipates its own ending and subsequent reiteration; that it anticipates the mortality we have already read; all of this enacts the impossibility of any unique identity, any singular statement.

... narration and text ...

The nature of Henry Jekyll's predicament over the subject of self-narration and the narration of the self as other points up, somewhat acutely, the work of spatio-temporal difference that marks the autobiographical urge of first-person narrative. The writing of identity, and its written-ness, is a profoundly textual affair. A first-person narrator constantly writes of herself as being involved in a narrative of events. The narrator observes events and engages in those events in a more or less knowing manner. Observation (analysis or critical representation) and engagement (performance) occur in different and differing places and at different, differing times. Recognition of this double practice is crucial to understanding the doubled and doubling structure of narrative in general, where one is both author and character, one who is produced by one's own narrations but who also serves the narration directly. One's identity is thus doubled, although the doubling is never a simple separation between identities. The other of the narrator is also the other within the self-same. This is complicated when the narrator acknowledges that s/he is in the act of writing, when writing is foregrounded on the page, as occurs in those statements of Henry Jekyll's, or in Charlotte Perkins Gilman's *The Yellow Wallpaper*, in which the first-person narrator narrates and writes the desire within herself to write, while writing that she is constantly forbidden to write (as though writing could release some other, uncontrollable figure[8]). Such an act and acknowledgement plays between positions of actor *in* and analyst *of* cultural ritual (*ON* 3). These positions are never clear-cut, never wholly separable; as Derrida suggests, the boundary between being actor and analyst 'appears uncertain. Always permeable' (*ON* 3). There is always a textual movement, a slippage between roles and positions which undoes the stable identities of both.

As such a doubled narrator interprets, analyses, translates, she crosses the boundary between positions in order to narrate her role *in* the narrative. She participates in the rituals she analyses. She always observes herself as never quite herself and yet as a supplement of her own identity always refigured in writing. Such positions are multiple, *textual*. In such positions one writes oneself as someone other than the self which writes; one thinks of oneself as another person, divided from one's writing self, yet somehow connected.

The narrator who comments on herself in the act of writing herself as other interjects with her own commentary. Phrases such as 'I did write for a while in spite of them ...', '... he hates to have me write a word ...', '... I haven't felt like writing ...', and '... there is nothing to hinder my writing ...', all taken from *The Yellow Wallpaper* (*YW* 4, 5), alert the reader to the double act of inscription, these being *re*presentations *in writing* of the act of writing; the subject is read as writing of herself writing. The one who writes writes of her other self, writing and proscribed from writing. Such critical, self-reflexive analysis is never merely critical observation. In *re*presenting the self, the self as other performs itself in other words, between the self who writes and the self who is represented indirectly acting, whose actions are remarked in other words in the trace of writing. The subject or narrator is thus '*nothing other than* the formation of this movement' (I:D 17 n.9). As we see in *The Yellow Wallpaper*, writing is not that produced by a living, present subject; writing produces the subject, the identity of the subject. This necessarily involves and implicates the narratorial 'voice' in both performative role-playing and narrative, textual structures. There is a question here which refuses to be resolved by terms implying some simple presence, such as 'voice' or 'narrator', or even 'subject', for, as Derrida suggests, this is very much a question of what is 'at play in the subject, while being absolutely irreducible to some subjectivity' (I:D 16 n.9). Narration, self-narration, puts into play that subjectivity which is never definable as some unified subject, even under the premise of the proper name. The subject is therefore never singular in any act of narration. At the same time, this gesture demonstrates the constant overflow of 'narrative' and 'fictive constructs', which complicate our understanding of what we call 'real life'. The figures of the fold, of the weave, and of *the place between*, – between 'fiction' and 'reality', between actor and analyst, between distance and proximity, between supposedly identifiable positions – arc implicated in the irreducible figure of the narrator. The writing of first-person narration involves narrative functions which are constantly folded onto one another. In assuming that the figure of the narrator has some stability, we construct this figure in an effort to calm down the play of the figural in language. We assume a definable identity and give that identity the shape of an extra-textual 'real' referent or signified.

Yet, as Derrida can show us through his attention to the work of the figural, we cannot assume that the sign of the narrator – 'I', in *The Yellow Wallpaper*, Henry Jekyll in *The Strange Case of Dr Jekyll and Mr Hyde*, Marlow in Conrad's *Heart of Darkness* – is in fact merely a signifier within the text for some extra-textual 'real person'. The narrator's self-referentiality, her or his nods in the direction of acts of writing and narrating, all of which references signify textuality rather than the 'real', do not allow us that luxury. The (self-)revelation of identity's written-ness through acts of inscription is always textual, always involved in the production of the text and the construction of identity as being written. What we can comprehend from the narrator-function, and what the narrator makes us aware of, through the act of 'writing the self', is the inscription of being and its necessary relationship to the subject's identity, by the determination of the subject as a written being irreducible to any single identity. This clearly observable intrusion, of the gestures and traces of writing, makes the reader aware of the written-ness of both text and subject. A narratorial voice is never a voice at all, but a weave of inscriptions and articulations.

Such acts of inscription show how texts are not merely transparent media through which the reader has direct access to either the voice or the presence of the 'author' or subject. The allusion to textuality performs the supplementarity of writing itself, which is the inescapable gesture of all writing, and not merely the most obvious instances where the 'I' who writes appears to refer to or signify the 'I' being written. The 'I' who is in the act of writing of the other is already read as a written 'I', already a performance of the textual field.

But let's return momentarily to Chapter 1, and to Derrida's insistence concerning deconstruction and what it is not. Given that so many critics want to calm down and domesticate Derrida's writing by constructing stable identities or family resemblances for deconstruction (and an equally stable subject position for Derrida), it's worth reflecting further on what Derrida says concerning 'deconstruction'. It is to be stressed yet again that Derrida insists one cannot reduce the term 'deconstruction' to being just one more metaphor, a substitute or supplement, for analysis or critique. Deconstruction does not have a stable, single identity, if only for the very reason that 'it' is not reducible to the concept of an identity. The construction of a narrated identity is dependent on the discursive contexts which change with every text; yet the effort to analyse and construct an identity is predicated on the possibility that the contexts are themselves stable and knowable. For example, as others have sought to construct deconstruction's identity, so we seek to construct the identity of Henry Jekyll as we read, although the ways in which we structure his identity are not always in our control. Our reading may be influenced by other factors of which we are not aware. Similarly 'deconstruction' is a term the appearances of which are not governable, predictable, hence Derrida's insistence that the word is not merely some substitutable technological metaphor. And the reason Derrida gives for this is equally straightforward: the terms 'analysis' and 'critique' imply processes of interpretation whereby, through techniques of reading, one arrives at the supposed essence, the truth, or meaning of a text.

In the broader picture of Derrida's writing, this is a point on which he has always insisted. Through close reading of what are conventionally defined as 'philosophical' and 'literary' texts (that is to say, belonging to particular traditions, disciplines, fields or genres the parameters of which we often accept as given), Derrida has shown how we rely on unquestioned assumptions, values or truths, or what are referred to elsewhere as philosophemes. And, Derrida elsewhere argues, philosophical figures, philosophical language, philosophemes, are always present, even in literature:

> in literature ... philosophical language is still present in some sense; but it produces and presents itself as alienated from itself, at a remove, at a distance. This distance provides the necessary free space from which to interrogate philosophy anew; and it was my preoccupation with literary texts which enabled me to discern the problematic of *writing* as one of the key factors in the deconstruction of metaphysics. (DO 109)

One of Derrida's points here is that there is no thought, idea, concept which is not constructed out of, or contaminated by, groups of other thoughts, ideas, concepts. There is no idea which is not in fact textual through and through. This is the substance of a famous, but often misunderstood, line from Derrida's *Of Grammatology*, which in the French reads: '*Il n'ya pas de hors-texte*' (*G* 158; italics in the original). Translated as 'there is nothing outside the text' (a translation admitting to the impossibility of exact, precise, true translation, whilst also acknowledging that other translations are possible), the phrase has lead to misinterpretations of Derrida's thinking, which suggest that Derrida suggests that there are nothing but texts and that there is no such thing as reality.

This is incorrect, and points at the very least to the difficulty of translation, and what is lost between languages. We may also translate the phrase as either 'there is no outside-text' or 'there is no outside-the-text'. The latter has been used as the translation in an article, where Derrida attempts to respond to the misunderstanding of the phrase, and to clarify by stating that '"there is no outside-the-text" signifies that one never accedes to a text without some relation to its contextual opening' (BSDF 841). Such a suggestion complicates our understanding of the binary relationship between text and context, similar to our thinking on the figure of inside/outside. In the same article just quoted, Derrida suggests that 'there is nothing but context' (BSDF 873), while, elsewhere, he has said, more directly, 'there are only contexts without centre or absolute meaning' (*LI* 32). To reiterate an earlier point, in this context: a problem arises conceptually around the figure 'outside', as though this referred to 'reality' with the implication of 'inside' being that of a text itself. In the sections from *Of Grammatology* entitled 'The Outside and the Inside' and 'The Outside is the Inside' (*G* 30–44, 44–65), Derrida argues that, if one comprehends the system of writing in its proper sense, one comes to understand how concepts such as 'inside' and 'outside' become, at the very least, problematized, not least for the fact that inside and outside are not strictly separable, always being connected to each other, being part of each other, as with the figure (used by Derrida) of the hymen (of which more below), which, strictly speaking, is neither simply inside nor outside the body.

A problem arises also from a misunderstanding of Derrida's use of the term 'text' (another figure for Derrida with a broader meaning than its merely conventional sense, and a term which Derrida uses alongside others such as 'writing', 'trace', 'hymen', 'différance', and so on. Texts are the 'chains, the systems of traces' emerging out of and constituted by differences (*G* 65). These chains and systems – also announced in Derrida's writing by the term 'writing' – are constructed and articulated by both temporal and spatial deferment and differentiation. 'Voice' is also textual. In metaphysical thought voice has been the guarantor of presence and, therefore, truth. However, it is also, for Derrida, a writing because voice can only operate temporally and spatially. Even in the time it takes to hear one's own voice – this hearing which announces one as both addresser and addressee, as both self and other, always already divided from one's own presumed unity of identity – presence is announced as absent, not there, because of the spacing in articulation, a spacing which is also a temporal deferring. And this is to reiterate the nature of writing, it being a fabric of traces, comprehensible *as* writing due to spatial and temporal relationships, which make the fabric (and the comprehension of the fabric) possible.

As a textual system contaminated by the traces of other discourses and languages, 'literature' permits access to the workings of 'philosophical' language because the philosophical language is not hidden away within its own discourse or discipline, pretending to some truth-value or seemingly 'natural' logical progression. Similarly, what we call literary is open to questioning from non-literary vantage points, even while the 'literary' may contaminate 'non-literary language' (as though there were something so pure). The perception on the part of the reader of what Derrida calls philosophical language in literature is a perception of the structuration of thought. It is in this recognition or perception that one can recognize those moments which are paradoxical or contradictory, where aporia open up in the structure, and which upset the logic or quasi-organic quality of the text. Thus, in looking for, and displacing the operation of, the philosopheme, one witnesses the operation of what Derrida had momentarily called 'deconstruction'. Therefore, once again, deconstruction is not a way of reading which we can control or master in order to get at the truth.

This is not to say that there are no truths, but to put it in a somewhat convoluted manner, the truth of Truth is that there is no truth; this is Truth's truth. Truths are to be understood as moments in a structure of thought, or philosophy, where the process of articulation, or questioning, critique, or analysis, comes to rest. And it is, for example, a mark of our cultural and 'historical' (a term of which Derrida has always been wary because of the metaphysical baggage it carries) positioning that we assume a concept or value to be an absolute, incontestable or natural value. Derrida has insisted that deconstruction is not some absolute, value-laden term. It is merely one term amongst many, chosen at a particular time as a French translation of the German *Destruktion* (from the writing of Martin Heidegger), which he has used as a name for an event, a movement, rhythm or gesture, a moment of non-logical problematization, whereby a text reveals its own textuality. As we have sought to show through the discussion of the textual nature of the 'narrator'-function, the structure is revealed through internal paradox, contradiction, or textile tension which dispel the illusion of truth, origin or absolute value.

But how might we demonstrate this further, and particularly in relation to a certain concept? How might we also consider further the way Derrida can inform our acts of reading and writing, even while what Derrida does can be seen to be inappropriate, not appropriable, for the purposes of transformation into a general theory of reading, through the act of interpretation?

... the gift ...

Let's take a text from 1992 by Derrida, *Given Time: I. Counterfeit Money*, which will have a certain, strategic, though limited, relevance and resonance in relation to 'Snowed Up', a short story by Richard Jefferies, a late nineteenth-century essayist and novelist.[9] This story is presented in the form of a diary, kept by a young woman, Edie Audley. The story, unfolding over a number of days, and written intermittently across the pages of a diary (the form of which we will discuss further on, with reference to Jefferies' story), tells, from Edie's perspective, how she and her father and his guests are trapped in the Audley home in London because of a snowfall which has catastrophic effects on the everyday life of the city. Not only does all business and trade dry up, but food supplies disappear also. Importantly for us, Edie has been given the gift of a fur coat by one of her father's guests. The gift is in fact part of a series of negotiations which might eventually lead Edie to be married to one of Mr Audley's guests. It is this gift which interests us here.

In *Given Time*, Derrida takes a long, close look at the concept of the gift, of what it means to give gifts, and what is involved conceptually, 'theoretically', 'philosophically', in the process of giving gifts.[10] Derrida points out that no gift-giving is ever simply that, it is never just a giving. For Derrida, implied in the act of giving a gift, implied even in the concept and logic of gift-giving, is a moment of deconstruction; which is that the concept is always problematized by another type of logic which has nothing to do with gifts, gift-giving or 'giftness'. And this 'logic' is the logic of economy, of economics. For, argues Derrida, in the act of gift-giving and in its attendant concepts, in the philosophy of the gift, there is suggested and already in place the possibility, the implication of a necessary return and of indebtedness. If I give you a gift, you feel obliged, you *are* obliged (at least in Western culture) to acknowledge that gift, to give something back to me, whether that something is another gift, or merely thanks. This obligation, says Derrida, is economic in its condition, it has a structure similar to other economic forms of exchange. And so 'the gift' is deconstructed by an inherent troubling of its own premises, by that other logic which 'contaminates' the logic of gift-giving.

In the case of Edie Audley, the gift of the furs which is announced, preparatory to anything else, in the first clause of the first sentence of the very first diary entry (Jefferies 1996, 19) is shown as the story unfolds, as the pages of the diary are filled and turned, to be clearly overdetermined by an economic network involving free trade, the government, a potentially arranged marriage, and property. This network also involves house and home, for let us not forget the etymological double root of economy and its related terms *oiko(s) + nemein*, meaning 'household' and 'to manage' or 'to control'. Edie supposedly controls or manages the household, she is supposedly in charge of the domestic economy of her father's house.

Whoever marries Edie will, however, have control of her, through the economic arrangement which is figured indirectly in the act of giving the gift of furs. The entire story 'Snowed Up' can be unfolded according to the lost semantic horizon of economy in its hidden roots. Something forgotten in the English translation is the domestic scene inscribed in 'economy', of which the Greek reminds us. And 'Snowed Up' serves to bring back to us this very scene. For all of the 'action' of this story takes place in the house, in Edie's father's house; and all the action takes place, including the act of 'gift-giving', around the economic issue of Edie, whose house she is to be installed in, whose domestic economy she is to manage, once she is married. Although 'given away' by her father as though she were a gift, Edie's 'value' is in the fact that she can be recycled, reused. She is an economical figure and the narrative is economic through and through, the gift of furs being merely a sign of this economics written otherwise.

We can see this throughout 'Snowed Up'. Despite the rhetoric of gift-giving by which Edie receives the furs, her writing reveals such rhetoric by unveiling the various local economic mechanisms, direct and oblique, involved in the event of the 'impure' gift. There are extended references in the first two days' diary-keeping to economic matters (Jefferies 1996, 19–23). These are amongst the more obvious allusions to questions of economy and to Edie's position in the network of concerns. All of the characters are introduced, the reason for the gift of the furs revealed, and the entire marriage subplot laid bare in its relation to economics, power, and the question, the secret of the household. What we come to understand from this story is the primarily economic function of gift-giving, as we've already suggested. The fur coat is paid for, effectively, by Alderman Thrigg, who is keen to marry Edie Audley. As Thrigg had had dealings with Mr Audley at the beginning of the story which resulted in the purchase of the furs, so Edie is now subject to a similar deal between the same two men, she now being the 'commodity', the 'household property', which has supplemented the furs, replaced its narrative function as that which connects marriage and economics through a gift: Edie is circulated as currency between the various male protagonists in 'Snowed Up' until, finally, she is presented as a gift for Phillip Aurelles, a young, penniless officer whose actions have saved everyone in the house from starving as a result of the snow storm. But all this can only occur once the snow has gone, for the snow had stopped all commerce, all normal routes of exchange. In fact the snow had made it possible for Edie to write, while the return to economic activity puts an end to Edie's writing. These are merely the bare bones of the gift-economy at work in the text. However, we may supplant the gift-economy structure with a figure which cannot be spoken of in terms of economic exchange, a figure which pertains to questions of writing and identity, to the writing of identity as a performance based on difference. The figure in question is that of the snow. The concept of the gift, whether embodied in the furs or Edie, is always already implicated in economic circuits, as I have just shown. Snow, on the other hand, disrupts those circuits and introduces into the text an *aneconomic*[11] figure of excess, non-exchange, supplement. The snow provides the opportunity for the suspension of trading and economic exchange and for Edie to open her diary at a blank page and begin writing in her own terms. The snow is pure gift to Edie and maintains its giftness by being a secret gift. It is the blank page which effaces the operation, albeit temporarily, of all those textual traces which traditionally figure so prominently as the dominant structural features of the English realist narrative tradition, and which can be economically signalled under the terms 'Money' and 'Marriage', for which the gift has conventionally been a ruse. The snow disrupts not merely the local discourses of the story 'Snowed Up'. It also effectively snows up, partially erases, the dominant tradition of English narrative fiction. The snow is a gift without reserve, without return, turning the blank page, making possible writing *against* literature. The snow thus shows us through its intervention the aporia in the logic of gift-giving. Edie offers no gratitude to the snow, she hates it in fact, even though it allows her the possibility of writing herself as other than the economic definition given her by the men in the story.

What we can suggest then is that the idea of the impure gift is structured in particular ways by other discourses which determine gift-giving. Paradoxically, it is snow which gives to Edie the opportunity to write and thereby reveal the various economic mechanisms and her own position within those. Edie has always already entered into such economic discourses, and acknowledges her indebtedness, albeit obliquely. She is readable as being part of the annulment of the 'giftness'; for, as Derrida puts it, '[f]or there to be a gift, *it is necessary* [*il faut*] that the donee not give back, amortize, reimburse, acquit himself, enter into a contract, and that he never have contracted a debt' (*GT* 13), and Edie has already contracted the debt. Furthermore, as soon as Edie keeps the gift as gift, then, as Derrida says, there is no more *gift* (*GT* 15). Edie has thus entered into the 'circle of debt, of exchange, or of symbolic equilibrium' (*GT* 16). On the other hand, Edie owes nothing to the snow; she owes it only to herself to write, this being the gift of snow, which is to say the gift of the blank page which has erased the history of literary authority. And the snow maintains its purity as gift because its giftness is hidden from Edie, as its secret. It is the secret gift of being snowed up that brings Edie's being into writing (as well as her writing into being). 'Snowed Up' therefore gives us to understand that there is no true 'gift' value, there is no truth to the gift within the conventional narrative. As Derrida suggests, '[t]he gift *is not*. One cannot ask "what is the gift?"' (ATVM 15).

... the proper name ...

The analysis of economics, the gift, and snow just followed is clearly not abstractable into a method of interpretation. The brief discussion of Jefferies' 'Snowed Up' relies for whatever cogency and authority it might have on a certain analysis of Derrida's, and it works by taking the logic of gift-giving as described by Derrida and looking at gift-functions in the particular instance of the text of 'Snowed Up'. But this is clearly not a methodology which one can apply to all works of literature equally. Richard Jefferies' short story makes possible a certain act of questioning in the light of Derrida's comments. It is a fruitful text for the exploration of the issues with which Derrida engages, not least because it revolves around questions of identity: the identity of the protagonist as actor and writer, the identity of literature, the identity of textual forms in general. In placing Derrida's consideration of the gift in the service of literary analysis, I no doubt run the risk of doing some violence to his thought. In attempting to transform his interest in the figure of the gift, I run the risk of betraying his thought. This is unavoidable. At the same time, however, my recourse to the thinking on the gift is itself not determined by me alone; this is dictated, as is my response, by Jefferies' text.

If I am to be faithful at all to Derrida's statements concerning the impossibility of transforming his thought into a generalized theory or programme for reading then neither can I, as I have already insisted, use Derrida's reading of 'giftness' as a general principle of analysis. Nor can I call it a deconstruction, turning the term deconstruction into a metaphor or simile for analysis, critique or method. If I have recourse to any particular term or phrase at this point, that may well be the phrase 'Derridean', as in the sense of 'Derridean thinking' or 'Derridean interpretation'. But this still suggests a particular strategy, technique or protocol for reading, for interpretation or translation as a 'theological' process in search of an origin.[12] Also this is merely to use a particular proper name as you would use an author's name such as 'Richard Jefferies', 'James Joyce', 'R.L. Stevenson', 'Charles Dickens' or whoever as a metaphoric or metonymic figure in phrases such as 'Conrad says that ...' or 'Derrida suggests ...', when, in fact, you mean that you have read and interpreted the following in a text which has been attributed to the person bearing that name.[13] The name assumes, or is assumed to have, a framing function. Its use is economical, implying a closed system and intimating a unitary presence, origin or source.

Furthermore, such phrases are not strictly accurate, inasmuch as, instead of readings where the meaning or origin was a particular truth or value (such as Reason, Logic, God), the meaning or origin has now become the person named 'Jacques Derrida' or 'Richard Jefferies'. Proper names, standing in for the absent author, announcing that absence and yet appearing to guarantee a yet-to-come, always deferred presence, serve as origins or unifying signs, economical means by which various ideas, discourses, philosophies, ideologies which come to figure in any given text are gathered together, as though the name guaranteed the meaning or truth or definable source. They suggest, in the words of Geoffrey Bennington, 'a certain passage between language and world ... indicat[ing] a concrete individual, without ambiguity, without having to pass through the circuits of meaning' (Db 104).[14]

As Bennington points out (and here we return to the brief discussion of the signature, earlier in this chapter), 'Derrida's work' demonstrates how the signature should guarantee a presence, an origin or *telos* (an end, purpose, ultimate object or aim), the end or object as origin. Thus the signature is mistaken as a teleological guarantee, a guarantee of an absolute point or presence at which our interpretation aims and with which we can close our interpretation. However, as Bennington's analysis shows, the signature, being written, carries in its inscription the trace of the absence of the author, and therefore the trace of the impossibility of absolute presence: 'Like every sign, including "I," the proper name involves the necessary possibility of functioning in my absence' (Db 148). Furthermore, the signature, the proper name, in naming the absence of the one who signs, marks the death of that person, '[i]t already bears the death of its bearer' (Db 148) because, to restate a point previously made, the signature as writing will outlive the bearer of that name.

So, to talk either of Joyce or Derrida, for example, as the origins of a text or thought misleads. To take the example of Derrida, this thought, this writing and text, which we are calling 'his', itself has a history, several histories, from Derrida's own history, his education, to the intellectual history and tradition, and the intersection of cultures out of which Derrida's work may be said to emerge. This is apparent in a more or less encrypted fashion in the trace of the other philosophers, writers, literary and philosophical discourses to which Derrida has applied. Were we to suggest as short hand the proper names or signatures Kant, Hegel, Celan, Ponge, Artaud, Valéry (see the next chapter), Socrates, Plato, Saussure, Structuralism, Freud, Psychoanalysis, Heidegger, Merleau-Ponty, Shakespeare, Marx, Husserl, we would no doubt acknowledge certain textual traces 'in Derrida', so to speak (Db 4). We could do the same with 'Snowed Up', seeking out the source of particular 'literary' or other references, the origins of the 'style', and so place the text either in Jefferies's own oeuvre or within the wider field of literature itself. The same may be said for the reading of any text. Were we to take *Jekyll and Hyde* we could no doubt attempt to discern the influences of the writings of Cesare Lombroso, Max Nordau or Havelock Ellis, all of whom wrote at the end of the nineteenth century and were concerned with issues of racial degeneration. Such theories also find their way into other texts by Richard Jefferies, as they do in Arthur Conan Doyle's *Sherlock Holmes* adventures.

But still this would not be to exhaust all the traces in either Derrida or any of the writers mentioned – even were we to study the texts being signified here. Take an example from 'Derrida's sources': 'Freud' is neither an origin nor an end in himself; the 'Freudian' text is not a point either of genesis or destination, being informed as it is by both other intellectual and cultural philosophemes from its past, the 'present' moment of its production in the late nineteenth century, and the 'future' moments of translation, in, say, Derrida's or our readings of Freud. In effect what we work towards when we seek out similarities, correspondences, and relationships that the proper name appears to guarantee for us is nothing other than a family resemblance that, in being invoked, dispels difference and asserts the self-same. Tracing the sources belongs to an effort to construct an identity which has erased from it all signs of difference, all signs of the other, all those marks which disturb and disjoint.

To go further, using the proper name in a phrase such as 'Derridean thinking' implies discernible strategies, techniques, devices for interpretation across a range of texts which are predominant in the texts signed by the name 'Jacques Derrida'. It is perhaps true that we could, reading the writings of 'Jacques Derrida', see certain features in common. We might discern a certain Levinasian strain, the influence of Maurice Blanchot, or Stéphane Mallarmé. But what of the features that are different? What of a feature which might appear in a single text, but in no other? Would we merely write such a feature off as 'marginal', not a 'dominant' theme? And, as Derrida himself has suggested, there may always be that which escapes us in our reading, in our translation or interpretation of his work, that for which we simply cannot account in any account of what we call 'his' work.

I feel that I should acknowledge at this moment that seemingly most of what I have told you so far is what you should not do, or be wary of doing, even as I have avoided the pretence of (the) beginning (of) a reading, of, for example, 'Jacques Derrida', of 'Richard Jefferies', of 'Charlotte Perkins Gilman' in these justifications. Were you to push me as to what 'kind of a reading' this will have been, if it is not a deconstruction, I might be tempted to say that, following the programme and title of one of Derrida's texts, this aspires in a very limited fashion to being a 'grammatological' reading, inasmuch as my attention is directed towards writing, text, traces, the formation of these forms and structures, and (a few of) the more or less 'philosophical' or 'conceptual' ideas which articulate those forms and structures, which help weave the fabric, the text-ile. But I'm still not happy with defining this 'reading' in this manner, because that would still be seeking to be 'true' to Derrida, and thus fall short of truth. It would still imply the possibility of imposing a programme of reading, abstracted from the example of 'Snowed Up', ahead of an encounter with another text or group of texts.

Another possible, provisional definition of this reading, a definition which marks its singularity, and yet which also acknowledges the debt to Derrida's writings, is to describe it as a 'hymenography' (*D* 213), a term which is appropriate as a description, if not an explanation, of the diary-structures of 'Snowed Up'. The same consideration may also be given to a certain extent to *The Yellow Wallpaper* by Charlotte Perkins Gilman. This analysis is limited, however. Gilman's anonymous narrator, although keeping a journal or diary of sorts, does not provide us with the clear indications of date and page which are provided in the story of Edie. The only evidence of different days and different pages in the journal-keeping activities are the blank spaces between groups of paragraphs. We may 'read' such spaces as indicative of separate acts of writing, separate diary entries, but Gilman's narrator does not offer us dates (with the exception of the mention of the Fourth of July being over).[15] Importantly, that which concerns us here is the weaving and stitching which writing effects, the pages of journals and diaries being like tissues, pieces of material or membranes, textiles woven together. The question of dates, of dating as a form of signature and the meaning of the term 'hymenography' will be made clearer in the sections which follow. For now, it serves to introduce such topics. We still must keep in mind that, as Geoffrey Bennington has announced, the only way of respecting Derrida's thought is to betray it (Db 316).

... strategic justifications (an internal *passe-partout*, of sorts)...

Many of my justifications, concerning analysis, reading Derrida, resisting deconstruction, have, so far, seemingly been involved in negating, denying, deferring, avoiding. Why?

Some may say that this is 'typical of deconstruction' (just another way of pinning something down, of presuming to identify a resemblance, and, thus, a *telos or logos*), 'the kind of thing Derrida does' or 'typical of imitators of the Derridean text'. There may be a little truth to this, in that, as Derrida is scrupulous and rigorous in trying to announce all the possibilities of a textual instance, as well as announcing some of the possible contexts within which he is writing or presenting his ideas, in order to show the structures within which thought and writing are produced, so I may be seen as also having tried to be both scrupulous and rigorous. Except that this 'introduction' does not begin to measure up to the rigour of one of Derrida's textual transactions. Nor does it pretend to; nor could such a reading be feasible in the space here.

Furthermore, if I have not set out a programme of reading, if

Derrida does not set out a programme of reading, how can it then be claimed that this is typical of something or someone, something called deconstruction, someone called Derrida. You might just as well say that it is typical of someone called James Joyce, Joseph Conrad or Richard Jefferies that he doesn't tell you the end of the story at the beginning. Granted, this – this act of writing which you are now reading – is what is called or identified as criticism, and the writers named above write what we identify as literature, but the act of criticism is essentially an act of reading, and every time something different is read, is not the only responsible act of criticism one which writes according to what has been read, responding to the call or demand made by this text which is other? Is not the question of reading one of responding to the otherness within identity, rather than imposing an identity upon a text? Or are we only interested in mastery, in control, in making things safe and comprehensible?

Again, it is true that I will have tried, am trying, to expose some of the contexts and concepts involved in Derrida's writing as well as addressing those within which this chapter is written, within which I think. Such an approach I believe I may have learned in part from what we call the texts of Jacques Derrida, but this is not to say that this is a 'deconstructive' text. Nor is this to announce a 'kind of practice', in Derrida's words (SA 9–33). As Derrida points out, if his work and thought have been ossified into a kind of practice that is immediately recognizable, then they are already dead, of no use. The chance of 'deconstruction', of a 'deconstructive mode', of 'that kind of practice' is in transformation, translation from 'the same thing each time'. Derrida argues that one should be able to recognize the process without recognizing it, by which I take it that he means that there should be certain similarities which are recognizable inasmuch as the process involves the development of a kind of ongoing internal critique. Yet the transformation should involve something not recognizable as 'deconstruction' or 'Derridean thought', which 'needs to be transformed, to move elsewhere' (SA 28–9).

So, hopefully, there will be have been that, in both the introduction and interpretation (of 'Jacques Derrida'), which betrays Derrida and which is recognizably Derridean, which transforms 'deconstruction', directing it elsewhere. It is perhaps a question of negotiating with the non-negotiable, as Derrida puts it (ATVM 17). Throughout this work, in this introduction, in the citations and the marginalia of footnotes, I have, either directly or obliquely, announced certain themes which find themselves occurring in Derrida's texts: themes such as economic structures, writing, signatures, proper names, margins and the concept of marginality, limits, boundaries, borders and frames; what constitutes such figures, how we define, say, a margin as opposed to a centre. For instance, how do we read the following?

Trieste–Zurich–Paris,
1914–1921.

The Diary ends here. It's quite possible that a lady's fright may have exaggerated matters; but it is also pretty certain that if a fall of snow four feet deep occurred in London and remained on the ground – being supplied by fresh falls – for only one week, the great city of London depending as it does upon stores brought in by rail day after day, would find itself in a very awkward position.

Richard Jefferies
Author of 'A Midnight Skate', etc.

(*Remark:* the – written – text of
this – oral – communication was
to have been addressed to the
Association of French
Speaking Societies of
Philosophy before the meeting.
Such a missive therefore had
to be signed. Which I did, and
counterfeit here. Where? There.
J.D.)

J. DERRIDA

How are we to comprehend the first extract above, which appears to conclude Joyce's *Ulysses* (Joyce 1993, 732)? How do we read the short paragraph at the end of the story by Richard Jefferies which appears to be a commentary on both Edie's diary and her personality (Jefferies 1996, 29)? Or how do we come to terms with the marginal remark of Jacques Derrida's, which comes at/after the 'end' of his essay 'Signature Event Context', which is, already, doubly removed from any 'source', given that a printed – counterfeited – reproduction of Derrida's signature occupies that space to the right of the parenthesis and above the name in capitals (*MP* 330)? Are these external margins or internal parentheses? What status do we accord them? Are they crucial or marginal in our reading? What, in short, is the authority, and what authority, as readers, do we grant to these marginal annotations, and to the signatures, 'Richard Jefferies' or 'J. Derrida/J.D.'? How are such last-minute incursions meant to be taken?

As I have stated, the questions raised by such textual marginalia find themselves announced, in different contexts and with different emphases, throughout what might be conventionally termed Derrida's oeuvre. Writing in and at margins literally figured points to that with which we should concern ourselves. Such gestures as the three immediately above trouble any neat distinction between inside/outside, word/world. They play with the notion of presence and its absence signified in the trace that is given at the textual margin. Each remarking troubles a certain identity and raises questions concerning identity or identification; each is a supplement, in excess of the conventionally understood limits of the text. Each of these gestures in writing remark and perform an act of spacing which displaces any notion of presence. Each is a graphic rem(a)inder of the difference within identity. The three broach the subject of identity by breaching the illusion of self-contained identities. Although he does not put his signature to it, Joyce's inscription performs both spatial and temporal spacing/displacement. As Derrida puts it, in talking of the frame, of framing devices and the *passe-partout*, '[n]either inside nor outside' each trace, each *trait* in its singularity, 'spaces itself without letting itself be framed but it does not stand outside the frame. It works the frame…. It situates…. *Between* the outside and the inside, between the external and the internal edge-line, the framer and the framed, the figure and the ground, form and content, signifier and signified, and *so on* for any two-faced opposition. The trait thus divides in this place where it takes place' (*TP* 11–12). Each of these devices is a performative utterance which gives us to understand that there is no real binary separation which is ever simply that. The edge of any text is worth attending to because of the ways in which it divides identity, rather than guaranteeing it. Each of these figures, figurations of the *passe-partout* (which phrase, Derrida reminds us, cannot be written in the plural; we must respect its singularity), in their singularity divide identity through an act of spacing. As Derrida puts it with regard to the signature in his critique of linguist J.L. Austin, each spacing disrupts presence through the mark, the trace, or writing, in Derrida's sense of that word (*MP* 327). That marginal figure which we assume to be both marginal and central, as though it were the signature which identifies and guarantees the unity of an identity; that figure we encounter most frequently 'in' or, more accurately 'on', 'at the edge of', the literary text – at the dividing limit or double edge – is ...

... the title (and the question of literature) ...

In this section I want to discuss the function of titles and their relation to what we call literature and the literary. The title marks a certain frame, boundary or limit (this is true as a general principle of all titles), and we should perhaps begin there, titles being, after all, a conventional starting point. Titles exist as borders between the supposed 'outside' and the 'inside' of the text, borders to which we are called but which we may never actually pass, in some senses. This is so because, throughout our reading of a text, we always have the title – which had served as an entrance point, an official recognition of the 'beginning' of a particular text as opposed to 'textuality' in general – as the horizon, the *telos* or meaning (one of several, including the author's proper name, already discussed) of the text.

Thus while we keep the title of any work in mind, our reading habitually ignores the title, the title's function. All the while we are subject to the law of the title, the law which dictates the ways in which a title will work, to which law we submit ourselves unquestioningly.[16] There are several texts by Derrida which talk about the (question of the) title, many of which are named in abbreviated form by Bennington (Db 241–58). The question of the law aside for a moment, the title, its functioning, is significantly complicated by its relationships to inside/outside binary thinking, by its very condition of being a title, as (Bennington points out) Derrida points out. The function of the title is to act as marker of the beginning of the text, as I suggest above. It is thus a marker of the outside limit of the text. At the same time, however, it is also *of* the text, if not exactly *in* the text, conventionally speaking (we certainly don't read the title as we read the body of the text; we submit the title to a different reading). It is therefore at the outer limits of the inside that is the text. Effectively, outside/inside distinctions are shown to be not as clear-cut or discrete as we had previously believed; outside and inside are shown to be connected, part of a 'hymeneal' flow (again, on the figure of the hymen in Derrida's writing and its importance to this reading, see the section of this essay entitled '... hymenography: the example of the diary ...').

Derrida's essay 'Before the Law' takes its title from a parable by Franz Kafka, also entitled 'Before the Law', which is to be found in Kafka's *The Trial*.[17] In taking the title as his own Derrida brings to our attention the laws of literature governing the use of titles, including those laws which determine the placing of titles and our understanding of the place of the title. Derrida uses this process of questioning the title as a way of raising the question 'what is literature?', a question he has constantly addressed. As Derek Attridge puts it in his introduction to the essay, Derrida 'focuses on the institutional, ethical, and juridical implications of any such question' (*AL* 181). What makes matters more complicated is that the words 'Before the Law' (in the original German as well as in the English translation) appear as the first words of the first sentence of the parable; thus the meaning of the words – as used in the sentence, as used by Kafka as a title, and as used by Derrida, also as a title – shifts according to the various laws they have to obey in their relative placings. The destabilization which occurs because of this shows for Derrida how, again in Attridge's words, '[t]he strict notion of the law [which] is predicated upon its absolute separability from anything like fiction, narrative, history, or literature ... cannot be sustained' (*AL* 182). This means that the Law is 'contaminated' by fictionality, narrativity, textuality; there is no pure essence to the Law, no originary status. The problematic (function of the) title, if not disproving the desired status of the Law directly, does serve to question any supposed certainty we may have about the laws of literature. As Derrida says, a 'title occasionally resonates like the citation of another title. But as soon as it names something else, it no longer simply cites ...' (*AL* 183). We see contamination, confusion, citation and undecidability at work in titles such as 'Snowed Up', *The Yellow Wallpaper* or, more recently, in the title of a short novel by French writer Sylvie Germain, *The Weeping Woman on the Streets of Prague*. Each of these titles have their functions and values problematized through being put to use in various ways within the texts they name, and by which function the text's identity is supposedly stabilized. Each title, like the proper name, supposedly gives us to understand something of what is *in* the text. Yet, in each case, the title is deployed within the body of the text. Edie talks of being 'snowed up' in 'Snowed Up', without the slightest awareness that when she does so she wrests the title from its place and breaks the law of the title by having the phrase operate as a remark on the weather. This in turn throws into doubt the propriety of the title as a title. In *The Yellow Wallpaper*, the narrator concerns herself with the yellow wallpaper, the peeling paper in a room at the top of the house. It is not only an object of interest, it is also the principal subject of her writing. In *The Yellow Wallpaper*, the narrator, who is a character within *The Yellow Wallpaper*, writes about the yellow wallpaper, within the patterns of which she discerns a character who is trapped, and struggling to escape – even as she struggles to escape from within the narrative in which she is confined. *The Weeping Woman on the Streets of Prague* involves a narrator who, like Edie and the narrator of *The Yellow Wallpaper*, is both actor and analyst, and who also cites the title of her text, not as title but as signifier of someone in that text. In this case, the figure being named throughout *The Weeping Woman on the Streets of Prague* is a weeping woman on the streets of Prague, whose unpredictable movements and appearances throughout the city cause the narrator both to write and walk, following in the weeping woman's retreating footsteps. In every case, then, the title in being complicated exceeds the function of the title, that function which Geoffrey Bennington describes as its 'irreducibly "legal" status' by which 'it identifies the text *for* the needs of the law' (Db 245). That which exceeds escapes its placement, displacing itself, and taking place as an improper citation of itself. The citation has become improper because, in the various examples of re-citation of the title as having a function other than as title, each text ignores not only the law of the title but also the law of citation.

The question of the title is, then, a double question concerning both function and placing, function being a result of placing, and placing, in turn, being an indicator of a possible function or several functions. There are certain identities involved in and troubled by the act of writing, as we can see. The very possibility of discerning the 'outside' and 'inside' of the text has been, even at the self-same moment that the title is put in place, suspended in its 'proper place' at the head of the text. But function has already been problematized. Although a title is not placed within quotation marks the question has to be asked, following Derrida's remark concerning citations cited above, do titles not appear to function as citations? This all raises other questions, bringing into focus a degree of undecidability. What had been previously the sign of a certain knowable referent, the title, has become, through the simple act of reiteration, unstable. Its context shifted, the title's meaning is affected. To what exactly am I referring when I cite a title? To what does the title apparently refer? All of these troubling issues begin to demonstrate through disproof what Derrida calls a few axioms or presuppositions concerning what we think we know of literature and its laws (*AL* 184).

These axioms or suppositions are:

1. That a text has a unity or singular identity which we consider, *a priori*, before the event of reading, in Derrida's words, 'inviolable' (*AL* 184). The accepted, conventional function of the title, its supposedly immovable place at the border of the text, is supposed to prove the text's unity, to assure us of the uniqueness and identity of the text being named. Yet *Middlemarch*, for example, while being the title of a novel, is also the name of a town within that novel. The title in this case names the novel and, simultaneously, cites the town (as well as referring to itself).

2. The text is supposed to have an author, another so-called guarantee of unity and singularity. This author is understood not as a fiction, or a character of fiction, but as 'real'. Indeed, the manuscript of 'Snowed Up' is signed 'Richard Jefferies, author of "A Midnight Skate" etc.', much as we find Derrida's signature and name at the conclusion of 'Signature Event Context'. Jefferies, in a private moment of composition, asserts his right to be recognized as an author, which is doubly asserted through the act of naming another text composed by him. That 'etc.' implies a number of other texts. The title of an absent fiction supposedly asserts and guarantees the author's property and authority. Richard Jefferies has provided the sign of what Derrida calls a '*presumed* reality' (*AL* 185). This at least is assumed on our part as readers. As Derrida says, there is a cultural consensus as to the these 'qualities' of literature.

3. The third axiom of 'literature', writes Derrida, is that all the events within the text gathered together by the name 'Snowed Up' are related and that 'this relation belongs to what we call literature' (*AL* 186). Yet, once again, this consensual opinion can be challenged when the text is partly represented as a journal or diary, amongst other forms not immediately gathered together necessarily under the heading 'literature'. Diaries do not always belong to the category of literature; nor do all diary entries relate to one another, and certainly not in the same manner as events governed by narrative logic in literature are supposed to do. We can consider both Richard Jefferies' short story, already mentioned, or we might

question the concluding pages of James Joyce's *A Portrait of the Artist as a Young Man* (Joyce 1992, 270–6). There is something in the diary as a form which exceeds both the generic distinctions and requirements – the laws – of 'literature'. The diary, as a supplemental structure – a structure always predicated on the potentially infinite supplement of yet one more day always arbitrarily following previous days without narrative economy – overflows literary form. Indeed, Jefferies anticipates the modernist nature of James Joyce's *A Portrait of the Artist as a Young Man* which relies on diary entries to mark the arbitrariness of formal closure and to exceed the 'literary' fiction of closure. Stephen Dedalus's diary entries could continue beyond the formal limit of *A Portrait*. Indeed, his figure, as a reminder of Daedalus in Greek mythology, is the figure of supplementarity, of the son supplementing the father, becoming a creator in his own right.

Now it can be argued that Derrida points out in the axioms what seems obvious. But that which seems obvious needs pointing out nonetheless: that there are forms of narrative, fiction, history, parable and so on which we use all the time which cannot be defined as literature, according to conventional or institutional definitions of what literature is; these forms or types are not specifically 'literary'. My turn to diary form at the end of Joyce's novel, its use in Jefferies' story, and the journal form alluded to in *The Yellow Wallpaper* seek to demonstrate, through an understanding of the various levels of ambiguity and undecidability of textual form, how what we take for granted as 'literature', what we assume unproblematically to have a unity, is always already problematized by its non-literary relations. Furthermore, what this essay proposes is reading which, through attention to moments of undecidability, refuses and resists the desire for mastery, containment and authority, which titles try to install, and which is signalled by such complicating and contaminating devices. In each singular case, whether the example be Jefferies, Gilman or Joyce, the narratorial voice exceeds the limit of the text. More prociocly, we should suggest that it is writing which exceeds the laws of the text, for, in each case, and implicit in the use of diary form, the question is one of a general writing which promises to continue beyond the margins of the 'literary' text. But for now we need to return to the title.
     The title conventionally serves a purpose similar in its performance

to the signature and the proper name (see Bennington, Db 241ff.). The title installed, a law is enforced. Let us see what Bennington, in discussing Derrida, has to say:

> Whatever its grammatical form, the title of a text functions as its proper name. Inscribed on the outer edge of the limit or frame that circumscribes the text (and whose empirical figure is the cover) the title identifies the text, and, like any proper name, permits one to talk about it in its absence. Without a title, be it only a classification number in a library, or the recitation of the first words of a text with no title, or even the word 'untitled' ... one would be unable to make external distinction between one text and another and all the disciplines of reading would collapse. The title, more still than the attribution to an author's proper name, is the very operator of textual normality and legality. (Db 241–2)

Fine; axiom No. 1, the title guarantees unity and singularity. Except that, as Bennington goes on to show, titles while acting in the name of the Law of language are, nonetheless, not as unequivocal as we would like to believe. Notice that, above, Bennington talks of both library call numbers and the institution of the title 'untitled' as manifestations of institutional normalizations – laws – of the textual frame, that which marks off the 'inner' and 'outer' places of the text. There is in Bennington's discussion the acknowledgement of the text-become-public, the propriety of the text, the text as public property, and the text institutionalized *qua* singular, unified text, available for certain functions, types of performances; and all this through the title.

This raises another question however: what of the 'private' text, the text which is either not yet published, or is not necessarily ever destined for publication, as in the examples, say, of a previously unpublished manuscript, intended perhaps for publication, but 'silenced' for a certain time (perhaps initially rejected by a publisher and subsequently forgotten)? Or what about diaries? We certainly make the assumption that 'Snowed Up', for example and as I have suggested, is a short story, a work of literature, because of certain marks which, through the already-in-place consensus about what constitutes literature, govern our interpretation of the text. In this particular case, there is the signature of 'Richard Jefferies', a name we have been taught to associate with literature, with the production of novels, novellas, essays and short stories, journalism concerned with agriculture, and other forms of 'documentary', 'imaginative' and 'journalistic' prose. We also understand 'Richard Jefferies' as the proper name assigned to a relatively minor figure in the literary canon. We therefore judge the text as literature because of the signature rather than through a translation of any other 'internal' textual elements, and we assign that literature (and its author) to a certain position within the general economy of what we know as 'Literature'. These are not merely idle questions or overstatements of the facts, as Derrida has himself reminded us elsewhere, through his critique of Jacques Lacan's reading of Edgar Allan Poe's short story 'The Purloined Letter'.[18]

This particular text, which also talks at some length about the question of the title, takes the Lacanian reading to task for having overlooked the literary form of Poe's text, and having simply assumed 'The Purloined Letter' to be an example of writing in which the 'Truth' of psychoanalysis is found, supposedly. Without going into detail about Derrida's reading at this point, this particular essay serves as a highly important argument for always bearing in mind the formal conditions of the text; how does it present itself, what are the recognizable markers of the genre to which it seemingly belongs, and, to go back to the question raised by the essay 'Before the Law', what is literature?

Is a diary 'literature'? Do we give diaries titles as we would novels? For those of us who keep diaries for private purposes or the registration of engagements, probably not. Diaries of this kind, which belong to one of those forms of narrative alluded to by Derrida in 'Before the Law' not commonly understood as 'literature', share a common, generic title: Diary, the very generic quality of which in its generalizing economy hides the singular, the unique, and all the possible intimacy contained therein. The Diary (of this kind) does not even require the presence of an author's signature, being the anonymous temporalization and spacing of the self-made-writing, writing-as-identity, identity as (marked by) *différance*. The title 'Diary' announces privacy and acts as a border patrol. At the same time, by its very generic impersonality, it keeps its specific identity secret and, in doing so, effaces its possible idiomatic literariness. If we read someone else's diary, in this case Edie Audley's or, arguably, Stephen Dedalus's, we are transgressing the laws of the diary. The inclusion in the novel or short story of the diary also challenges the identity of 'literature' and confuses distinctions between 'public' and 'private' forms of writing. The binary distinction is dismantled through the contamination of the one with the other.

In a certain way, this question of the title, as it is articulated in relation to the idea of the diary, raises the problem of acts of narration and our comprehension of them as readers. This is especially the case in narrations such as Charlotte Perkins Gilman's *The Yellow Wallpaper*, Sylvie Germain's *The Weeping Woman on the Streets of Prague*, or Richard Jefferies' 'Snowed Up'. In each example (although always in a singular fashion), the first-person narrator has a double role, which can be described as 'a narrating narrator and a narrated narrator' or the 'inscriber and the inscribing', to borrow Derrida's phrases from that discussion of Edgar Allan Poe's 'The Purloined Letter', already mentioned (*PC* 431). As the narrator narrates, s/he tells and writes the events, s/he is their 'author' and s/he also narrates her/himself inside the events, as one of the characters of her/his narration. Her/his status is different, however, from that of other characters whom s/he makes speak and act. The narrator has consciousness of her/himself, and this consciousness involves a consciousness of her/himself as a writer. S/he writes of her/himself, and writes of her/his ability to write, acknowledging the limits of her/his authorial powers. Importantly for us, though, we see that the narrator remarks her/himself as always doubled, as both her/himself and as other than her/himself. Furthermore, with her/his writing, s/he also tells us that s/he is telling us the events.

Understanding this we comprehend that there occurs through these various narrator positions, whether of the anonymous narrators of *The Yellow Wallpaper* or *The Weeping Woman*, or of Edie in 'Snowed Up', what Derrida calls, again in relation to the Poe text, 'a problem of framing, of bordering and delimitation, whose analysis must be very finely detailed if it wishes to ascertain the effects of fiction' (*PC* 431). The narrator's various comments mark out the different kinds of commentary, which allow us to see the levels of narration, while complicating further the outside/inside boundaries of which I have already written, and which will again be taken up below, in relation to an exposition of Derrida's use of the figure of the hymen.

For now, though, and to return to the question of the title, we see, as Derrida has suggested, that 'the same group of words would not have the value of the title were they to appear elsewhere, in places not prescribed by convention, for example in a different context or in a different place within the same context' (*AL* 189). The title, rather than being simply, purely, a point of origin, is readable as a supplement to a text, played with and disturbed, disjointed from its conventional location, identity and function by the self-aware narrator. This articulation, which is also a disarticulation, plays with, and unsettles, the 'truth' of literature. Above I outlined three axioms or presuppositions put forward by Derrida in his essay 'Before the Law'. I omitted the fourth, even though I have talked about it more or less throughout this part of the text. Let's now turn to Derrida, as a way of summarizing, and returning to the point of departure, as another strategic justification:

> We think we know what a title is, notably the title of a work. It is placed in a specific position, highly determined and regulated by conventional laws: at the beginning of and at a set distance above the body of a text, but in any case *before* it. The title is generally chosen by the author or by his or her editorial representatives whose property it is. The title names and guarantees the identity, the unity and boundaries of the original work which it entitles. (*AL* 188)

There are certain titles which appear not to acknowledge this guarantee. Indeed, reading the title shows how the guarantee is there in order to be troubled.

Titles are made equivocal by their reiteration in different contexts. Phrases such as 'Before the Law' or 'la pleurante des rues de Prague' are homonyms of the titles they replay; they sound exactly the same when read out, yet cannot be taken as the same (by implication then the meaning of all language is unstable). Reading those texts in which the titles recur shows that each title certainly does not serve the same function twice in any of its manifestations. If we argue that the context *is* the same – that the phrase appears in the supposedly unified context of a diary, a novel, novella or short story – we must still acknowledge that its placing alters its sense, a sense even more altered precisely because the contexts are so different. In the overall context of the example of the diary-text, we may say that these contexts are also composed by various discourses, traces or threads, in the writing, which surface repeatedly, the value of the discourses altered each time they make an appearance, while yet causing an accretion throughout the text. What we are witness to, then, and what our reading produces, or seems to produce, is the resistant nature of the text, its resistance to the search for a single meaning. And we are therefore also witness to the text's affirmation of its text-ness, and of a certain otherness within its identity, through its resistance.

Yet this otherness, an otherness resistant to the naming of a particular identity, can be found in the very act of writing. In the essay 'Force and Signification', Derrida suggests that such resistance, such otherness, is the very 'thing' in writing, or in any structure, whether biological, linguistic, or literary, which denies the effort of certain procedures or protocols of interpretation, as in a structuralist reading for example, to reach closure in the act of interpretation (*WD* 27–30). The structuralist reading aims to bring together all the elements of a text and account for them through demonstrating that the text has a structural unity. Furthermore, such readings aim to replicate certain aspects of a text's movements, structures and trajectories as part of a homogeneous whole. Literary interpretation seeks to perform a teleological act of reading which produces wholeness and unity, closing up the text in the production of a single meaning, where all that is seen as significant in the story is said to aim at generating this single meaning. And this is effected by placing various elements of the text in particular places relative to other textual elements, while, at the same time, ignoring, overlooking, other textual elements and figures which cannot be interpreted along the lines proposed by the particular protocols of that type of interpretation.

The very idea of literary interpretation is conventionally organized around philosophical and conceptual principles (such as 'aesthetics', 'truth', 'value', 'meaning') as we've already suggested earlier in this chapter, and as are other areas of thought in our culture. Thinking on literature and literary criticism, literary theory and related matters thus becomes shaped and oriented according to broader principles. We seek, conventionally, to orient ourselves, our identities, through acts of reading in relation to the textual structure, the goal of which is a centre, a central, unifying meaning. As Derrida suggests, 'classical thought concerning structure could say that the center is, paradoxically, *within* the structure and *outside it*. The center is the center of a totality, and yet, since the center does not belong to the totality (is not part of the totality), the totality has its center elsewhere. The center is not the center' (*WD* 279). The title is one such possible 'center' which is not the center. If we accept what Derrida has to say, then we must acknowledge that:

> ... the entire history of the concept of structure ... must be thought of as a series of substitutions of center for center, as a linked chain of determinations of the center. Successively, and in a regulated fashion, the center receives different forms or names. The history of metaphysics ... is the history of these metaphors and metonymies. Its matrix ... is the determination of Being as *presence* in all senses of the word. (*WD* 279)

The title, the author, the signature or proper name: all are examples of those 'metaphors or metonymies' of which Derrida speaks. Importantly, this passage addresses the relationship between the idea of the system or structure, and the idea of writing, both of which have been mistrusted in the history of Western thought. Speaking of a 'series of substitutions of center for center ... a linked chain of substitutions', Derrida is alerting us to the very condition of writing itself, and the way in which meaning is produced by the movement of difference and the play of writing.

As we see from a reading of the title's possible reduplication and disjointing function, any connections which are made do not provide a sense of unity. The title, the *idea* of the title, like other figures and the conceptualization which stands behind the example and re-enforces its function, comes to operate as one of that series of possible substitutions, one figure for the centre. The working of the title allows us to make such connections. Yet it is the very connectedness which, when read carefully, tends to dissolve and dismiss easily identifiable 'positions', such as 'inside' and 'outside', 'author' and 'character', 'narrator' and 'narrated', 'economics' and 'pleasure', 'private' and 'public' writing, 'fiction' and 'documentary', 'fiction' and 'truth', 'narration' and 'performance'. Meanings slide and shake, and are unsettled from a secure location because they are not discretely located or stable. Nor, as I hope I am showing, can they be thought of as such. Theirs are chance meetings, connected and yet arbitrarily divided.

... dating ...

In order to explore Derrida's writing further, and given the talk of diaries and journals, I want to look in this section at the dates of the diary and the manner in which they function. Dates and their function are a feature largely passed over in considerations of the literary. They are one of those marginal traces which have much to say, yet which remain silent. The diary as one possible narrative form dictates that we must respond to the dates in our acts of reading, instead of examining only the more obvious features of the narrative and its contents. From examining the dates, and exploring the date-function, I will then turn in the final section of the chapter to the figure of the hymen, to the diary as hymenography, and the figure of writing in the broad sense, once again.

'[D]ating', says Derrida, 'is signing' (*AL* 259). Yet what, we might ask, is being signed? Every date, like every signature, marks that which is dated or signed, with an apparent uniqueness or singularity. Yet we can re-read the date, as we can the signature, and thus the date and the signature are paradoxically re-markable outside of the singular context of their initial inscription. Derek Attridge explains the paradoxical logic of dates further:

> ... all writing is a dating (as it is a signing) ... the date, like the signature, exhibits the counter-logic of iterability: serving to fix for the future a specific and unique time and place, it can do so only on the basis of its readability, which is to say that it has to remain open to repetition and reinscription; its repeatability is a condition of its singularity. (*AL* 371)

Inscribed in the very singularity of the date is the possibility of its being reinscribed elsewhere. The condition of the date is, therefore, an enigmatic condition according to Derrida (*AL* 378), precisely because it resists thematization and cannot be theorized due to the paradox or aporia in its logic. Yet the memory of the date is 'rooted in the singularity of the event' (*AL* 381). For us to recognize the singularity of those events, we have to be able to re-read them, to reiterate them outside of their singularity. We cannot therefore theorize or make a general, totalizing rule from the singular example concerning how each day, each date, functions. This holds true for all single works of what we term 'literature'.

Each date already speaks of itself, to paraphrase Derrida (*AL* 382). Yet the date, in the act of 'preserving its memory ... by the inscription of a sign as memorandum, will have broken the silence of pure singularity' (*AL* 382). The act of writing the diary signals the writing of our identities as a heterogeneous and discontinuous collection of entries.

We locate our Being as already other, marked in writing and remarked by difference. Being is not simply the construction of the subject of a 'given year, month, day, or hour', it is also located at a 'given place' (*AL* 387). This otherness is not a simple opposition, part of a binarism, but dispersed among a series of arbitrary days and locations. Writing a diary entry, we confirm the date's and our own iterability through the 're-marking of place and time, at the point of the here and now' (*AL* 391). At the same time, our acts of inscription also reveal the constructedness, the structuration, of all narrativity. Dating merely reveals to us the truth of narrative, or, to put it another way, narrative truth. Yet it is not only a narrative truth but also the truth of Being: which is that there is no original, no single unified identity, no centre from which all is generated.

Each diary entry performs the contingent strangeness of identity, the reiterated estranging of identity from itself. Identity is never fixed, but written and rewritten – re-marked – by the discourses which trace it and which memory traces in turn. Each date of the diary thus signs an other I who is reiterated through the act of re-reading as other than the I who writes. This act is one which brings us back to ourselves as always already other than we are. And we can connect ourselves to the date so precisely, without theorizing either, yet still noting that both are subject to inscription, by acknowledging, along with Derrida, that the date is 'always bound up with some proper name' (*AL* 390).

Each date of a diary, each date which has its hitherto blank page filled in acts as a form of key or cipher for memory. We are given access through dates to memory and to the memory of Being manifested, not as a presence, but as a written trace. And this access is to a series of discontinuous events. Being is always remarked as strategically incomplete, fragmentary, and therefore strange, contingent, provisional. This provisionality is attested to by the possibility of future pages, future blank spaces, awaiting the act of inscription, but also understandable as having already been written, the subject yet to write those pages already possibly dead. The writing of the diary thus dispels any possibility of a full presence, haunting us and our identities through the fragments by which it is composed.

In talking of the relationship between Being and the dates of the diary I seem to have shifted ground from talking about 'literature' to talking about what is ostensibly a far more 'philosophical' topic, 'Being'. This might in itself strike you as inappropriate to 'literature'. But this is exactly the kind of argument levelled at Derrida; for some literary critics he is too 'philosophical', while for philosophers he is not philosophical enough, bringing literature into his discussions (as we saw in Chapter 1, with regard to Gasché's response to Derrida's essay on James Joyce). Yet what is going on here is a fundamental questioning of the ways in which we read and write, the ways in which we ask questions. In discussing Being in relation to the diary entries as dates, I have pointed to diary as being fragmented within itself because of its blank pages, The diary is, like the subject who writes, a non-unified Being or identity composed of a non-predictable series of signatures of Being and, specifically, *Being other*. The diary as *textual identity* resists theorization as unified entity. The diary is randomized through the possibility of continuation, elision, omission, absence, unpredictable difference within itself. This is understandable whether we consider the short story by Richard Jefferies already mentioned, Gilman's *The Yellow Wallpaper*, or, for that matter, *The Weeping Woman on the Streets of Prague*. All in some manner consider or invite the good reader to respond to the condition of writing in relation to identity and Being. And each resituates one's comprehension of iden- tity, displacing the illusion of unity through the articulation of inscrip- tion. It may further be suggested, beyond those works of 'literature' which most obviously assume the episodic form of journals and diaries, that we also consider the structures of the epistolary novel, with its multiple acts of writing, dating and signing, whether we take Tobias Smollett's *The Expedition of Humphrey Clinker*, Richardson's *Clarissa, or the History of a Young Lady*, or *Les Liaisons dangereuses*, by Choderlos de Laclos. Indeed, the epistolary novel complicates matters further by its frequent inclusion not only of 'private' letters and dates, but also a variety of signatures, which call into question the fictional unity supposedly guaranteed by the title *and* the author's proper name.

We cannot, therefore, define the journal, diary or epistolary novel unequivocally by their generic definitions, any more than we can say that they are simply, unquestionably 'literature'. In each singular instance the generic identity is troubled by the singular example of the text in question. Form and content are iterable, yet not wholly definable. Indeed it is iterability which defers definition, as well as those 'marginal' features which are not conventionally assumed as 'literary'.

Immediately above I wrote of the contingent strangeness of Being. Comprehending the writing of Being unveils for us the relationship between identity and its difference, its supplementary otherness. Otherness is not merely one half of a self/other binarism, and we should not make the mistake of thinking of it in this fashion. The reason for my describing the otherness within identity as supplementary is as follows: this supplementarity, the excess and overflow of Being, is traced or remarked not only by the unpredictable diary entries but also in the oscillation across the non-fixable positions between actor and analyst, and narrating narrator and narrated narrator in narratives. Such supplementary otherness is figured in the movements of writing. The possibility of the date yet to come, the writing yet to be inscribed on the blank page, the unpredictable writing is understood as always in the future, always to come, and always on the way to Being. We can thus imagine the possibility of an other identity, one more supplement in excess of the identity we read, always yet to be written in the future, never having presence or being present as such.

... hymenography: the example of the diary ...

> The hymen is thus a sort of textile
>
> Jacques Derrida

Writing is what connects, making connections without necessarily unifying. It is the trace which makes connections between apparent opposites, seemingly discrete and disparate, self-contained positions: outside and inside, word and world. As this section will explore, we may suggest that writing offers a series of connections which can be read as hymeneal, in the sense given the word by Derrida. In this section, we will consider Derrida's use of the figure of hymen

Since 1968 at least the figure of the hymen has been appearing repeatedly in Derrida's writing, from the influential essay 'Différance' onwards. In this essay Derrida produces the figure of the hymen as one of what he calls the 'nonsynonymous substitutions' for the key term *différance* (*DR* 65). Other terms used by Derrida are 'archi-writing', 'archi-trace', 'spacing', 'supplement', *pharmakon*. It is important to stress that such terms are *nonsynonymous* substitutions. While no term has any precedence over any other, each term can be substituted for any of the others, within specified contexts. However, this does not mean that they carry with them the same meaning. Each figure describes a certain movement or spacing, both spatial and temporal, by which any signifying system comes to be constituted. Each term carries for Derrida the trace of its own differentiation within itself, so that none of the terms in question can be read as holding the promise of a unity. Such figures in Derrida's writing point to the ways in which the production of meaning is spatially and temporally organized. Derrida again discusses the figure of the hymen in the poetry and writing of Stéphane Mallarmé in *Dissemination*. 'Hymenographies' and 'hymenologies' are described in this work by Derrida as writings, treatises, on membranes (*D* 213). In the 'Letter to a Japanese Friend', where Derrida tells us that deconstruction is neither an analysis nor a critique, he even suggests that, in certain texts of his, 'deconstruction' is replaceable by 'hymen' (*DR* 275). In attempting to introduce Derrida's work, then, as a source for critical-interpretive insights, it is clear that we must come to terms with 'hymen'.

Geoffrey Bennington stresses that 'hymen' 'names "economically" the relation between inside and outside ... "hymen" says separation *and* the abolition of this proximity' (Db 226). The figure of the hymen can name economically precisely because it carries within it the possibility of contradictory and oppositional meanings simultaneously. It is not reducible to a single meaning, and neither is such a meaning decidable. The figure of the hymen figures its own division within itself. The term 'hymen' therefore figures in a certain manner that which is between apparently definable concepts while simultaneously naming both their separable spheres and their interdependent connectedness. (Consider for instance Derrida's remark that the history of literature constitutes 'the hymen ... *between* literature and truth' [*DR* 65].) Bennington also tells us that the term has an immediately comprehensible 'sexual register' (Db 226), while Peggy Kamuf states that Derrida's use of the term acknowledges a certain thinking about the subject of femininity on his part (*DR* xxxvix–xl). The term has of course led feminists to question Derrida over the use of the term. However, Derrida has cautioned, in 'Choreographies', that '"hymen" ... no longer simply designate[s] figures for the feminine body' in his work (*EO* 181). Indeed, in *Dissemination* Derrida pursues the Latin and Greek etymology of 'hymen' and related words to show how hymen is related to stitching, tissue, sewing, weaving, textile, spider web, net, the text of a work, the weave of a song (a wedding song or song of mourning) (*D* 213). So, the 'meaning' of the hymen for

Derrida is in the fact that its complex semantic and textual relations mean that it cannot be pinned down or confined to a single meaning. Neither simply sexual nor non-sexual, hymen itself comes *between* the two places, as it were, complicating our understanding once more. The hymen does not simply name something and cannot be defined as such.

For Derrida, then, hymen is marked by a double meaning. It is, in his words, '… a sign of fusion *between* identities' (*DR* 209; emphasis added). This figure marks the difference, and also the connectedness, between two places, two identities, between, let us say as Bennington does, outside and inside. Hymen, in Derrida's writing, is the graphic expression of the margin, limit or border which connects opposites, binary oppositions such as inside and outside, and allows their meaning to be understood in relation to one another, while reserving to itself a non-determined place for which a univocal meaning cannot be given. Absolute meaning cannot be found in the figure of the hymen and interpretive acts cannot control its meaning. If we think of the actual tissue of the hymen, the 'veil-like tissue across the vagina that remains intact as long as virginity does' (*DR* xxxvix), we understand how it connects the 'inside' to the 'outside' of the female body, and yet is neither, strictly speaking.

The hymen is thus *in-between* and hymen names this in-betweenness. In making and marking or re-marking such a connection (to name 'hymen' is always to re-mark its betweenness), and in being 'in-between', hymen names its own betweenness. At the non-place of the margin, the border, the limit not simply of one but of both figures in opposition – the hymen is the limit of both inside *and* outside – hymen betrays the fact that inside and outside are never simply or completely separate. Writing may be said to be hymeneal in that it betrays the connection between pairings such as gift and property, or gift and economic exchange. Writing-as-hymen folds back the various economic interweavings, the network or web of interdependent economic functions and their philosophemes, and thus reveals the hymeneal function of/as a written trace. Writing is always written *between*: it is written *between* the reader and the characters of a narrative. Writing as a *hymenography* offers a *text*-ile weave which traces for the reader numerous interconnections. It is the hymenography, the hymen as writing, which both traces identity for us while also leading, seemingly inexorably, to the partial erasure of identity – an identity which is apparently self-spun. This hypothesis on my part becomes clearer once we remember that marriage is the joining of two identities and that hymen is an archaic synonym for marriage itself, as Kamuf points out (*DR* xxxvix). The act of consummation will abolish the hymen by breaking the virgin's membrane. This effectuates the partial erasure of one identity through the interpolation of the rights of an other identity.

In discussing the hymen I have named only the spatial relationships which writing grafts through being between. It is important that we acknowledge that Derrida also insists on the *temporal* spacing effected by the figure of the hymen. As well as being a spatial figure of undecidability, the hymen is also a temporal trace. The difference between virginity and non-virginity is defined by the temporal spacing. The hymen, writes Derrida, is the figure of 'a series of temporal differences without any central present, without a present of which the past and future would be but modifications' (*D* 210). Here we have what amounts to a possible definition of the structuration and writing, for example, of a diary. The diary is particularly and often intimately associated with the self, with the ideality of identity and the assumptions of writing's relation to presence. The very form of the diary itself – of any diary – accords to this description of Derrida's. There is no central present moment either in a diary or in keeping a diary. Each day is a temporary present, with each previous and succeeding day being past and future modifications of the idea of the present. No single day can be said to be an absolute present, the origin, source or organizing, generative moment from which all others are engendered. Even the act of writing on a given day only serves to announce not the present as such but the memory of the present as past narrative. With a diary, the 'future (present) and past (present)' have no 'mother-form' (*D* 210) of a constant present which gives birth to them. Writing a diary reduplicates this deconstruction of the idea of a constant, central present, which the blank pages of the diary have always already implied. Writing only serves to re-enforce the deconstruction of a centre, a presence. The writer's identity emerges as a series of identities out of this act of writing. Writing performs identity. Acts of writing to oneself about oneself guarantee that one is no more a presence to oneself (despite the desire for that reassurance) than one is to others; writing acknowledges that the writer may already be dead and is certainly absent, but always already a trace or trait. The diary impresses the condition of writing on us in a particularly intimate and irresistible fashion. The diary, and thus one's identity, is hymeneal therefore precisely because of the dated sequentiality of the diary, its temporal spacing, and its spatial relations, each date signing the never-being-present of the present.

The diary as the text of Being is hymeneal in another fashion also. Writing is woven together out of the weaving or stitching together of culturally accepted foreign phrases, discursive allusions, rhetorical devices, philosophemes, so-called literary or semi-literary phrases, terms, quotations and paraphrases, clichés and modish terminology, all of which form the textile network of both writing and identity. As the figure of the hymen folds outside and inside onto one another, so writing folds numerous traces into the identity it maps, connecting identity to the text of the 'outside world', determining that identity as a series of traces from that world. The word and the world are sewn together in the folds of writing. Writing is thus hymeneal not only because it traces the margin between 'exterior' and 'interior' 'worlds', but also, importantly, it shows those 'worlds' to be textual, folded onto one another. Identity is thus the application of writing. Writing a diary refers to the condition of all writing and performs identity as a series of related folds while making it possible for the reader to see that identity is not a source or origin from which a truthful representation of the world emerges. Rather, identity or being is seen as performed, composed out of a web of traces which are both woven and written, textile and textual. In writing a diary, and in writing of a 'self' in a diary, as a character in that narrative which is performed from memory in the act of keeping a diary, the act of performing that identity is necessarily strategic, unstable and always incomplete, in process.

In effect, then, such a 'hymenography' unsettles the very idea of stable origins, centres, sources, or meanings, whether these are sought after 'locally' in literature or in the desire of a full presence. Writing plays with the very idea of fixed meanings. At the same time as writing unsettles (writing causes little tremors which expose semantic dependence on hymeneal traces) writing connects places, times and events. Writing does this in the place of the diary, across the blank pages which may also be considered as margins or spaces, the spacing of the hymen *between* the signatures of the dates. Writing connects and, in so doing, partially erases the difference between '[n]onpresence and presence' (*D* 209). Writing, if it is one name for 'hymen', is also a name which names *différance*. The figure of the hymen, like that of the date, gives us to understand the following: in writing of oneself every day, the subject not only writes of her self as always other than herself, but also she writes of her identity as always already a series of supplements without any discernible originary starting point, each inscription of identity being yet another 'nonsynonymous substitution', to recall Derrida's phrase for the hymen-function. Her writing, her identity, thus promises through its hymenographic movements a supplement or overflow beyond the possibility of finite interpretation or full meaning. Furthermore, the dated entries of the diary-form, even as they remind us of the impossibility of presence, also speak not only to the potential absence of the reader/writer, but also to the subject's death.

We should pause however, to consider the hymen further, rather than accepting it uncritically as an unproblematic figure. Were we to do this, we would merely be falling back onto an economical theorization of the 'hymen' useful for explaining a particular textual form or narrative technique. We would thus institutionalize the figure, making it a safe tool for literary analysis in much the same way as some have done with the term 'deconstruction', and it is precisely against such institutionalizations in acts of reading and writing that Derrida warns us.

If the blank pages figure the figure of the hymen, then they – like the figure of the hymen – are only to be recalled after the act of writing, after the act of penetration. For the act of writing effectively abolishes the blank page, leaving it only as a memory. If we can think the possibility of blank pages to come in the future, it must also be possible to imagine them as being no longer blank. Similarly, for us to imagine writing on the blank page is to imagine the breaking of the hymen. The act of writing is paradoxical then (as is the very figure of the hymen itself), especially it would seem with regard to its temporal spacing. The act of writing is marked by its own double function. Writing is not a form of representation which can be described in hymeneal terms; it is hymeneal rather because it confuses and connects; it offers continuity between the supposed signifieds, the exteriority of which it confuses by re-marking them as signifiers, *in writing*. Any page in a diary always refers to every other diary page, past and future, within a particular diary or throughout the idea of the diary. The double function of diary writing – the doubling of the narrating and narrated narrator, the analyst and actor – is the confusion of the hymen between positions through and through, because such spatial and temporal confusion means that we can no longer differentiate between poles, not simply between signifier and signified, but between the identity of one signifier and another.

This confusion-effect, which is also an effect of contamination, is intensified by possible references to literature and the literary, to the *belles-lettrist*'s techniques, as well as to other possible discourses and philosophemes. Writing is thus a constant folding, veil after veil, tissue after tissue, which is, to quote Derrida, 'located between present acts that don't take place. What takes place is only the *entre* [between], the place, the spacing, which is nothing' (*D* 214). And it is precisely because the hymen figures the *between* that it carries within it the possibility of opening up a gap in coherence, logic, identity, meaning and explains *why* we can comprehend it, following Derrida, as a marginal figure, a figure of the border. This also explains *why* the hymen is (albeit nonsynonymously) an *aneconomic* figure. Hymenography shows the proximity as well as the gaps in textual logic, it figures the transitions between poles, between inside and outside, text and 'reality', imitation and representation, signifier and signified. Writing does not 'outline' or 'trace' a portrait, image or representation; it obscures, covers up, hides.

All of which leads us to further considerations of 'hymen' in the text of Derrida. Let's look at three different expressions, taken from different texts, of the function of the hymen, in relation to writing and economic value:

> The graphics of the hymen withholds *a margin* from the control of meaning. (*DR* 371; emphasis added)

> This entire syntax is made possible by the graphics of the margin or the hymen, of the border and the step ... (*DR* 544)

> Anything constituting the value of existence is foreign to the 'hymen.' And if there were hymen ... property value would [not] be ... appropriate to it. (*EO* 182)

We can discern a certain movement of thought here across these texts which we must acknowledge if we are to comprehend the ways in which Derrida approaches questions of interpretation. As has already been stated, for Derrida the figure of the hymen is one possible name of a margin or space wherein what is written, what is signified by that space and spacing, does not allow itself to be fully interpreted or translated.

Derrida's second remark suggests that, for meaning to be possible at all, for the syntax to be in the least significant, there must be the margin, border, the movement or oscillation *between* which allows us the possibility of discerning any meaning between positions or statements. And what makes interpretation at all possible is the undecidability, a certain question of force and tension, between say writing and reading. We use the author's name as a signature with special properties in order to locate and situate writing properly, in order to determine the literary from the non-literary, as I have just said; this involves us in trying to turn writing into Literature through the supposed unity and identity given by the signature as a figure for an absent presence.

However, the author's proper name should not be taken to be a signifier to a real person. The name on the cover or title page is one more textual sign, albeit it of a possibly different order than other signs. As Derrida puts it 'proper names ... are not real references but indications for the sake of convenience and initial analysis' (*DR* 173). There is at work in the proper name certain privileged textual effects; yet the proper name does not offer a truth. As Derrida puts it

> ... the effects or structure of a text are not reducible to its 'truth,' to the intended meaning of its presumed author, or even its supposedly unique and identifiable signatory. (*EO* 29)

Contrary to such a notion, writing exposes, against the effect of the proper name, a condition of otherness within identity, the otherness within being which writing expresses. Writing-as-hymenography constitutes a range of nonsynonymous identities through a series of supplements which serve to mediate against the truth and univocity which conventionally we are led to understand the authorizing title or proper name as expressing. 'Performances' of narrating and writing acts unfold for us the excessive overflow of positions which all writing implies in itself. The spatial and temporal deferral and differentiation of meaning which any act of writing enacts mediates against all desires for presence, truth, origin and uni(voci)ty. The writing subject announces the conditions of both writing and identity, announcing nothing less than the writing *of* identity, writing *as* identity, and the differentiated identity of writing form itself. And we are given a particularly cogent demonstration or performance of this in the writing of a diary. For the diary form announces the hymeneal condition of identity's writing.

Writing is, then, a question of identity, writing always being enfolded into itself, yet differentiated from itself as such. It is a writing which announces the act of writing *as* an act of performing the subject. Subjectivity is provisionally given, contingent upon context, and without a permanent presence, without a centre. The subject thus doubles her identity through writing, dividing that identity and re-stitching it. All inscriptions are therefore not about the subject's 'reality' but about the inscription of Being, Being's trace. Each diary entry, each dated page is another fold of the hymeneal tissue, folding back on itself at one and the same time the acts of temporally, spatially self-differing and self-deferring inscription and the deft spacings of identity as difference. Even as the subject writes to keep the hymen intact, so she penetrates it once again, leaving at once both memory and future anterior possibility, the possibility of the blank page, the blank margin of the page, awaiting annotation: and is that, after all, not exactly what a diary is, the annotation of identity in all its differential re-markings?

The subject of the diary therefore offers us a series of margins, interwoven *betweens*, broken and re-made, re-marked as so many hymeneal figures: *between* writing and the psyche, *between* writing and gender; *between* writing and culture, writing and ideology, writing and identity, writing and history, writing and structure, writing and form. Between writing and reading. *Between writing and literature.* Perhaps more than anything the form of the diary as a hymeneal writing brings to us the *between* which connects, while re-marking, re-tracing writing and literature, literature and non-literature. Such writing is the border, the limit, the margin, the blank page, the space which makes the place between so undecidable, which creates a tension and a play between places we call the literary and non-literary. Writing is that marginal figure which confounds such definitions and any supposed certainty which 'literary theory' might believe it brings to interpretation. Writing is that ill-named thing deconstruction, which escapes the instituting question of literary theory: 'what is ...'?

Thus what we are left with is writing – and reading. Without presence, without institution, without programme. The subject is always already a kind of writing and a kind of reading. There is a passage from Derrida's *Dissemination* which is pertinent:

> There is writing without a book, in which, each time, at every

moment, the marking tip proceeds without a past upon the virgin sheet; but there is also, *simultaneously*, an infinite number of booklets enclosing and fitting inside other booklets, which are only able to issue forth by grafting, sampling, quotations, epigraphs, references, etc. Literature voids itself in its limitlessness. (*D* 223)

The hymen names a writing which has no formal opening, no formal closure, no deliberate narrative device motivated by particular characters. The diary is thus a writing without a book, without the formal properties of literature. Yet, at the same time, even as writing a diary verges on the edge – the border or margin – of the literary, even as it is a writing at the margins, it also plunges literature into its own limitlessness, placing 'Literature' under erasure.

Part II

Preparatory to Anything Else: Singular Examples or, Identity, Spectrality, Undecidability

3 Writing (of) Identities: Facing up to Derrida or, the Example of Paul Valéry

... this complicity with the 'French' or 'Parisian' context also meant conflict, opposition, rupture, estrangement, a certain uprootedness.

P... 416

We are beginning to glimpse that the disruption of these categories is also the effect of what was written by Mallarmé.

AL 112

In the previous chapter I mentioned how historical and biographical sources, hidden or otherwise, were not my primary concern, if they were a concern at all, in gathering together and exploring certain perceived – and supposedly perceivable – relations concerning Derrida's writing and those of other authors and thinkers. This holds particularly true for this chapter. The question of identities, and of identities' relationships to signature effects, is never discernible exclusively in terms of the biographical or the biographical source. Recalling Derrida's opening gambit in his essay 'Qual Quelle: Valéry's Sources', from *Margins of Philosophy*, I would say just now that I am not seeking to unearth various sources, tracing them back to their supposed origins or performing some kind of archaeological-histori-cal act which 'would chatter on about heritages, readings, borrowings, biographical inner springs' (*MP* 275). To use Derrida's advertised phrase from the same passage, the '"discourse of history"' is not the concern of this critic. As Derrida's essay on Paul Valéry suggests, there is never traceable a source as single point of origin.

In this chapter we will interest ourselves instead in what might be called a rhetoric of identity. As already announced, this is a rhetoric which is an abiding concern in Derrida's texts, although hardly ever explicitly stated *as such*. I might suggest that the identities of Derrida's texts are caught up in the explication of the principle of identity, as that very principle is traced by difference. Identity for Derrida is never just identity *per se*: the identity of identity is never conceived in purely abstract terms, as though identity were definable according to some abstract or idealized conceptualization. Identities are always and only identifiable as identities *of*: some one, some thing. Whatever the identity, this is only recognizable through the play of writing, text, *différance*. By identity, then, we might also be allowed to suggest otherness, otherness within identity, the relation of otherness to identity, whether either alterity or identity refer to, directly or indirectly, personal, poetic, literary or even national identity. The rhetoric in question is then one of uprootedness and disjunction, a rhetoric of disjointing which crosses boundaries, undoing the certainties concerning a certain identity, say for example between self and other, French and not-French.

These sometimes clear, sometimes oblique identities and *their* relationship to questions of place and of what takes place in the name of such relationships – and in the relationship that literary critics sometimes explore between larger questions of identity (cultural, poetic, national) and proper names such as Paul Valéry and Jacques Derrida – are what interests me here. In beginning the exploration of this complex and highly over-determined rhetoric, I have in front of me questions asked by Derrida of the poet Stéphane Mallarmé which become my departure point, and which I paraphrase as the questioning and open-ended thesis of this chapter: is there *a place* for Derrida in a 'history of literature'? Or, to begin with: does his text take place, take its place, in some overall picture of French literature? In a picture? of literature? of French literature? (*AL* 111–12).[1] By bringing together the two authors named in the title I hope to catch, in their wake, and after reading them in various ways, what, if anything, might be said either to haunt Derrida and Valéry, or traverse them, which disturbs any simple historical, personal or national location, yet which has a certain bearing on the very question of French contexts and identities.

Let's start over again with three quotations, from Paul Valéry and Jacques Derrida.

Looking/writing: for example, Valéry?

Intérieurement, s'il y a voix, il n'y a pas vue de qui parle, et qui décrira, définira la différence qu'il y a entre cette phrase même qui se dit et ne se prononce pas, et cette même phrase sonnante dans l'air? Cette identité et cette différence sont un des secrets essentiels de la nature de l'esprit – et qui l'a signalée.[2] (Paul Valéry, *Cahiers* xxii, 304)

[Within the subject's consciousness, if there is a voice, there is no sight of that which speaks, and who will describe, define the difference which is there between that very phrase which speaks itself and does not pronounce itself, and that same phrase which sounds in the air? This identity and that difference are one of the essential secrets of the nature of spirit – and which has signalled there?]

[In Algeria] ... the source, the norm, the authority of the French language was elsewhere. And, in a certain manner, confusedly, we learned it, I learned it as the language of the other – even though I could only refer to one language as mine, you see! And this is why I say that it is not a question of language, but of culture, literature, history, history of *French literature*, what I was learning at school. I was totally immersed, I had no other reference, I had no other culture, but at the same time I sensed clearly that all of this came from a history and a milieu that were not in a simple and primitive way mine. (*P*... 204; emphasis added)

La personne qui parle est déjà autre que moi (Paul Valéry, *Cahiers* xx, 15)

[The person who speaks is already other than me]

If the picture or, at the very least, the subject of French literature *qua French* is destabilized in Derrida's wake (he being only the latest of a number of writers who disturb the certainty of French identity through the French language), then, tentatively, we might suggest that Derrida's thoughts on the subject, wherever they are encountered, are driven by an ekphrastic impulse – an impulse which is also a pulse, a rhythm, a certain heartbeat. The quotation of Derrida's given above locates importantly the situation of non-correspondence and the manifestation of the other within the same, which divides identity and finds itself discussed wherever Jacques Derrida encounters Paul Valéry, whether directly or indirectly. Derrida gives us to see the limit of the transformation between a certain act of looking and a certain event in writing. This event occurs in encountering Valéry over the issues of the figure, the face, and the French language. It can also be intimated that Derrida's writing is never a reading as such, at least not in the sense that a reading brings to the text in advance of the encounter a programme. Instead, this writing, I would argue, can be seen as a form of performative and transformative, radical ekphrasis, which in looking at the text of the other also views itself both as other and from other, equally destabilizing positions, breaking down the simple binary opposition of constative and performative utterance, already mentioned in previous chapters and discussed by Derrida (in his transaction with Ponge's 'Fable') in 'Psyche: Inventions of the Other' (P 30–40).

What Derrida observes from that place of the other within the French language and French literature in which he so often seeks to position himself in relation to a text, a thought, a subject, a painting, a poem, is the gaze of the other, the other writer, the other's text focused on that which is never absolutely interpretable because of its singularity and the necessity of its 'internal' alterity. This singularity, which Derrida so frequently and faithfully traces in all its contours, denies the possibility of making an example of the given text, as an example which can be taken to offer an identity claiming to offer a universal model. Following Derrida, we can *see* the text in all its exemplary singularity, but this is not translatable into a written programme for a general textual economy. This is equally the case whether Derrida is talking of an identity expressed through a poem or whether the subject is national or cultural identity. What Derrida thus sees – and offers to show us in his gaze, from his other location – is a form of writing which does not permit itself to be read. This is the case even as this writing is also not a reading, strictly speaking, but rather a transformative and performative event. In such textual transactions, Derrida traces the textual identity so as to transform its identity by allowing the other identities of the text to emerge.

Such an impulse as the (re)generative rhythm(s) of Derrida's writing often means that we will encounter in Derrida's texts writers and *their* texts with which we believe we have some familiarity, yet who, in the wake of Derrida, strike us as never quite themselves, as somehow other than the signatures with which we assume ourselves to be on nodding terms, at least. If Derrida's Baudelaire, for example, of whom he writes in *Memoirs of the Blind*, is a certain less well-known Baudelaire than the author of *Les Fleurs de mal*, then the same may also be said, while acknowledging the singularity of the idiomatic example, of Paul Valéry. The Valéry encountered in Derrida's texts is not (simply) the poet Valéry, but an other Valéry, Valéry the political or philosophical essayist. This is not to say that the several Valérys are absolutely separate; this is to suggest an impossibility of the order of the supposed separability between constative and performative utterances. Instead we would suggest that the Valéry who we see through Derrida's eyes can never be read as quite the same as the writer we may have encountered before the event of reading in Derrida's wake. The affirmation of an other Valéry, an affirmation of an other identity *for* Valéry, is also potentially a denial of a Valéry who we believed we had read. (The same might also be said for Baudelaire, Mallarmé, and, indeed, of Derrida himself, albeit all in highly different contexts.)

And it is Paul Valéry, this other Valéry within the familiar poet, side by side with himself, but never as quite himself, who dictates the triply remarked phrase in the opening of Derrida's essay 'Qual Quelle: Valéry's Sources', given first as a lecture on the centenary of the writer's birth, in 1971. Three times, then, in different, differing and self-deferring, self-dividing ways, Derrida writes of the writing of the subject:

I – mark(s) first of all a division in what will have been able to appear in the beginning. (*MP* 275)

– I mark(s) the division – (*MP* 275)

– again I mark (s) and multiply (multiplies) the division – (*MP* 276)

These statements in their reiteration perform the division and dispersal of the subject, tracing a regenerative fragmentation of any possible identity (identities) even at that moment which appears to be the beginning of something so conventional as an essay or lecture. As Derrida puts it in the very same essay, the source is already divided (*MP* 277), and this is as an acknowledgement of a certain 'repetition of Valéry's' (*MP* 278). If this is a repetition of Valéry's, something already installed in Valéry's own writing on the subject of the source, as Derrida intimates, then it is also in a certain way a reiteration and transformation of Valéry: a performance of Valéry's implied practice, as well as a précis of what Valéry does, *in other words*.[3] I spoke just now of the (re)generative rhythm(s) of Derrida's writings. To claim this as a particular identity for Derrida, however, is to miss how such a movement or pulse 'in Derrida' is also that similar – though never exactly the same – 'power of regeneration', claimed by Derrida as Valéry's interest in 'Qual Quelle' (*MP* 278). In performing Valéry otherwise, Derrida displaces his own beginning *and his identity* in an essay on the impossibility of the source as a knowable single site, producing his own otherness.

The passage from which the claim concerning the 'power of regeneration' comes is itself quite astounding in its opening, as are the subsequent folds of what is a very long paragraph. Derrida begins with a moment of return, a certain folding back upon himself in the section entitled 'rebound':

> I had not *reread* Valéry for a long time…. in going back to the texts I thought I knew … I asked myself in what ways a certain relationship had changed. Where had the displacement, which in a way had prevented me from taking my bearings, been effected? (*MP* 278; emphasis added)

The act of rereading places a number of identities – a number of looks or gazes: the I who rereads now, the I who reread then, I asking myself – into a somewhat indeterminate relationship which disturbs and displaces the possibility of either a stable identity or any simple communication as the self-affirmation of an identity to itself. The look, looking back, looking at oneself as other than oneself, and asking oneself certain unanswerable questions, can never be represented straightforwardly as 'I', the inscription of a self-presence (and this, of course, has been announced already at the beginning of the essay). Rereading already places the writing subject in a certain other relationship with/in himself, while partially erasing, denying, the possibilities of a first or original reading, forever displaced in the passage by that 'first' redoubling verb. Doubleness, displacement, dislocation of the subject. 'I' is prevented from 'taking its bearings', and the source of that displacement can only be located in the unanswerable question, which leaves the subject all at sea.

Paul Valéry thus arrives and returns, arriving as he returns – *l'arrivant* as *le revenant* – to disturb identity. He turns up on a number of occasions in Derrida's writing, and often in a quite haunting fashion as the spirit at the wake of identity which Derrida has been rehearsing, certainly in later texts with regard to the question of national, spiritual or cultural identity. From 1971 to 1991, Derrida returns to Valéry, even as the poet returns to Derrida. Between *Margins of Philosophy* and *The Other Heading*, the question is, specifically with regard to Valéry, never simply one, but is always a doubling and regenerative question of identities and the impossibility of first or final locations. He – Valéry – may well be everywhere, at every turn of the page, but the occasions to which we limit ourselves here are those involving discussion, citation, exegesis, passing reference, the deferral of authority. There is the essay, already briefly cited at the opening of this chapter (and immediately above), 'Qual Quelle'. There are also references in *Glas*, 'Psyché: Invention de l'autre' (already mentioned), *Specters of Marx*, *The Other Heading*, *Of Spirit*, and as a signature in a footnote to 'Ulysses Gramophone'. Many of the references to Valéry, and the citings (or sightings) of him, concern themselves with questions of identity and the spirit of identity, even with spirit or spectrality itself.

In particular, there is the question of Valéry's passing appearance on the stage of European identity in Derrida's *The Other Heading*. In this text, Valéry makes the kind of spectral appearance discussed in *Specters*, where Derrida situates Valéry in a 'tradition' of spectral discourse tracing itself back to, and in the wake of, Shakespeare, via Karl Marx (*SM*, 5–6). Insistently, Valéry's text returns via some of Derrida's most extended endnotes, which endnotes serve to acknowledge the coming of the other as other and the desire to do justice to the other.[4] Thus the structure of Derrida's text is doubled, as if in homage to Derrida's Valérian (dis)orientation in 'Qual Quelle': arriving so insistently in the notes, the poet and essayist arrives in Derrida's wake, while Derrida acknowledges, both in the body of the text and, especially, in n.6 (*OH* 118–22), that all he can do is to write on the subject of European cultural identity *after* Valéry, giving up commentary and giving himself over in this footnote and those which follow to extended quotation. This thereby allows Valéry's haunting trace to double Derrida's own text, to disrupt the certainty of its own European cultural identity. We will come back to *The Other Heading*, but for the moment must take a look at Valéry's spectral trace in 'Psyche: Inventions of the Other'.

As with all ghostly apparitions (*AM* 64), Valéry's appearance is swift though somewhat significant in 'Psyche'. This essay, which treats of inventiveness in the work of Paul de Man, and offers a sketch for a reading of Francis Ponge's 'Fable', offers to confuse the identities of the constative and performative in language. The opening sentence of the essay is both '*used* and *mentioned*, as an example of an opening sentence', as Derek Attridge points out in his note to the text (*AL* 311, n.1).[5] Following Derrida's argument in the essay, Attridge also alerts the reader to the French 'original' of the opening sentence, 'What else am I going to be able to invent?' (P 25), which is: *Que vais-je inventer encore?* In its final word, the sentence is marked by a multiple ambiguity. *Encore* carries in it numerous identities, none of which are made any more certain in their meaning by the sentence having been framed as a question. The collapse of the use/mention binarism itself anticipates Derrida's comments on Ponge's text 'Fable', a text which allows Derrida, typically, to recall yet one more anterior, other identity, in a seminar given at Yale. As Derrida recalls, remembering such a beginning allows him to mime a 'starting over', which simultaneously calls up Ponge's text as a 'myth of impossible origins' (P 31), and which 'presents itself ... as the invention of language as the same and the other, of oneself as (of) the other' (P 31). Although Valéry is not mentioned, there are clearly discernible in these statements some of the concerns of 'Qual Quelle', especially in that phrase 'myth of impossible origins', which Derrida explores through Valéry's use of the word 'source' and the homonyms 'Perrier / Père y est'.

Following this, Derrida continues to regard certain situations or relationships by recalling a possible line of Valéry's: 'In the beginning was the fable' (P 32). This is described as 'miming but also translating the first words of John's gospel ... a performative demonstration of the very thing it is saying' (P 32). It is this – which, as we suggest, is Derrida's own practice/performance – which leads him to comment on that mark which divides 'I', the 'invention of the other in the same' (P 33). Ponge's text involves a particular narcissistic desire and the breaking of a mirror. Importantly, this figure of the mirror in Ponge's text offers us the sight of the possible gaze of the other, from the other to the other. We describe it as the figure of the mirror rather than the mirror because of Derrida's use of *figure* in the French text of 'Qual Quelle', which means both a figure in writing and the face or visage (to which we shall return). The subject is marked by a division in identity between writing and the look, of which Ponge's inscription of the looking-glass as poetic figure serves to remind us.

It is possible to catch the doubleness of *figure* in the figure of the echo's relationship to identity elsewhere in 'Psyche', where Valéry's echo finds Derrida in the wake of the poet once more. Derrida moves from the consideration of the invention of the other in the same to point out that Ponge's first line has no metalinguistic function (in this, Derrida's 'first' sentence in 'Psyche' has anticipated it). It is its own repetition and only that, an echo without origin (P 34), the echo of Narcissus. Although Valéry, strictly speaking, is not mentioned throughout this essay, other than that brief memory of Derrida's already cited, nonetheless, and arguably, Valéry returns and retreats again and again as the other of Derrida's words in the narcissistic commentary. The line in question which haunts Derrida's words is from Valéry's notebooks: 'It must be confessed that the self is nothing but an echo.'[6]

It is worth a momentary digression here, into Philippe Lacoue-Labarthe's thinking on the subject of identity, in order to suggest the communication and displacement between word and image which is at work in Derrida's writing on/after Valéry. In his reading of Theodor Reik and Jacques Lacan's analysis of the subject, Lacoue-Labarthe comments on the 'theoretical' consequence of thinking the subject at the limit of the theorizable that:

> the figure is never *one*. Not only is it the Other, but there is no unity or stability of the figural; the imago has no fixity or proper being. There is no 'proper image' with which to identify totally, no essence of the imaginary ... the subject 'desists' because it must always confront *at least* two figures (or one figure that is *at least* double), and that its only chance of 'grasping itself' lies in introducing itself and oscillating *between* figure and figure....
>
> Everything seems to point to the fact that this destabilizing division of the figural ... [connects] it, as a result, with the autobiographical compulsion itself. (Lacoue-Labarthe 1989, 176)

As one can see from Lacoue-Labarthe's remarks, the situation of identity involves both writing and the gaze, as well as what is located by the gaze of the other, misrecognizing the image as itself. Identity's (self-)destabilization is caught up in, connected to this 'autobiographical' compulsion: the desire to write oneself, to imagine and see oneself, but always seeing oneself from an other place (a self-displacing situating of one's identity caught by Derrida in the term 'autobio-photographies', from the title of an interview already quoted, a term which brings together the graphic, the figural and the look, the image). The complex strands woven together here are clearly discernible in Derrida's writings on identity, and especially in those places where the issue of cultural identity – in relation, say, to a 'French' writer or the French language – is at stake. We may even suggest, then, following the subject of fragmented identity and the echo of the subject as the other within the same, the other which places the self-same (identity) under erasure, that the interview just mentioned – 'There is no *one* Narcissism: Autobiophotographies' (a title which echoes Valéry's Narcissus fragments; *P...* 196–216) – is Derrida's clearest commentary on his otherness within French culture and within the French language, an otherness always being performed in every act of writing.

If otherness is not always or only the most appropriate word, exteriority might be. In response to a question concerning a certain Judaic-Greek-German traditional axis within his work, Derrida suggests that there is 'certainly ... a feeling of exteriority with regard to European, French, German, Greek culture.... I have the feeling that I am doing it from another place that I do not know: an exteriority based on a place that I do not inhabit in a certain way, or that I do not identify' (*P...* 206). Thus there is, for Derrida, a constant sense of placing himself in certain ungovernable situations in relation to perceivable dominant identities, and allowing that 'taking place' to dictate to him. Derrida's writing thus takes from Valéry's own texts (as it does with regard to Baudelaire, Mallarmé, Artaud, among so many others) the task of acknowledging the self looking at its other self within itself.

This is the very kind of 'situating', of placing or letting take place, with which we interest ourselves with regard to the question of the instability of identities: a situation which is neither an exhaustible nor definable context, but one which, once comprehended as a possibility, itself makes possible certain readings, certain writings (of Derrida's, our own), and certain ways of *seeing* involved with complicity *and* conflict, as the first epigraph to this essay announces. There is, thus, a relationship or situation marked by what Derrida, with reference to Mallarmé, has called '*suggestion*, ... undecided allusion' (*AL* 120), which relationship, in remarking the place where something takes place, announces a certain liminality and, with that, a question of undecidability concerning identity. The question of the undecided allusion is not only a question posed by Derrida to cultural or spiritual identities writ large but, as we know, at a particular lexico-conceptual level also. When, in 'There is no *one* Narcissism', Derrida comments that the word 'deconstruction' imposed itself on him (*P*... 211), he is acknowledging his relationship to French; importantly, however, he also points out that the word 'plays on several registers, for example linguistic or grammatical, but also mechanical or technical' (*P*... 211). This 'play' is precisely the play which moves between the lexical, the conceptual, the philosophical, cultural and, even, national registers as the disjointing of any simple identity, but from within its own structures. It is the effect of disjointing which occurs in Derrida's encounter with Valéry. Derrida's 'reading' of Valéry is concerned with the double question of spirit and identity, and the troubled relationship between these.

That triple parenthesis which spaces, displaces, and defers the unity of identity at the beginning of 'Qual Quelle' performs the play on several registers, and is reinvented by Derrida twenty years later, in his next significant transaction with Valéry, in *The Other Heading*.[7] As different as their respective topics may appear to be – the impossibility of locating a source, the question of Europe, *today* – both essays treat of the unfolding and fracturing of identities, demonstrating the necessity of thinking the other within the same as a precondition of thinking identity only on the condition of its non-identification with itself.

Before mentioning or citing Valéry in *The Other Heading*, Derrida opens himself to his audience in Turin, allowing them a particular view of himself, by confessing and confiding about his doubled relation to European identity.

> Je vous confierai pour commencer un sentiment. *Déjà* au sujet des caps – et des bords sur lesquels j'ai l'intention de me tenir. C'est le sentiment un peu accablé d'un vieil Européen. Plus précisément de quelqu'un qui, n'étant pas tout à fait européen par sa naissance, puisque je viens du rivage méridional de la Méditerranée, se tient aussi, de plus en plus avec l'âge, pour une sorte de métis européen sur-acculturé, sur-colonisé.... C'est peut-être le sentiment, en somme, de quelqu'un qui a dû, dès l'école de l'Algérie française, essayer de capitaliser la vieillesse de l'Europe tout en gardant un peu de la jeunesse insensible et impassible de l'autre bord. En vérité, toutes les marques s'une ingénuité encore incapable de cette autre vieillesse dont la culture française l'avait très tôt séparé. (*l'ac* 13–14)

> To begin, I will confide in you a feeling. *Already* on the subject of headings [*caps*] – and of the shores on which I intend to remain. It is

the somewhat weary feeling of an old European. More precisely, of someone who, not quite European by birth, since I come from the southern coast of the Mediterranean, considers himself, and more and more so with age, to be a sort of over-acculturated, over-colonized European hybrid.… In short, it is perhaps, the feeling of someone who, as early as grade school in French Algeria, must have tried to capitalize, and capitalize upon, the old age of Europe, while at the same time keeping a little of the indifferent and impassive youth *of the other shore*. Keeping, in truth, all the marks of an ingenuity still incapable of this *other old age* from which French culture had, from very early on, separated him. (*OH* 6–7; last two emphases added)

We notice in this gesture the moment of 'autobiographical compulsion' spoken of by Lacoue-Labarthe, along with a gesture of 'autobiophotography', the snapshot of the self as other, a polaroid snapped from some other place. It is a gesture which Derrida doubles when speaking of Valéry's 'origin', reiterating (auto)biography as other than itself: 'Valéry is a Mediterranean spirit.… this Mediterranean shore also interests me – coming as I do from the other shore if not from the other heading (from a shore that is principally neither French, nor European, nor Latin, nor Christian) …' (*OH* 36–7). That question of a certain exteriority finds itself repositioned, allowing Derrida the opportunity to speak, in the wake of Valéry, from the other's situation, with the gaze of the other, towards Europe, about European identity and its own perception of the other.

If 'I' had marked in 'Qual Quelle' the division of the subject, here, twenty years later, in the longer quotation given above and in the remark on Valéry also, identity is remarked, once more, as always already doubled, self-divided from itself by being both old and young, European and Mediterranean, European and not (quite) European, and having a certain relationship to a particular intellectual, philosophical, cultural axis, which in Derrida's case is Judaic-Greek-German, and which, with the example of Valéry, is that of a 'European from the Greco-Roman Mediterranean world' (*OH* 36). And all the while there are in Derrida's remarks a number of folds which are also unfoldings, realizations and confessions. There is that sense of gazing at Europe as the other, but from the complicated self-realization of the difference within identity, of being already other, viewing that other old age from the other shore, the shore of the other. We see Derrida (and are we not also being invited to see Valéry in a similar situation?) gazing back on his other self, seeing his otherness within European, Francophone culture, from a number of distinct positions, all views of the other within the same. The beginning is not really such in this passage because the confidence which Derrida shares with his audience, and then again with us, is already [*déjà*][8] marked, remarked by the subject, viewed from particular shores: the question of Europe seen from some other place. French cultural identity both divides the subject and is divided by it. It leaves its mark on the subject's identity – 'I' marked by that division – while remarking those insoluble ties between binarisms already mentioned. The very liminality of the eyes as they mediate between self and other is what comes to be remarked through Derrida's recollection, his memory of otherness determined as never quite the same as any of the dominant cultural traces, his memory of otherness, imprinted, colonized, by the culture of the other.

Yet this division and doubling is the necessity of identity, the possibility of a future 'European identity', as Derrida comments. As he puts it in the second axiom from *The Other Heading*, the entire problematic of European identity can be expressed as: '*What is proper to a culture is to not be identical to itself*' (*OH* 9). What Derrida calls self-difference, difference to and from itself, is the internal possibility – the other within the same – of cultural identity. There can be no 'culture or cultural identity without this difference *with itself.*... a difference at once internal and irreducible to the "at home (with itself)" [*chez soi*]' (*OH* 10). How may we relate this to the autobiographical compulsion, to the gaze of the other from within the apparently self-same, and also to the very question of deconstruction as being intimately tied to the question of French identity as never quite itself?

Derrida continues by stating that what has been said of a cultural identity 'can be said ... of all identity or all identification; there is not self-relation, no relation to oneself, no identification with oneself, without culture, but a culture of oneself *as* a culture *of* the other, a culture of the double genitive and of the *difference to oneself*. The grammar of the double genitive also signals that a culture never has a single origin' (*OH* 10). Having strategically signalled in these passages following the autobiographical confession the shift from 'I' to 'we', Derrida announces the impossibility of saying 'we' alone, moving through the act of memory from cultural identity, through one's relation to one's own identity and the culture(s) which determine that identity, to the very question of grammatical doubling which affirms doubleness and heterogeneity, while denying a single source or location. To quote a line from 'Qual Quelle' – for surely this is one of the possible texts to which Derrida's recollection and consideration of identity's otherness returns us – '... the source cannot be reassembled into its originary unity' (*MP* 279). What is at stake here on the subject of identity's duration and discontinuity for Derrida is what he describes in that earlier essay, in Valéry's wake, as 'the duration and return of a writing' (*MP* 279). In Valéry's words (cited by Derrida), the question is one of 'the plurality of the singular' (*MP* 282).

The plurality of the singular is what marks and is marked by 'I'. It is that which is performed by the figural, by the figure of writing, and the figure of the face. As Alain Finkielkraut points out in his study of Lévinas, *The Wisdom of Love*, it is the face which constitutes for the 'I' who looks and desires to read the 'alterity of the Other' (Finkielkraut 1997, 29). The face is that 'tangle of signs' which remain other through being unreadable, even though seen (1997, 31). Derrida's writing on Valéry amounts to a response to this alterity. It constitutes a tracing of and, up to this plurality within the singular, the trace of the other within the same, of difference within identity. Derrida's writing comes face to face with Valéry's text and offers us at times transformative paraphrase and, at others, transformed citation, where Derrida's writing gives way to the other's text, and the other of the text being written. This is of course a performance as well as an analysis, as the following passage from 'Qual Quelle' demonstrates/enacts:

> The I has 'no relation with a face.' That which sees and is seen first of all, that which yields (itself to) seeing, the face, then elevates the source to an initial displacement. In this figure an initial metaphoricity perhaps places on view that which has no *figure*. (*MP* 283–4; emphasis added)

The figural is always that which is self-displacing. Here we read both Derrida's commentary and his simultaneous placing of his own I/eye in the place of the other, regarding or yielding itself to seeing, with regard to Valéry, in a manner which does not comment on its own processes directly, yet which unfolds itself in the act of seeing. The initial displacement has always already taken place, so that Derrida writes in Valéry's wake, miming and giving himself up to the metaphorical or figural relationship. The division and plurality which is marked by the commentary/performance of the text's singularity in relation to its other is remarked by Derrida in the negated term *figure*, which in French is self-dividing between the figure in writing and the face (the face which does the looking and the face which is seen). The deconstructive movements here are traced by Derrida throughout Valéry's essay on the source (and throughout the essay on Valéry). It is, however, chiefly Derrida's focus on the face/figure, sighting/writing torque which interests us here, and which connects 'Qual Quelle' to *The Other Heading*. Derrida follows the movement in Valéry from the consideration of I as source, as pure presence (*MP* 280–1), through its function as that which names itself (in Valéry's words) as the '"universal pronoun, the appellation of which has no connection with a face"' (*MP* 282). On this, Derrida amplifies significantly:

> That which has no relation to a *face*: let us understand this equally as with a particular subject ... and with the system which defines the face, to be reconsidered further on as a source which receives: the eyes, the mouth, the ears which yield (themselves to) sight, speech, hearing. (*MP* 282)

Once more, Derrida maps the other place of the self already marked in the self-same, a gesture summarized three pages on from this comment: 'Glance of the figure, figure of the glance, the source is always divided, carried away outside itself.... As soon as it *performs* Narcissus's turn, it no longer knows itself. It no longer belongs to itself' (*MP* 285). If Derrida writes from a certain exteriority he does not quite know, this in itself is the gesture of the division, the plurality of the singular and the trace of writing within identity, performing itself as never quite itself, seeing itself as other than itself. Even as we catch sight of the other, so the other has already given us over to being seen.

The figure and the face, the fraught questions concerning identity as the negotiation between (not) seeing oneself and seeing the other, return to note 6 in *The Other Heading* (*OH* 118–22). This note marks for Derrida what is arguably the most sustained turn towards Valéry's text, a turn which is continued across the rest of *The Other Heading's* notes. The double 'figure', that of the figure and the face, is raised through the engagement with Valéry over the issue of 'thinking Paris', and what it means for Valéry to think Paris, as a figure for a particular intellectual, spiritual and cultural identity. In this note Derrida actively doubles Valéry's cultural identity in the first sentence: 'Valéry the Mediterranean, Valéry the European ...' (*OH* 118 n.6). The writing

performs the gesture of the division of the self and parallel relationship between a certain self and other mapped in the textual gesture
which affirms hybridity and also speaks imminently to Derrida's own
situation and to the problematic question of French cultural identity
as a self-sufficient identification. The note moves through a series of
reversals and inversions of thought which mime Valéry's own strategies. As Derrida shows us, the other author's thinking on the possibility of thinking Paris evolves around a series of performative folds
whereby the effort to think Paris is shown to be part of the production
of an identity wherein one is already thought by Paris. This inverse
movement is shown by Derrida to be predicated, immediately prior to
this moment in Valéry's 'Paris is Here', by 'the "figure" of the face [la
"figure" de la figure], [which] had guided the analysis of this capital of
capitals. One actually *looks the capital in the face*. One distinguishes
the face, the head and the forehead' (*OH* 119).[9] As the French parenthesis demonstrates, the figure is already doubled, and redoubles
itself in its ambiguities, and this in regard to the situation of a certain
pre-eminent cultural identity as the capital, the head, of Europe and
also the capital on which to build as the model for a particular
construction of cultural identity. But the face does not see itself; it is
seen from an other place, from within Valéry's text, for example,
which unfolds for Derrida 'insistent ambiguit[ies]' and the 'abyssal
potentialities of this equivocation' concerning Parisian identity (*OH*
121).

  Paris thus becomes a certain figurehead for a spiritual identity and
yet also, in another text from 1937, a concentration camp which
consumes every Frenchman who distinguishes himself, to paraphrase
Valéry (*OH* 122). We recognize through Derrida's citations a gesture
which cannot quite be read, even though we see it so well. Ten years
apart, Valéry's texts produce Paris as *pharmakon*,[10] determining,
writing, performing identities constructed out of contraries. Twenty
years apart Derrida returns to Valéry, writing around the subject of
identity's own dissemination, its difference from it-self. It is Valéry's
own writing which unfolds the disseminative gesture, tracing the
question of identity with all its 'abyssal potentialities', but perhaps
most insistently over the doubling which occurs in the figure and the
face, the figure of the face, looking and looked at. Looking into
Valéry's I/eye, Derrida draws an other reflection, seeing himself, yet
not able to read himself in an ambiguous relationship with French,
Parisian, cultural identity.

Perhaps it is for this reason that Valéry maintains for Derrida so significant a role, even though his trace is only ever imminent. As Derrida suggests in *The Other Heading*, justifying his citation of Valéry, the other writer's text 'bears the marks of an urgency, or, more properly, an *imminence* ... whose repetition we seem to be living' (*OH* 61). This gesture retains the autobiographical trace while moving it beyond the purely personal. Derrida's own writing lives out the trace of this imminence, not only in the figural gestures of the two writers' arguments but in the image we glimpse of them both, as both European and not European (*OH* 64), as speaking and writing in French (*OH* 49), and yet finding this situation fraught with paradoxes, tensions, and estrangement (*P...* 416). Indeed, as he moves towards his conclusion, Derrida points to the Valérian comprehension (at the end of the 1930s) of the paradox of claims to universal importance for French cultural identity, which Valéry sees as both ridiculous and fine (*OH* 73). In having drawn on the doubleness, the division, in Valéry as both European and Mediterranean, in having located Valéry along the margins of his text as that other trace within the French heading, Derrida comments:

> Mais je ne suis pas, ni ne sens *de part en part* européen.... je ne veux pas et ne dois pas être européen *de part en part*.... Mon identité culturelle, celle au nom de laquelle je parle, n'est pas seulement européene, elle n'est pas identique à elle-même.... Si je déclarais pour conclure que je me sens européen *entres autres choses*, serait-ce être par là, en cette déclaration même, plus ou moins européen?... Aux autres, en tout cas, et à moi *parmi eux*, d'en décider. (*l'ac* 80–1)

> I am not, nor do I feel, European *in every part*, that is, European through and through.... I do not want to be and must not be European through and through.... My cultural identity, that in the name of which I speak, is not only European, it is not identical to itself.... If to conclude, I declared that I feel European *among other things*, would this be, in this very declaration, to be more or less European.... It is up to the others, in any case, and up to me *among them*, to decide. (*OH* 82–3)

Returning to the resistance that always lies at the heart of the autobiographical impulse, a resistance which is also the necessary tracing of affirmation and otherness, Derrida once more collapses the distinction between comment and performance, as he simultaneously marks the fragmentation of the I, locating himself in some other position, in the position of the other, and seeing himself – me *among them* – among those European others, in the midst of European identity, as the other within the same. Or this is one possible reading, at least. Thus Derrida always writes in Valéry's wake, seeing the poet as an other who returns in a ghostly fashion to disturb the (question of) identity of (in) Derrida's writing. Seeing the other, Derrida's writing performs that act of tracing the *trait* which divides the identity of the writer as a self who recognizes himself in his other. Clearly, this is the gesture in the early essay 'Qual Quelle', where Derrida gives himself up to the other in the discussion, especially at those moments when he considers the dream or 'lure of the I' (*MP* 297) conjured by hearing oneself speak. One does not see oneself, one is blind to one's location; but the event of speech convinces us that we are present to ourselves, our identities complete and self-sufficient. As Derrida points out, '[w]hen I speak (to myself) without moving tongue and lips, I believe that I hear myself, although the source is other; or I believe that we are two.... this [is] the possibility of a "normal" double hallucination' (*MP* 297). Yet it is possible to sight oneself otherwise, as the concluding comments from *The Other Heading* demonstrate. Instead of maintaining the 'possibility of the double hallucination', Derrida's quasi-autobiographical gesture doubles the '"normal" double' in a movement, a rhythm which prohibits the European 'we' speaking itself to itself alone.

All of which is to follow in Valéry's footsteps, to *see* in Valéry that which divides identity and thus holds itself up as other than itself, performing its own deconstruction. In seeing Valéry's blind spots, as Michael Naas puts it, in 'Qual Quelle', Derrida displaces himself and, in encountering Valéry, transforming Valéry, transforms his own acts of writing also, performing as other than himself through acts of ventriloquization. In doing so, Derrida demonstrates what Naas calls 'the irreducible singularity of Valéry's discourse [with which] ... Derrida identifies himself, his situation, and his time' (Naas 1992, lv). Hence, the frequent, though fleeting appearances of Valéry throughout Derrida's writing, as the haunting example which disjoints the notion of the exemplary, illuminating the return of the other and the impossibility of the source as an origin, explored in 'Qual Quelle'. For Valéry is, for Derrida, the figure whose texts make it impossible to know the status of the poet and, by implication, unsettle the identities of both Derrida and, in turn, the reader. In the wake of Valéry (as merely one singular example among so many others) Derrida performs that work which is the most necessary, seeing and situating identities against the most imposing dominant identities, those which are, in his own words, 'the most solid ones in some way, of the culture, the philosophy, the politics in which we live' (*P...* 215).

In coming to comprehend this, we may perhaps begin to understand that Derrida's work, while never reducible to the comfort of a programme, is, nevertheless, relentlessly political, speaking as it does from some other place to the negotiations we must enact in our acts of critical engagement. This might mean that in the act of reading we must never bring to bear an identity ahead of our textual encounter. Facing up to Derrida means losing face, giving way as a response to the alterity of the other, as the only responsible gesture in the act of writing (of) identities.

4 The Hauntological Example: The City as the Haunt of Writing in the Texts of Iain Sinclair [1]

'can you seriously expect *anybody* to understand these things?'
Mike Goldmark to Iain Sinclair (*LT*)

Who wrote this book?

Iain Sinclair (*RD*)

L'avenir est aux fantômes

Jacques Derrida (S)

First apparition

The dread word, GHOST, recalls me. (Dickens 1985a, 246)

Charles Dickens uses these words near the beginning of 'The Haunted Man', a seasonal ghost story set in London. The topography of the sentence is interesting, not least for its own spectral, self-haunted doubling. The narrator is apparently troubled by a spirit which anticipates or haunts the narrative which is to follow. The sentence is marked by an excess, a displacement within itself that troubles the stable location of any identity. There is haunting within the very architecture of the sentence. The emphasis rests on that already troubled and troubling sign – ghost – as signifier of a signifier, rather than by the always already absent thing itself. This differential emphasis is redoubled in Dickens's own written stress and marked by the printer's use of small upper-case letters for the word 'ghost'. Then, that troublesome phrase 'word, GHOST' may be read with a little – but only a very little – forcing as 'word-ghost': a ghost composed of words, the trace of a trace inscribing words; not a ghost at all but the ghost of a ghost, a spectral signature or trace, haunting the very words on the page and referring, if at all, to an apparitional trembling.

Also of interest in Dickens's sentence is that call or impression which the word makes, the trace of the other left on the memory of the subject. There is too that strangely emphasized focus in the syntax of the statement on the trace of the call as *recall*, as a double act of memory and writing, where GHOST comes to map the space between writing and memory, troubling both. The subject awaits the chance or event of such a re-call, with the word, GHOST, being that which returns. He awaits its arrival, the spectre being, as Jacques Derrida has brought to our attention, the *revenant*, the one who only ever comes in coming back. Even and especially if, in Derrida's words, and as Dickens reminds us,

> ... this, the spectral, *is not*. Even and especially if this, which is neither substance, nor essence, nor existence, *is never present as such*. (*SM* xviii)

Which is nothing other than to suggest that the spectral is that which is written, and that writing, the trace, *différance*, are spectral through and through. We are not in the presence of a spectre, then, but are attended by a haunting rhythm which is nonetheless strangely familiar. There is written on to the same space, the mark of the uncanny, and yet, simultaneously, the domestic scene of haunting, haunting's familiar domesticity. As Mark Wigley points out in his own reading of the haunted house as a recurrent spectral trope in the work of Jacques Derrida, 'a house is only a house inasmuch as it is haunted' (Wigley 1993, 162). As we shall see in the context of Iain Sinclair's mediation of London, the same can also be said for the city, for its institutional, architectural and topographical spaces. Ghosts return to disturb the idea of structure. To understand the city is to understand its being haunted, its being-spectral. The city's identity is thus always already disturbed from within by some other, haunting trace.

Second apparition

This chapter proposes an introduction to the importance of the spectral in Iain Sinclair's writing, specifically his most recent publication, *Lights Out for the Territory*, although also with reference to other works by Sinclair.[2] This approach to Sinclair is governed in part by my response to Jacques Derrida's interest in spectres, spirits and other haunting traces, and, to a lesser extent, the interest shown by architectural theorists in the writings of Jacques Derrida, especially where issues of architecture and spectrality overlap. A poet and novelist, Iain Sinclair focuses most, if not all, of his energies on the nature and condition of his adopted home, London. Particularly, his texts, from the poems *Lud Heat* and *Suicide Bridge* to the novels *White Chappell Scarlet Tracings*, *Downriver* and *Radon Daughters*, explore in aleatory fashion the various energy flows of the city as he maps out what he calls in numerous places the 'psychogeography' of London. The psychogeography which Sinclair traces raises spectres which are always already there, revenants of the city, endlessly recalled through walking, memory and writing. Drawing on the various histories and narratives of gnomic mysticism and urban violence that haunt the structure of the city, from the Temple of Mithras and the alchemical writing of John Dee and Elias Ashmole, through William Blake, Charles Dickens, and Jack the Ripper, to Jack 'the Hat' McVitie, the Kray Brothers, and Margaret Thatcher,[3] Sinclair's texts are to be considered not so much as representations of London in any facile sense as they are attempts on the part of the writer to be faithful to the psychic nature of the city as he comprehends it. Areas of the city such as Lambeth come to be comprehended as particularly spectral.

The act of writing the city is, then, for Sinclair, always an act of responding to ghosts, to the traces of ghosts. Writing London involves acts of fidelity to memories which are not our own. As Sinclair puts it, '[f]urious displacements of energy are capable of damaging the membrane of what we call "the past". The past is an optional landscape. We are gifted with unearned memories, memories on which we have no moral purchase' (*LT* 214). The work of such displacement, or what Jacques Derrida calls 'ghostly disjunction' (A*M* 81), means that, for Sinclair, '[w]e are [written as] the fiction of vanished lives and buildings … misremembered and ineradicable' (*LT* 237). London is, then, the city of the eternal return of the haunting, haunted trace, where the texts of William Blake and Jeffrey Archer (novelist and sometime member of Thatcher's cabinet), for example, intersect, never quite themselves, returning to haunt our comprehension of the urban space. Even the Thames is understood as a temporal trace and projection, retaining 'its special status as a ribbon of memory' (*LT* 178).

Writing allows ghosts which have left an indelible or 'ineradicable' (*LT* 145) mark on the structure of the city to return, to 'stalk' Sinclair's writing even as he 'stalks' the city streets, whether in a fictional guise or as himself. Sinclair's writing is informed by a range of texts which express faithfully the always haunted architecture of London, transforming the space into architexture and *an*architecture, as that within the structure which both haunts and solicits the framework. Most immediately, Sinclair's debt is to the ghosts of Blake and Dickens, as his writing constitutes on occasions the partial palimpsest – but also the equally partial erasure – of texts such as *Jerusalem, Milton, Sketches by Boz, Bleak House* and *Our Mutual Friend*, to name merely a few. There is readable a reciprocal spectrality between Blake, Dickens and Sinclair, as his narratives come to seem like ghostly variants of his literary predecessors, even as they are haunted by those earlier writers of London.

The reciprocity between the three writers is most remarked, most easily traced, in those places in Sinclair's text where writing assumes a spectral effect of redoubling what are discernibly Dickensian and Blakean rhythms of urban inscription. In Blake, we read the lists of place names, those otherwise arbitrary catalogues of London locations, which today seem most like the arbitrary wanderings of the No. 19 bus, which runs from Islington to Lambeth, north-east to south-west. William Blake, who is named a number of times (*LT* 96, 103, 128, 143, 150, 154, 189, 214, 215; whereas Dickens is not, unless as the absence which drives the textual shape at given moments) as the ghost whose city-spectres haunt not only Sinclair but a number of his contemporaries, is manifested most powerfully in two places:

> Aldgate, Bishopsgate, Moorgate, Aldersgate, Cripplegate, Newgate, Ludgate, Billingsgate, with the Tower, Barbican, and Castle Baynard: eleven wounds in the electrical circuit.... The city as is proper, is one gate short of holy Jerusalem, of symmetry. (*LT* 103)

The conceit is positively and, I feel, undeniably recognizable as Blakean in the power it conjures. Sinclair's invocation of gates, already partly traced in the earlier *Suicide Bridge* (*SB* 183), and no longer in existence, suggests a spectrality to the city, a haunted trace as *retrait*, part of that London always already gone, leaving only its trace. The abyssal figure of the always missing gate which breaks the symmetrical circuit might well be traced, I would argue, from Blake's *Jerusalem*, with its suggestion of the golden pillars of Jerusalem rising from Lambeth, the house of the lamb. The gates now remain as only absent signifiers of signifiers for, as Sinclair tells us, '[T]he meaning of the gates has been carried away with the brickwork' (*LT* 103). Blake is then invoked as the 'godfather of all psychogeographers' whose verse dictates possible walks through London, ahead of their happening (*LT* 214). Finally, Blake is found haunting the work of Sinclair's contemporary, graphic novelist Alan Moore, in his sequence *From Hell*, which considers the *bête noire* of Sinclair's own *White Chappell Scarlet Tracings*, the Jack the Ripper murders. Speaking of Sir William Gull who appears as prime suspect in Moore's text, Sinclair writes:

> A lecture tour of the lefthand path. King's Cross gives way, as Gull munches through a bag of black grapes, to Hackney. 'Albion Drive. 'Twould seem auspicious in that we aspire to probe the ventricles of London, England's heart. Regard the London Fields...' Snippets of Blake, brief asides on the Dionysian ... and the cab rolls on to Bunhill Fields; Hawksmoor's obelisk at St Luke, Old Street (pencilled crosses on the map); then Cleopatra's Needle, the Tower of London, St George-in-the-East and Christ Church, Spitalfields ... (*LT* 128)

This is Sinclair's précis and citation of Moore's text, the words of Queen Victoria's surgeon promising the ghost of Martin Amis, while the city becomes mapped through another of those locations-become-citations. When we read 'Snippets of Blake' we know we're in the very heart of such snippets, and in the very heart of the spectral city, the trace of which is confirmed by those haunting structures of Nicholas Hawksmoor, the subject of both Sinclair's *Lud Heat* and Peter Ackroyd's *Hawksmoor*.

More than this, however, there is readable a certain ghostly transference between the Blakean signature-topography and the anarchic and ungovernable taxonomic traces of the city which are to be found so often in Dickens. (Think of Krook's window, in *Bleak House*, which we might fancifully imagine as an anagram and signature for London, and which, without too much trouble, we might rewrite as Blake's

House, bringing us both to Soho and Lambeth simultaneously.) Dickens frequently writes descriptions of the city and its various locations according to unorderable lists, taxonomies of forced and heterogeneous concatenations which speak of the condition of the city. It is such taxonomy which whispers the word-ghost of Dickens in Sinclair's writing. The ungovernable taxonomy as trace of the city is to be found in all Sinclair's works. There is for instance the following list (one of many) in *Suicide Bridge*: '... broken razor-blades, vaseline, offal, sheepshead soup, / copydex, panatella, gammon' (*SB* 193). Lists such as these proliferate throughout Sinclair's writing, but one more must suffice for now, from *Lights Out*:

> Alignments of telephone kiosks, maps made from moss on the slopes of promotional bills from cancelled events at York Hall, visits to the homes of dead writers, bronze casts on war memorials, plaster dogs, beer mats, concentrations of used condoms, the crystalline patterns of glass shards surrounding an imploded BMW quarter-light window ... (*LT* 4)

And so the list goes on according to the dictates of the city. Dickens understood how necessary it was to record such images as the debt of fidelity the writer owes to the city, and so does Iain Sinclair. It is this double-trace, the Blake–Dickens axis, as axiomatic inscription that the city imposes, which any reader of the city may find and must pay attention to when travelling on foot through London.

Sinclair seems indebted to Blake and Dickens as the most obvious but by no means exclusive literary executors of the city (the ghosts of Verlaine and Rimbaud demand our attention in Sinclair's work but must for now be neglected). Like them, he comprehends what is dictated to any writing on the city by London itself. This is seen in Sinclair's example of the 'cosmic egg' entwined by a 'dentated snake' from the Sealy tomb in St Mary's Church, Lambeth (*LT* 193–4). Beneath the verse which appears on the egg, Sinclair notices, 'on closer examination, ... the ghost of another poem, or earlier version of this one, ... hidden beneath; the letters filled in and partially obliterated' (*LT* 194). So, the trace of London: palimpsest and haunting, or, in Sinclair's own words (describing the work of Brian Catling), 'iteration, transformation, erasure' (*LT* 261). The ghosts who return via Sinclair's writing give us to understand what the writer describes as 'the unedited book of the city ... filled with a cacophony of quotations ...' (*LT* 232).

The structure of *Lights Out for the Territory* is that of an apparently loose collection of essays, the shared subject of which is London or, to be more precise, a series of Londons. The subtitle of the work is '9 Excursions in the Secret History of London', and the essays move from a consideration of randomly observed graffiti through the observation of Ronnie Kray's funeral, some caustic critique of Thatcherite piracy, to the possibility – or otherwise – of filming London; from anonymous writing, then, to the lyricism of the image, as the trajectory of the city's traces. As with Sinclair's other writings, the nine essays which comprise *Lights Out* offer a range of sometimes cryptic, sometimes journalistic considerations of aspects of the culture, the history, the textuality and, most importantly for us, the spectrality of London. Yet the loose structure of this present text is precisely that: loose or, at least, always resonating. We're on shaky ground when we write about London, and Sinclair knows this. Such resonance in the textual field is, we are made to realize, a disturbance inherent in the structure itself, so that the very act of writing about the city of London always involves its own dislocation, that which leads the writer and reader astray.

The book begins with an apparent consideration of graffiti, the ostensible purpose of the first essay, 'Skating on Thin Eyes: The First Walk' (*LT* 1–54), being that Sinclair and his photographer, Marc Atkins, will trace a V-shaped route from Abney Park in Hackney, south-east to Greenwich, and then to return north along the line of the River Lea to Chingford Mount, 'recording and retrieving the messages on walls, lampposts, doorjambs' (*LT* 1). Graffiti is defined as 'reproduced words [which] join the rest of the trumpeting exotica in the encyclopaedia of the city' (*LT* 16). The 'walls, lamposts, doorjambs' recall and are haunted by numerous Dickensian accounts of urban architecture in all their arbitrary chaos, while the phrase 'trumpeting exotica in the encyclopaedia of the city' seems itself haunted with Wilkins Micawber's description of London to David Copperfield, who suggests to his young companion that 'your peregrinations in this metropolis have not as yet been extensive, and that you might have some difficulty in penetrating the arcana of the Modern Babylon in the direction of the City Road ...' (Dickens 1985b, 211). Despite the fun that Dickens is clearly having with Micawber, there is a sense that, when encountering London, we all become haunted by Micawber's words, as Sinclair's writing makes clear.[4] Yet, to return to the question of the graffiti, the writing on the wall also belongs to an act of exorcism for Sinclair: words reiterated on different walls, in different streets and neighbourhoods, suggest a form of ghosting which transforms one place into another, while turning the walker into a ghost to be exorcised in the act of reading (*LT* 16). Sinclair's perception arises out of his conviction that '[f]ragments of London are perceived [in the act of walking] as Polaroid epiphanies; signed and abandoned' (*LT* 2). The instant of the Polaroid image suggests the haunting trace and the 'instant without duration' spoken of by Jacques Derrida in his comment on the appearances of ghosts:

> Ghosts always pass quickly, with the infinite speed of a furtive apparition, in an instant without duration, presence without presence of a present which, coming back only *haunts*. The ghost, *le re-venant*, the survivor, appears only by means of figure or fiction, but its appearance is not nothing, nor is it mere semblance. (AM 64)

This instant of the *revenant* is precisely what haunts Sinclair and what is captured momentarily in his appreciation of graffiti; this instant always determines the *trait* as *retrait*, as we see from the statements quoted from *Lights Out*, leaving the writer – and the readers – witness to the trace of spirit in a state of 'uncertainty and indirection', to recall a phrase of Geoffrey Bennington's (Bennington 1994, 202).

Spectrality is implied once more when the writer observes that '[s]prayed messages are meaningless, having no programme beyond the announcement of a non-presence' (*LT* 3), and that walking can easily turn into a 'phantom-biopsy' (*LT* 4). Even though I spoke earlier of a trajectory from writing to film, this is anticipated already in Sinclair's prose, both in the earlier image of the Polaroid epiphany and when he describes graffiti as '... "open field" semiological excesses on the wall ... [looming] like the back projection of a middle period Godard film' (*LT* 18). Walking London is then already a complex textual affair of drifting and transference, an affair of haunting in short, driven by random inscriptions, projections and traces, with the suggestion that something about the city could be known through reading its chance signs in an unpredictable fashion. Reading the graffiti as cinematic projection alerts us to the fact that while the spectre may be visible, it is never tangible, as Derrida reminds us (S 129). Sinclair is quite explicit on the point that the twin movements of walking and writing might be closely linked: 'I had developed this curious conceit while working on my novel *Radon Daughters*: that the physical movements of the characters across their territory might spell out the letters of a secret alphabet. Dynamic shapes, with ambitions to achieve a life of their own, quite independent of their supposed author' (*LT* 1). What is clear already is that mapping the city in such a fashion disjoints any simple oppositions such as walking/writing or observing/remembering. This disjointing is clearly spectral, for, as Derrida points out in an interview with Bernard Stiegler, the logic of the spectre disrupts all oppositions, between the sensible and insensible, the visible and invisible (S 131). Sinclair's folding of a previous text onto the current essay announces such spectral logic, while his narrative draws together for the reader apparent oppositions (only to unveil their deconstruction).

Iain Sinclair maps his unpredictable walks across London, writing his movements as memory's responses in the wake of what he describes throughout *Lights Out* as *stalking* the city. Stalking is a clearly overdetermined term which Sinclair tries to appropriate for his own purposes. It is necessary, however, to make a number of points concerning the idea of stalking, so as to avoid misunderstanding. Stalking and haunting are sometimes synonymous – roughly – in Sinclair's writing. Or they may be understood as nonsynonymous substitutions. While stalking seems oriented towards a future purpose or goal, haunting offers a figure of temporal return, which leads to a temporal tension. However, stalking the spectre means moving towards a trace always ahead of us and always already in retreat, always having retreated and leaving only its trace in its wake. Stalking intimates a form of drive or desire and what brings such a drive to manifest itself is the haunting nature of the city, which in turn turns the urban stalker into a ghost, as Virginia Woolf acknowledges in her wonderfully spectral essay, 'Street Haunting: A London Adventure' (1965, 23–36), in which a search for a writing implement is the pretence or conceit by which the writer allows herself to remember in the trace of her own writing her ghostly other drifting through the wintry twilight of London side streets. The spectral condition of the city thus returns to the writer as other to his or her memory of the city, thus turning the writer into both a stalker and a ghost at one and the same time.

The other issue raised by the terms 'stalker/stalking' is that of gender. It might seem, at the close of the twentieth century, that stalking is a specifically gendered activity, and one associated with fear and potential violence. Were we to accept such a reading unequivocally, the equation would mean that for Sinclair to be the stalker, London must, as object of desire, automatically become feminine. This, however, is to impose determinate meanings on Sinclair's writings in particular ways which themselves are violent. Although Sinclair's desire is clearly a desire driven by a will to know London, the fact that what is desired is so often described as a centre or a presence (see in this essay, below) would seem to suggest a desire for phallocentrism, which, as Sinclair is forced to acknowledge repeatedly, is always frustrated. This is because, when reading from a 'Derridean' perspective, it is possible to see that Iain Sinclair recognizes the city as the accumulation of a number of writings and traces. Seeing the city in this fashion, as a textual/textile composite, ineffable in its relationships, does not automatically suppose that the city is feminine. As I have already suggested, Sinclair attempts to transform our understanding of the verb 'to stalk'.

Stalking – which the author opposes consciously to *flânerie* – is movement with a purpose but without a goal, dictated by the city in advance of expedition, and an act which Sinclair acknowledges as being intrinsic to those writers and artists who most faithfully respond to the spectral return of London in their works; artists such as Brian Catling, Gavin Jones, Rachel Lichtenstein, Rachel Whiteread, Aidan Andrew Dun, Sinclair's photographer Marc Atkins, Alan Moore, Chris Jenks, Arthur Machen, Angela Carter, Robin Cook (or Derek Raymond), Allen Fisher, and Richard Makin, whose description of graffiti cited by Sinclair – 'a transparent and resonant superimposition of word and place' (*LT* 6) – provides an aphorism for the haunted space that is London. Stalking is the rhythm imposed by the city, on both the feet and the pen. Stalking becomes the means by which the numerous and wholly unpredictable city spectres are encountered: by chance and, often, quite violently, because unexpectedly. Once encountered, however, the ghosts leave their mark, their traces in the trace of Sinclair's writing, even as they retreat. Stalking makes possible, then, the city spectres who return via Sinclair's prose to haunt London, even as the writer has occasion to cite and paraphrase those already mentioned, a handful amongst many others, demonstrating that the act of stalking is, once again, dictated and imposed by the condition of the city. Iain Sinclair uses 'stalking' in a way which transforms the word in a manner which cannot be predicted. To stalk usually implies that someone is being followed for a purpose, as in the case of the stalking of Eugene Wrayburn by the deranged schoolmaster Bradley Headstone, perhaps the city's first stalker from Dickens's *Our Mutual Friend* (a novel in which London is described as a 'sooty spectre' [Dickens 1991, 420]).

However, what is being stalked by Sinclair is nothing less than the condition or spirit of London which haunts Sinclair, not only in *Lights Out for the Territory*, but also throughout his writing career. Thus stalking itself becomes a term roughly synonymous with haunting, which term Sinclair uses a number of times as a figure for walking the streets (*LT* 145, 253, 268). Sinclair himself haunts the streets and returns via the pages of his own text as the stalker, moving and always ahead of the act of tracing such ghostly movements in the act of writing London. Sinclair's stalking is the ghostly trace always to come, always ahead of any other urban movement or memory. Stalking, we learn from Sinclair's writing, is, then, a ghostly process, the haunting nature of which is reciprocally reduplicated through writing. In this case, inscription performs the spectral trace of the random movement, urban aleation never present as such but re-presented as a deferred, constantly deferring topographical trace which both marks and retreats.

Most frequently in Sinclair's movements and inscriptions of London, the act of writing as the trace of memory – the trace of a trace – of London, finds itself being recalled by other texts of the city, texts which are themselves others' memories and the memory of otherness of London, whether these textual traces are 'historical' or 'literary' in any simply defined sense. To reiterate an earlier point: the spectral nature of the metropolis collapses any neat distinctions or oppositions between the real and the textual, the historical and the literal, walking and writing, witnessing and remembering. For example consider the following passages:

> And yet, outside the City, beyond the influence of the walls, this millennial fear persists, the flood at the end of time. There is a decayed Unitarian chapel at 49 Balls Pond Road; a ghost with an interesting history, hidden behind corrugated sheeting. Once this was the headquarters of Oswald Mosley's legions – from which they ventured out for acts of provocation in defiance of Dalston's long-established aliens: a skirmish in Ridley Road market. The kind of affair that was witnessed by the young Harold Pinter. (*LT* 98)

> Piecing a walk together along the craggy remnants of the London

Wall – Ragstone blocks, brick bonding courses – is like retrieving a
false memory, the visual evidence for truths we prefer to forget. The
Wall defines the limits of the imagination of Roman London – and is,
in this, an act of modesty. To try to get a sense of the original shape
by tapping its accredited ruins, following the designated route, is
futile. You are contradicted, misinformed, fenced out, overseen for
every inch of your journey. But the perversity of that desire, to pick up
on the energy field, is as strong as ever. I am haunted by a mythology
of gates: as metaphors and as facts. (*LT* 102–3)

Both of these passages suggest the textual play within the architectural and historical fields; both suggest a certain ghostly disturbance
which rewrites shared memory according to the dictates of the
spectre. Both also suggest the need to write and to remember and the
futility of the attempt, governed as all acts are by the voice of the other
which can neither be predicted nor contained. What we come to
understand is that, as Derrida suggests: 'La logique spectrale est *de
facto* une logique déconstructrice [spectral logic is *de facto* deconstructive logic]' (S 131). We also understand from passages such as
these that, again in Derrida's words, this time from Ken McMullen's
film *Ghost Dance*, 'to be haunted by a phantom is to remember something you've never lived through; for memory is the past which has
never taken the form of presence'.[5] The condition of London is both
ineradicable, to use Sinclair's reiterated term, and simultaneously
indefinable. Both passages cited above gesture towards the desire to
read, to interpret, and yet, paradoxically the affirmative resistance to
such gestures, which haunts any attempt to impose a structure.

We see further evidence of the play of spectral logic in Sinclair's
graphic text, 'The Griffin's Egg', a collaboration and contest with Marc
Atkins's photographs and the artwork of Dave McKean over the
editing of the uneditable city. The text might itself be taken as the
trace of *Lights Out for the Territory* or a possible ghost of that text.
'The Griffin's Egg' presents a struggle for the memory of the city
between Sinclair and his collaborators on this tale. The narrative is
structured as a series of photographic and sketched images which
blur, bleed into and ghost one another, while Sinclair's text strains to
compete with its own ghosts, but chiefly that of the fictive Axel
Turner, a photo-journalist belonging to Sinclair's tale, but resistant to
Sinclair's desire to write or edit the city. The photos and sketches play
out the dialectic, as phrases such as 'Who needs a writer?' or 'More

spirit less taste', 'Pin down the true images and words are redundant', and 'Stick any two postcards to a wall and you've got a narrative' (GE 46–7) initiate a series of displacements already registered in the frame. At one point the furious photo-journalist resurfaces after suffering a stream of Sinclair's aphorisms, to announce: 'Alright I'm back on the case. Fucking writers. Think there's no emory without language' (GE 49). No doubt this riposte has been engendered by the earlier accusation that 'Turner's camera has a mind of its own. Instead of reporting, it invents. An unreliable instrument of fiction, cursed with memory' (GE 45). Perhaps that's the problem: the camera, cursed with memory, brings back the ghosts which writing tries to keep at bay, to play with. The camera makes the spectral possible in a way that writing can perhaps only imagine. Sinclair's projected movement – from writing to film – in *Lights Out* might seem to support such a thesis, but whatever the truth, the partial erasure of 'memory' in Turner's statement presents us with the workings of the spectral logic *in words*, but never spoken as such, when memory breaks down and the emery is all we're left with, with which to file away at the past.

The egg in question in the title of the graphic story is that same egg from the Sealy Tomb in St Mary's Church, Lambeth. Even as the egg carries its own partial erasure and palimpsest, so the pages of 'The Griffin's Egg' are ghosted through with words and titles from Sinclair's previous works, such as 'Lud Heat', barely discernible, yet undeniably there on the first page. Thus Sinclair's text enters into London's ghostly condition, becoming and performing one of those 'partially erased memorials ... [and] an intriguing set of broken texts, ... signifiers, symbols' (*LT* 191). The fictional photographer, Axel Turner, who is responsible for making manifest the traces of so many of the writer's ghosts, has a fascinating and haunting pedigree, explained by Sinclair in *Lights Out*:

> The name 'Turner' drifting away from the visionary London painter to the wrecked rock star hiding out in Powis Square for the film *Performance*. And on again to a fictionalised disguise for Marc Atkins in my novel *Radon Daughters*. Axel Turner: a cheap pun to christen a compulsive punster. (*LT* 169)

The figures of Turner become part of the psychogeography of the city itself, countless ghosts recycled through a single signature, always other than itself, tracing its own otherness as part of what Sinclair describes as the city's '[s]erial composition' (*LT* 2). Seriality implies iterability, the possibility of the city becoming a 'shape-shifting place not an actual city', in Brian Catling's words to the author (*LT* 258). As the eternal re-Turners show, because of this condition, the city's spectral citations are multiple, haunting one another endlessly. There is dictated by the city spectres, whether fictional or historical, a disjointing otherness which, in Sinclair's language, becomes 'a museum of memory from which another London, disturbing and demented, could be reassembled' (*LT* 253).

Turner–Atkins's work is given further consideration by the author, towards the end of *Lights Out for the Territory*, as he becomes one of Sinclair's fragmented, ghostly subjects, one of the many London artists on whom the text turns its gaze. We see the way in which the city haunts the artist, for we are told that Atkins, 'drained by the sheer mass of city imagery ... has started to deconstruct his catalogue ... But scraps of language are tautologous: there is already a powerful narrative element in the image. Each frame provokes the next, implies movement ... [Atkins's] work ... was heavy with active contradictions: substantial spirits. A crowd of absences and negations, contrails, entrails, mud, paint' (*LT* 274). Here are to be found some of the elements present in 'The Griffin's Egg', transformed. It is Atkins who, we learn, invents the name Joblard, a character who appears in Sinclair's *White Chappell* and *Downriver*. The name is given on the spur of the moment, when attending an outpatients' clinic, and is, according to Sinclair, 'a reckless procedure: plunging into metafiction, sub-text, the fantasy world of spectres, doubles, half-resolved literary projections' (*LT* 275).

Atkins is not alone in such procedures, however; we have the feeling someone called Iain Sinclair has also indulged in such acts, and that, when he speaks of other London-artists, he is also speaking of himself. If we turn briefly to *White Chappell Scarlet Tracings* we will see such haunting disturbances engendered by the city.

What disturbs, what is unpredictable and impossible to define is nothing other than the spectral, and the possibility that, in the words of Derrida, 'we've got a ghost story on our hands here all right. But we should wait until there are more than two of us before we start' (*TP* 257). All stories are ghost stories effectively, of course; Sinclair impresses this upon us. It's just a question of whether you choose to recognize that fact, and so give yourself up to the undecidability which is dictated to you. When you walk in London, through London, you have to abandon yourself to this; writing about the city should recall such abandon while leaving itself open to chance. Waiting until there are 'more than two of us' is unnecessary, it seems, for, as Iain Sinclair puts it in *White Chappell Scarlet Tracings*, '[w]hen two men meet, a third is always present, a stranger to both', a phrase which later finds itself not quite itself, giving up the ghost as, 'where two men are' (*WCST* 36, 97). These remarks which invoke the ghost already on the scene arise in different strands of the same narrative, one of several, and it is at moments such as these that we encounter the Sinclair spectre. The narrative involves a first-person narrator, known as Sinclair, and his colleague Joblard (one of Marc Atkins's others, as already mentioned). Whether this narrator is the same narrator as the one identifying himself as the narrator – and also 'the Late Watson' (*WCST* 15) – in the narrative strand concerning the dubious posse of second-hand book dealers who begin the narrative, is never absolutely certain. But then, as our narrator, one of several possible ghosts, informs us as he comments on the plethora of spectres and suspects haunting the Jack the Ripper murders, '[t]he medium does not choose who he will serve', and 'our narrative starts everywhere' (*WCST* 61). These conditions are, once again, dictated by the haunted city.

Things become no clearer when George Meredith, in the guise of Chatterton, plagiarist 'of the unwritten' (*WCST* 66), is invoked in a South London pub (in Southwark to be precise, a place with numerous Dickensian ghosts, not least those traced in street names such as Little Dorrit Court or Quilp Street, along with the ghost of the Marshalsea, which haunts Sinclair's text) in a three-way conversation between Sinclair, Joblard and the Landlord. We are informed that Chatterton, the shadowy absent figure, and not the textual variant provided by Meredith for the purposes of identity and posterity, 'became a presence, *manifesting* himself in other men's plays and novels. Francis Thompson. Dangerous ground in which to get lost' (*WCST* 66; emphasis added). Chatterton leaves behind a trace of spectacularly troublesome provenance. Indeed, Chatterton is, arguably, only ever this trace, and one which occurs again in *Lights Out for the Territory* three times (141, 154, 158), belonging in the second instance to a 'cheesy triumvirate of ghosts' in the work of Barry McSweeney (the other two being Blake and Milton). This one scene points to the problems attendant in reading the city in Iain Sinclair's texts. Even that 'dangerous ground' is a spectral doubling, occurring earlier during the narrator's self-introduction (*WCST* 15). Such doubling is everywhere, so that, as we attempt to read, we find ourselves lost in the city, lost in its text, getting spooked by chance, by the event that the city figures. It is that gesture of displacement and undecidability, where the unassimilable haunts in phrases such as: 'Grantham's Daughter, this is your vision!' (*WCST* 12). All at once a malignant poltergeist becomes inscribed into a ghostly approximation of a line which seems to suggest Blake's apocalyptic urban texts, *Milton* and *Jerusalem*. Yet if this is the case, then the ghostly apparition arrives from Milton's future. Here is the *revenant* bang up to date, returning to haunt both Sinclair and his readers.

Third apparition

As we see from the examples of Sinclair and Atkins, the artist is one possible figure of the spirit medium who might be attuned to the energy fields of London, and to what returns via them to us. Rachel Lichtenstein, 'an artist who specialised in not-forgetting, [and] the recovery of "discernible traces"' might well be an 'unjustified survivor, a ghost with no substance' (*LT* 238). Gavin Jones paints 'in negative', conjuring spectres in his reverse field images (*LT* 254). Brian Catling admits to constructing spectres, while his poetry is described by Sinclair as 'acts of mediumship' (*LT* 263). Catling is also described as 'haunting' the city, 'like one of Wim Wenders' terrestrial angels' (*LT* 268). Aidan Andrew Dun's *Vale Royal* is, for Sinclair, one of the most important London texts; Dun 'wills himself to disappear into his text. He recovers it, rather than inventing it.... [*Vale Royal*] was the present articulation of the ineradicable benediction: an incarnation of the numinous on the ground of the city' (*LT* 144–5). It is *Vale Royal*'s cast of London characters – Blake, William Stukeley, Chatterton, St Pancras Old Church – which were to become Peter Ackroyd's ghosts (*LT* 141). And Rachel Whiteread's *House*, appropriately enough a Turner prize winner, is described by Sinclair as a 'solitary representative of all that ... [Hackney] had once been. It mocked the destruction of so many hectares of East London; this self-elected survivor, ugly ghost' (*LT* 226). Whiteread had transformed an abandoned house in London's East End into the ghost of itself, first by using the house as a shell or mould into which concrete was poured; then the house was removed, brick by brick, to leave its simulacrum in its place, entitled

House. When torn down, *House* remained only as a series of concrete traces; it was a 'white ghost ... seen in negative' (*LT* 232), and '[a]n absence, a brick outline in the grass ... a removed structure' (*LT* 237). The ironies around Whiteread's project multiply (as all good spectral tropes should do), when Sinclair points to the irony in 'Tarmac sponsoring the genesis of Whiteread's revenant' (*LT* 226–7), having already discussed Whiteread's previous project, a Turner prize nominee, entitled *Ghost*. A revenant as recipient of the Turner prize, a ghost as a runner up; we need say little more.

Through Sinclair's meditations on those who respond to London, we come to see that the city-artist is 'an involuntary shaman.... S/he develops strategies of derangement, activates some small part of the map.... The city, with its possibilities of random meetings and discoveries, its gift of anonymity is his [or her] space and ... subject' (*LT* 269). But then, as the author admits, 'I'd long held the fancy that the skin of London should be divided up by poets and seers as much as by families of gangsters....They would service the ground they stole from, haunt a particular territory, tune themselves to notice everything, every irregularity in the brickwork' (*LT* 145). In these two city-citations, we read certain trembling connections, connections which also disjoint, between tuning in, haunting, and the subsequent 'irregularity', the manifestation of disruption in architectural form. The resonance between the artist and the gangster spelled out by Sinclair is a certain disturbing vibration available only to poetry and violence. The poetry of the city effects a kind of violence on the map, even as the gangland violence of the Richardsons, the Krays, Tony Lambrianou,[6] has always been, for Iain Sinclair, the manifestation of an urban poetics.

It is no wonder, then, that the author should become side-tracked by the last gangland funeral. The witnessing of the Kray funeral emerges by chance out of a consideration of the pit bull as the symbol *par excellence* for, at one and the same time, the working-class Eastender – 'Dogs confer status, even at the bottom of the heap' (*LT* 56) – and Thatcherite cupidity. It is the idea of the dog, and Ronnie Kray's occupation listed in his passport as 'dog breeder' (*LT* 68), which allows Sinclair to reflect on chance concatenations as the condition of the city. In observing the funeral procession, Sinclair becomes interested in the traces and memories written in floral tribute, a kind of organic graffiti:

RONNIE. THE COLONEL. THE KRAY TWINS. Spelled out in pink carnations, with scarlet tulip crowns for emphasis ... Fresh pinks with broken veins. THE OTHER HALF OF ME: as if Reggie had been interred with his brother. (The crowds outside St Matthew's call for his release, an end to this unnatural punishment. Which can never happen. That would be like rewriting history, opening the grave to make us see the spectre of our past wasted by time, pinched, crook-backed, shrunken.) (*LT* 87)

The passage slides into parenthesis as it considers the impossibility of a reprieve from the Home Secretary. Sinclair's vision of the disinterred spectre makes us aware of an unpalatable connection between the violence of London's past and the economic thuggery and selective amnesia of the current administration. However, another ghost is also present at the funeral, that of William Blake:

Four pall-bearers – Charles Kray (North), Freddie Foreman (South), Johnny Nash (West), Teddy Dennis (East) – would symbolise the homage paid by the four cardinal districts of London. The conceit was Blakean, the Sons of Albion 'dividing the space of love with brazen compasses'.

The route too, as the clerk previewed it, came straight out of one of those odd, but effective listings in Blake's *Jerusalem*. Districts linked by will, not logic. (*LT* 74–5)

Sinclair forces upon us particular spectral relationships between poetry and violence, while reminding us that this is, more than anything, a London funeral. The Krays are 'natural born killers on the spectral plane' (*LT* 72). Blake's brazen compass dividing love offers a haunting figure for what will come in Sinclair's text, the Thatcherite drive to obliterate the spectral city, which Blake himself sought.

Curiously, this chapter on pit bulls and gangland funerals – 'The Dog and the Dish' (*LT* 55–89) – is the only essay in *Lights Out for the Territory* where Sinclair stands still for any length of time, observing the funeral, and where there is hardly any mention of ghosts, of haunting, or any other spectral manifestation; unless, of course, the ghost of Ronnie himself can and does return via Sinclair's prose, if not as a poltergeist in the form of a pit bull, then as the displaced zeitgeist of Thatcherism – the pre-eminent Tory power broker, *avant la lettre*, a symbol of what Sinclair describes as 'Bill Sikes Thatcherism, with the pit bull as its proud emblem' (*LT* 62), and now as anachronistic as

'Norman Tebbit tattoos'[7] (LT 62). Of course, it's a grimly humorous and entirely ghostly opportunity for Sinclair that Ronnie 'the Colonel' Kray shares a first name with that other Ronnie of pit bull culture: Reagan, Maggie's slightly less demented oppo, a kind of Tony Lambrianou to Thatcher's Mad Frankie Fraser.[8] Sinclair recalls his gruesome twosome – Reagan and Thatcher, not Ron and Reg – immediately following the Kray street party, via Reagan's last film excursion, Don Siegel's The Killers. The gathering momentum in this episode is focused around death, murder, burial, savaging, and we begin to see Sinclair's discourse moving towards a critique of what some have tried to make of London at the expense of its ghosts, its others. It is against such acts of exorcism and monstrosity – the pit bull as the protector who will howl at demons – that Sinclair begins to turn in search of other Londons, other traces of the haunted city. Early on in the episode, Sinclair feels the need to describe the dog's opposite, which 'must have a special quality; a quality that by its nature will be impossible to define. We can look for movement in the air, an unpredictable shift in the intensity of light' (LT 60). The author might be describing nothing more than the city's atmosphere, but there's a sense here, early on and despite no overt references, that Sinclair has found himself in the presence of ghostly traces. Poetry offers such ghostly traces because it is 'the hard stuff, the toffee of the universe. The antimatter that granted validity to the Thatcherite free-market nightmare by steadfastly manufacturing its contrary: a flame in the dark. There never was a better period in which to be unknown, off the record, ex-directory' (LT 134).

The need for the ghost becomes apparent once Sinclair gives voice to his concerns for the attempted murder of the city and the exorcism of its ghosts during the 1980s, a time when there was a furious entrepreneurial effort to bury the ghost, to give the city monumentality, and a centre. The corporate vision for London had as its logo 'the imago of Margaret Thatcher' (LT 90), where Thatcher was 'the window-dressing, ... while [Denis] got on with the real task, amassing wealth, shoring up the immemorial "liberties" of the Square Mile' of the City of London (LT 112). We can catch a glimpse in that phrase, 'the immemorial "liberties" of the Square Mile' the merest trace of Blake's 'Charter'd streets' and all which that implies, and against which Blake and Sinclair, in his wake, position themselves. The corporate desire was to erase London through reinvention, to create 'the new Hong Kong, Venice, the Pearl of the River. The towers of Manhattan rising out of swampland, Unlimited on-line credit. A city of electricity. A giant slot machine with clouds in every window. An *inverted* centre. A conceptual city. A centre that could be anywhere and nowhere' (*LT* 227). Sinclair sees such a patently metaphysical conceit opposed to the other Londons. Composed of 'compromises and epiphanies worked out through the centuries', the city spectres, whose whirling anticipates the shape of the traffic cones which constitute markers of the current Capital paranoia (*LT* 104), have been 'wantonly and, mindlessly set aside by an attempt to turn the zone of the City into a privileged playground. Legoland with shoulder-arms and extendible nightsticks' (*LT* 104). He writes also of the City's faux-pastoralism with its 'sick trees feeding their blight into a sealed system. The plashing of a plurality of fountains in mustard brick courtyards, heavy with the ghosts of labour' (*LT* 91). The hermeticism of the new City reminds us of a coffin, or a crypt at the very least; yet even the environmentally controlled tomb cannot keep the spirits at bay. What becomes discernible through the spectral traces – a Blakean sub-text as the voice of the unconscious other manifesting itself through Sinclair's metaphors – is that haunting is a profoundly political affair. The contest over the survival of the spirit becomes a question of whether one gives up the idea of a centre or whether one needs the idea of a centre desperately, as a concept with which to keep the ghosts at bay. When seeing the sign 'Dalston Town Centre' earlier in his walks, the writer responds, 'I love the chutzpah of that. Can a ghost have a centre?' (*LT* 12–13). From this we read the impossibility of assigning centres to so spectral a place as London. Naming the town centre becomes an act of a politician driving a stake through the heart of the spirit of place. But spectral logic is that for Sinclair with which to counter political logic.

Fourth apparition

'London is begging to be rewritten', suggests Iain Sinclair (*LT* 141). Such rewriting is already underway, always in processes of recycling and remembering otherwise. London is seen as 'a network of coincidences and cyclic collisions' (*LT* 156), a definition with which Dickens would surely have agreed. Apart from the writers already mentioned, Sinclair cites Allen Fisher, whose London is a 'fragmentary, multivoiced schizo – openly invaded by a consciousness of "the other"' (*LT* 151), while Richard Makin's verse is composed of 'revenant diction geistraum' (*LT* 154). Sinclair concludes repeatedly that the city has no centre; it obfuscates, and is only revealed when it reveals itself as 'an erasure, an absence' (*LT* 107, 117, 130). At best, London is for Sinclair, '[t]he unheard voice that is always present in the darkness' (*LT* 162). Citing Chris Jenks on the necessity of 'alternative cartographies of the city' (*LT* 145), Sinclair sees that the only hope for London is in writers who are willing to 'wrest it from the grip of developers, clerks, eco freaks, and ward bosses' (*LT* 146).

Such an idea and much of that which I have addressed, it might be suggested on the part of those seeking to criticize a hauntological or spectropoetical analysis, is merely a question of intertextuality given a ghostly guise. But I would respond that in purely – simply – intertextual forms, the structures of the texts which resonate remain in place to a great degree as citations more or less; never quite disjointed, never quite subjected – or subjecting in turn the trace or structure of the 'principal' text – to reciprocal haunting and erasure, cross-hybridization or uncanny contamination. Intertextuality never quite gives up the ghost of a structure. Intertextuality behaves as though quotation, paraphrase and pastiche were the normal order of things. The haunting urban palimpsest carries in its own trace its own erasure through which emerges the ghosts of other writings, other memories and traces, memories not our own but which resurface as the traces of an other London. The inscription of the city's ghosts succeeds, to paraphrase Derrida, only in effacing itself (*RM* 29). Sinclair's writing acknowledges the return of the ghostly trace, the revenant of the city, always unpredictable, always already other than itself. Against monumental exorcisms and cut-price burials, Sinclair invokes the ineradicable trace of the trace, an impossible cartography forever haunting our steps. The city in Sinclair's writing, or rather the writing of the city, marks the limit of what one can say, as the knowability of the city withdraws before the stalking steps and pen. The city is nothing as such, in Sinclair's text; it is only the trait, the ghostly remainder which fragments the map of the city through what Derrida calls fraying and 'a differential splitting' (*RM* 28), which *traits* (for there are always already more than one) sign the 'irreducible difference' (*RM* 28) of the city's haunting citations. His writing acknowledges all the while that, in the words of Edmond Jabès, 'Only in fragments can we read the immeasurable totality' (Jabès 1993, 42).

5 *Heart? of Darkness?* Reading in the Dark with J. Hillis Miller and Joseph Conrad

A question of reading

Heart? *of Darkness?* We might think that we know how to read this title, although after Derrida's unpacking of the function of the title, we can no longer be so sure. We might believe that we understand what the terms of the title of Joseph Conrad's novel mean. We assume for example that we know what a heart is, whether we choose to consider the term literally or metaphorically. We also assume we know the meaning of 'darkness'. No doubt, in unfolding the meanings of these two words, we will inevitably work towards definition, defining them by reference to that which they are not, that from which they differ, and that the meaning or value of which is deferred in seeking to assign value to the terms 'Heart' and 'Darkness'. But none of this can adequately answer the question I seem to hear being asked – it's another of those 'improper' questions of which I spoke in the first chapter – which is: what is a 'heart of darkness'? Such a question inevitably causes other equally difficult questions to proliferate. For example: how do we locate a 'heart of darkness', if indeed what seems to be required is some navigation aid, a compass perhaps or a map (how do you map the unmappable?)? Where, in the dark, can you hope to find a heart, or even the heart of the darkness itself? Can/does darkness, whether literal or metaphorical, have a heart? Is it the heart itself which is dark, and is such a thing possible? At this juncture, before we go any deeper into the dark, we may be forced to acknowledge that the question surrounding this title is a double question of indirection and reading. Indeed the title does nothing other than alert us to everything which occurs in the novel of the same name, even as that very title signifies indirectly the form and content of Conrad's text.

The degree of undecidability which the title articulates is symptomatic of the text as a whole. Even that little *of* is profoundly problematic. It disarticulates the title, so that we cannot be certain whether the question is one concerning a location in the dark or the darkness of a heart. To borrow from a commentary of J. Hillis Miller's, how does the genitive in the title work (Miller 1987, 9)? What does it do to either or both of the terms of the title? Once again, we are back with the question of reading and its (im)possibility, which calls to mind the words of Paul de Man, who says of Marcel Proust's work, 'Everything in [the] novel signifies something other than what it represents';

> it is always something else that is intended. It can be shown that the most adequate term to designate this 'something else' is Reading. But one must at the same time 'understand' that this word bars access, once and forever, to a meaning that yet can never cease to call out for its understanding. (de Man 1979, 47)

Although de Man is speaking of Proust's writing (of which Mark Currie writes in his volume in the Transitions series), his claims concerning reading are forcefully pertinent to the title of Joseph Conrad's short work, as well as to the texture and levels of that text as a whole, as we shall see. *Heart of Darkness* is nothing other than a series of confrontations with reading and with 'something else' which constantly unfolds throughout the various layers of the text ceaselessly, while never allowing the reader access to a full meaning, or indeed to the centre, the heart (if there is such a thing) of the matter. If, as Hillis Miller has claimed, and as we have already seen in the introduction, deconstruction can be defined as the 'rhetorical analysis of works of literature' (1987, 9); and, furthermore, if deconstruction is 'nothing more or less than good reading as such' (1987, 10), then such rhetorical analysis, such good reading, must always proceed in the dark.

The problem I seem to have above with the title is, then, a problem with the text as a whole, as well as being a problem with reading. The title and the way in which it fails to communicate – or, rather, the fact that it communicates its failure to communicate except in the most indirect manner, so that it installs undecidability in the very act of communication, a quality reiterated throughout Marlow's narrative – can be described provisionally as a figure of negative anastomosis.[1] Anastomosis names interconnections, intercommunications between parts. Miller describes the genitive *of* as such a figure. Yet this title, *Heart of Darkness*, singularly fails to connect, even while *of* appears to connect at the moment which it disjoints, and *even* while the title operates in such a way that it is wholly typical of the language of the novel. Throughout the novel there is to be found everywhere a desire to connect: the narrators seek connections between themselves and their audiences; Marlow, the second of the narrators, seeks to connect with Kurtz, to make connections about Kurtz through the fragments of information he is given or otherwise digs up for himself; various waterways are invoked as forms of intercommunication between one place and its other, becoming immediately metaphorical and alerting us to the nature of all textual passage; the different narratives seek to form intercommunications, as do the various remarks made by a number of minor characters. Yet despite this constant activity, despite the ceaseless work to understand, which we as readers are also engaged in, the problem remains that we all, characters, narrators, readers, language itself, endlessly find ourselves communicating incommunicability and undecidability, butting up against the limits of reading and the limits of writing.

How then are we to proceed, if at all? How do we steer ourselves in such a murky atmosphere? Do we not find ourselves as readers in a hopeless place, the co-ordinates of which are unknowable, yet constructed from the very event of reading, and trying to guide ourselves much as Marlow does, in both the jungle, along the river, and in *Heart of Darkness*?

Impossible topographies

Before moving any further, I'll continue by addressing some of the issues explored in this chapter and already implicated in what I've said so far, trying to map out the territory a little, at least in order to pretend for the moment that a map of the unmappable is possible; that is, that it is possible to pretend the darkness is discernible. This chapter will move forward through a brief consideration of some of the themes of J. Hillis Miller's reading of *Heart of Darkness*, which is presented in a collection of essays on that novel as a 'deconstruction' of the text.[2] I will question this definition of Miller's reading, in order to assert, once again, that there is no such thing as deconstruction understood as an interpretive methodology. In pursuing this line I will suggest that Miller's essay needs to be understood in all its singularity. While Miller's work has a particular intellectual heritage which it shares with certain aspects of Derrida's thought, what Miller does cannot be said to be the same as what Derrida does; neither man's work offers the reader a methodological framework which is shared between them or even throughout their numerous writings, even though there are discernible overlapping concerns and interests (as there are, arguably, between Paul de Man and the two men, or between Derrida's writing and that of Jean-Luc Nancy and Phillipe Lacoue-Labarthe, as already mentioned in the introduction to this volume). Nonetheless, Miller's reading is exemplary of his own demands to pursue rhetorical analysis and good reading.

This chapter will also attempt to put to work (as have the previous two chapters) certain of Derrida's interests as we encounter Conrad's novel. By indirection and analogy, I will seek to make interconnections, as if I were navigating a course which is wholly unpredictable. I will seek to chart this course through the various layers of the text, as if they were so much jungle foliage, in respect of the questions which the text appears to raise about the condition of textuality, the construction of identity, the internal necessity of difference within the principle of identity as that from which identity is constructed as meaningful, along with a consideration of the various acts of narration out of which *Heart of Darkness* is woven. I will seek to explore how the text always complicates its own apparent gestures towards meaning, frustrating those potential meanings by performing indirectly at a number of levels the statement, *il n'y a pas de hors-texte*, to return to that phrase of Derrida's: there is no outside-the-text.

Heart of Darkness may be read, I will suggest, as a constant unfolding of this phrase while performing Derrida's suggestions that 'there is nothing but context' (BSDF 873) and that 'there are only contexts without center or absolute meaning' (*LI* 220), remarks which have already been cited in another context in this volume. In short, there is no heart in or to the text in the sense of there being a centre or absolute meaning. Reading cannot locate this. All of the text mediates against our desire to search for meaning, value or centre. It does so by putting into play constant heartbeats, rhythms, *tempi*, movements which rely on tension, paradox, ebb and flow, and the constant play in all that word's senses between reader and narrator, presence and absence, sound and silence, outside and inside. This is effected, we shall show, at the level of narration, at the level of form, and, especially, at the level of phonetic and scripted prefix, through a range of reiterated marks (none of which signify beyond themselves but only to each other, as signifiers of signifiers, traces of traces) and reiterated erasures and negations of possible, unequivocal meaning. In particular, we will be looking at the work of prefixes such as *in-*, *im-*, and *un-* which occur frequently throughout the text. These install the movement of *différance*, of deconstruction or disjointing, making the search for the heart impossible, the location of meaning undecidable, the discernment of a centre, a source or origin, unfathomable, and, simultaneously, interminable.

In reading the *im*possibility of reading *Heart of Darkness* except as an interminable movement which takes us in simultaneously contradictory directions (without a heading as such), we will relate the experience of the narration to the question of memory. The very interminability of the textual rhythm or heartbeat is an articulation, we will suggest, of trauma and suffering as part of the subject's identity. This in turn suggests that narration is seen in the text as a shared experience between narratorial voices. Precisely what is shared is the endless desire to communicate and the impossibility of communicating. Narration becomes no more than the disembodied projection of memory in the dark, as the narrators seek to communicate and so read and understand that which is unknowable in the narration. There is always an act of remembering the other, reiterating the other's narration and perplexity, and the effort to communicate incommunicability as the writing of a certain duty, an ethical bearing witness to that which haunts us all in the darkness, the alterity at the 'heart' of our identities. Narration can be seen in *Heart of Darkness* as ethical in that, despite its frustrations, it attempts to read, in an engagement where reading is, in Miller's words, a 'response to an irresistible demand' (1987, 43) for which the narrator must take responsibility. Narration as memory and the writing of identity open and unfold themselves as this response and responsibility throughout Conrad's novel. The reiteration of certain prefixes, negations and erasures mark this ethical response, while also leaving the mark of a 'repeated infliction of a wound' (Caruth 1996, 3). This wound has no meaning as such. Yet it speaks painfully to 'what remains unknown in our very actions and our language' (Caruth 1996, 4). What remains unknown, and yet what the text bears witness to, is that indefinable *Heart of Darkness*.

'Through a glass, darkly'

For J. Hillis Miller, *Heart of Darkness* is undoubtedly 'parabolic'. Its narrative accedes to the condition of parable in that – as Miller's reading goes – while the narrative seems to address its reader in one way, it nonetheless expresses 'another reading or truth not otherwise expressible' (1990, 181). The parable, all parables, work through indirection. We do not *see* the truth of the parabolic narrative but come to understand its secret truth as that is revealed or unfolded to us. Thus, we might suggest, Miller proposes a reading of *Heart of Darkness* which, in looking into that dark heart (which we've by no means begun to locate), sees nothing other than as 'through a glass, darkly' (I Corinthians 13:1). What is seen is nothing that can be viewed directly. But what looking into the dark will give us to understand is the possibility of the revelation of a mystery, which we must await and to which we must respond. Parable is therefore, for Miller, of the order of apocalypse, that other figure to which he likens Conrad's tale, in that it invokes 'an act of unveiling' (1990, 181).

Having positioned his contention concerning the parabolic status of Conrad's text, Miller then asks what it might mean to 'speak of *Heart of Darkness* as parabolic in form?' (1990, 182) His contention is that the narrative is wholly parabolic and partly apocalyptic. This allows 'much illumination to be shed ... in the light of these generic classifications' (182). What arrives for the critic is the revelation of 'how' the story means, though not necessarily 'what' it means. As support for such enlightening figures of speech – and it's no accident that Miller, being the good reader involved in rhetorical analysis, allows himself figures of illumination when face to face with *Heart of Darkness* – Miller points to Conrad's own use of metaphors and other figures of speech suggesting illumination, while simultaneously offering a definition of apocalyptic narrative as 'that [which] sheds light ... that [which] clarifies and illuminates' (182). This is exactly the gesture that Miller's own critical acts seem to perform. His use of the figures of parable and apocalypse apparently aid our comprehension of the text's means of production, while refraining scrupulously from trying to tell us what such a means of production would have us understand. This in effect is to unveil the rhetorical structure of the text, without attempting to have mastery over its undecidable play.

From the specific example of the definition of apocalyptic narrative, the critic moves to the universal claim that '[a]ll criticism claims to be enlightenment' (182; presumably that 'all' includes Miller's own reading). We may well be enlightened by Miller's definition of the text as parable, but this enlightenment or illumination will not serve to penetrate the heart of darkness itself. Such a thing is impossible, strictly speaking. Enlightenment allows us to see where we are, but not where we may be going; illumination reveals to us that we are in the dark. Indeed, looking into the light only serves to remind us through blinding us, or making us squint at the very least, that the darkness remains exactly that: darkness. In making us aware of this indirectly, Miller is of course doing no more than showing us, indirectly and in another manner, what Conrad already shows us, and what Marlow tries to show us, from a different heading. While it is Miller's intention to show how the illumination will come from that which is dark as a result of our patient concentration on the darkness, I would like to suggest that the density of darkness is such in *Heart of Darkness* that whatever 'spectral illumination' there might be, to borrow Conrad's narrator's phrase (and Marlow does not see that he cannot see; or, rather, what he can see is that he does not always see, while he sees that he may not always be able to make us see), its powers of enlightenment are greatly limited. The problem might well be in that figure of the light itself, and the accompanying tropes of enlightenment and illumination, which figures of speech invoke some Hegelian torch-bearer. Unlike parable, which is parabolic and works through the arc of indirection, light travels in a straight line. It does not bend but can only be refracted, throwing all else into penumbra and obscurity.

The question of enlightenment and indirection is raised by Miller. The critic quotes the narrator's assessment of the form of Marlow's narrative. Marlow, we are told, is not 'typical' of sea-going story-tellers. Quoting the manuscript variants, Miller offers us this passage concerning the description of Marlow's story-telling and the possible location of the meaning of the stories he tells:

> ... to him the meaning of an episode was not inside like a kernel but outside [*ms*: outside in the unseen], enveloping a tale which brought

it out only *as a glow* brings out a *haze*, in the *likeness of one of those misty* halos that *sometimes* are made visible by the spectral illumination of moonshine. (5) (Conrad [*HD* 138] cit. Miller 1990, 182; emphases added)

Miller picks up on the interdependent relationship between 'inside' and 'outside' in the passage, and is right to do so. As we will show, the movement between either 'position' is, in *Heart of Darkness*, simultaneous and contradictory, thereby creating, if not an aporia between discernible identities, at least confusion and the play of undecidability. Importantly, for the moment though, you should notice those words I have emphasized in the passage. All seem to suggest veiling as much as unveiling, illumination as diaphany, but also as the illumination of adiaphany, that which is non-transparent and opaque, and the 'limits of the diaphane', to borrow Stephen Dedalus's words (Joyce 1993, 37).[3] Analogy and simile operate in simultaneously contradictory directions here. Illumination, referred to indirectly, obscures as much as it unveils, and there is not that absolute enlightenment towards which criticism aims or tends.

Particularly interesting for me is Conrad's excised phrase 'outside in the unseen', now placed forever 'outside' *Heart of Darkness*. The excision itself suggests a desire for clarification which, in that moment of erasure, has obscured possible interpretation because the movement towards a place indicated in the phrase is now no longer unequivocally given, and we are forced to recall Derrida's dictum that there is no outside-the-text. That excised phrase of Conrad's is readable as desirous of the outside-the-text, the *hors-texte* as possible centre or location which, while absent, is still imaginable. The phrase is suggestive of a metaphysical location for meaning or value to which a reading of the text might aspire, were the phrase retained. 'Outside in the unseen' maintains a truth beyond the trace. Yet, as Conrad's writing performs for us, we become aware through the tension of writing, and the difference at / as its heartbeat if not its heart, there is no more an *hors-texte* for Conrad's narrators than there is for Jacques Derrida. The anonymous narrator's repeated exploitation of supplementary simile on simile, analogy on analogy, metaphor on metaphor (an exploitation shared also between identities in the text, the deferral and displacement of writing remarking itself across supposedly discrete narrators) only renders illumination itself unclear, fogged up. The tentativeness of expression only marks that 'limits of the diaphane'.

Miller unpacks for us all of this paradoxical undermining (1990, 184). Of the spectral illumination, Miller suggests, '[t]he meaning of a parable does not appear as such ... the figure is supposed to illuminate the reader.... The figure both illuminates its own workings and at the same time obscures or undermines it' (1990, 183). It is precisely this simultaneity which, we wish to suggest, is marked in the commonest prefixes in Conrad's tale. Also, as Miller indicates, Conrad's use of the figure of spectral illumination which is that hazy halo alludes, albeit obscurely, to the working of narrative tropes, figures and motifs (184). And here, as Miller puts it, lies the problem, the double paradox, as he calls it, of the parable: 'All Conrad's work turns on this double paradox, first the paradox of the two senses of seeing, seeing as physical vision, and seeing as seeing through, as penetrating to or unveiling the hidden, invisible truth, and second the paradox of seeing the darkness in terms of the light' (185).[4]

As Miller then goes on to say, much of the light in *Heart of Darkness* is indirect or 'twice-reflected light' (186); and, 'the darkness is in principle invisible and remains invisible. All that can be said is that the halo gives the spectator indirect knowledge that the darkness is there' (186). Following Conrad's figures, and principally the figure of the moon's reflection of the sun's light in its halo, Miller alerts the reader to the paradoxical conditions of Conrad's narrative as a parabolic narrative in particular, and to the condition of all parables: all that you can see is what you can already see. The story is never a 'plain statement of meaning' (187), but always an imperfect, reflected and refracted likeness of a likeness of a meaning which is inexpressible (187). In thus expressing the way in which Conrad's rhetoric operates, Miller's essay reproduces, albeit with an ironic distance (which is also already installed in the various narrative levels of Conrad's narratives), that impossibility of gaining access to meaning which, as Miller is at pains to show, *is always already there in Conrad's writing*.

As another indication of such impossibility Miller notes how '[t]his proliferating relay of witnesses',

> one behind another, each revealing another truth further in which turns out to be only another witness, corresponds to the narrative form of *Heart of Darkness*. The novel is a sequence of episodes, each structured according to the model of appearances, signs, which are also obstacles or veils. Each veil must be lifted to reveal another truth

behind which always turns out to be another episode, another witness, another veil to be lifted in its turn…. The relay of witness behind witness behind witness, voice behind voice behind voice, each speaking in ventriloquism through the next one farther out, is a characteristic of the genre of apocalypse. (188)

Through this 'relay' Miller adds his own critical performance to the chain of substitutions and supplementary commentaries (to which my own is another supplement). If I have a criticism of this figure it lies in that 'behind' and the implicit image of a depth-model on which Miller's description seems to rely. Instead, given our insistence on the condition of textuality and writing, it should be possible to comprehend the figural form of the text in terms of surface metaphors, of the intersection of planes. Be that as it may, Miller nevertheless offers a model which effectively retraces the movements of unveiling, movements which paradoxically unveil only another veil, another plane of refraction and obscurity. Far from offering illumination and clarification, all we are made aware of is that we are in the midst – without being in the heart – of darkness.

Therefore, we cannot say that Miller's 'reading' of *Heart of Darkness* (if it is that at all, Miller's essay offering explanation more than interpretation) is, in any sense, an attempt to adduce a meaning for the narrative so far. Nor can we suggest that this is a deconstruction of *Heart of Darkness*. Miller does not deconstruct the text. We cannot learn from his essay how one might deconstruct a text, if only because the essay, in all its singularity, is always seen to be responding to the demands put on it by Conrad's text. Unless of course we see – 'see through' rather than merely see – that Miller's rhetorical explication is the faithful act of the good reader, who carefully and scrupulously responds to what is already constructed by the text. This is not to say, of course, that at a certain level there is what Miller describes as a failure to read, in discussing Paul de Man's work. This 'failure' is, claims Miller, a 'universal necessity' (Miller 1987, 51). In Miller's understanding of de Man, the ethical reading is the reading of unreadability. This is our responsibility as 'good readers': in order to read what the text says to us we must read against what is said in the text, to paraphrase Simon Critchley (1992, 46). The only 'meaning' we can offer in the wake of the critic is to suggest that, at a certain level, *Heart of Darkness* is a story about something, something else other than what it seems to say, even while it does appear to be saying that it is saying that it cannot say directly anything about that something else. And Miller as the good reader points out that saying the impossibility of saying something else, unless it be through indirect allusion. All of which, if you'll forgive the apparent circularity, is what we read Conrad already doing. If Marlow 'makes explicit his sense of the impossibility of his enterprise' (187),[5] then so does Miller, albeit through stating this explicitly through the implicit imitation of the rhythms and gestures of Conrad's prose.

Having sketched the various rhetorical manoeuvres by which the text displaces any movement towards clarity, even as it pulls back the veils apparently, through the various relays and layers, Miller's reading comes momentarily to rest on what seems a 'curious' moment of definition. I've alerted you to this 'curiosity' for reasons which will be explained and explored more thoroughly in a moment. For now, however, let me quote Miller:

> There is another reason beyond the necessities of revelation for this structure. The truth behind the *last witness*, behind Kurtz for example in *Heart of Darkness*, is *no one can doubt it*, death, 'the horror'; or, to put this another way, 'death' is another name for what Kurtz names 'the horror.' No man can confront that truth face to face and survive. Death or the horror can only be experienced indirectly, by way of the face and voice of another. The relay of witnesses both reveals death and, luckily, hides it. (1990, 189)

What I find so curious here is that absolute certainty of Miller's which apparently brings to a halt the movement of his text, so seemingly focused is it on establishing a determinate value. This leads me to ask three questions:

- How can we be certain that Kurtz is the 'last witness'?
- Why can no one doubt the truth to which Kurtz bears witness, naming it 'the horror, the horror'?
- Why is death the truth?

Taking these three questions in turn, let's respond to Miller's comments.

Kurtz as the last witness: He is Marlow's 'object', his goal. Arguably, however, Kurtz is merely one more relay in the unveiling, who is failed by Marlow, inasmuch as Marlow has lied to Kurtz's intended. Marlow becomes one more relay – after the event of meeting Kurtz which has already occurred prior to our encounter with the text.

No one can doubt it: This truth which Miller claims no one can doubt Kurtz bears witness to, how is it possible not to doubt what occurs when the words 'the horror, the horror' are uttered? Marlow immediately bears witness to Kurtz's utterance, which we as readers are encountering at a double remove. He can offer, however, no explanation, to 'truth'. That to which Kurtz bears witness is undecidable.

Is death that truth? The question raised between this and the previous question circles around the issue of the possible meaning of those words: 'the horror, the horror'. As Miller reminds us, Marlow himself has stated that the 'inner truth is hidden'. The 'unseen' had, in that erased line from the manuscript, been outside. In this remark it is 'inside', reconfigured as hidden and, therefore, unknowable. There can be no certainty that Kurtz's reiterated words signal death as such. We might equally suggest that 'the horror, the horror' could be taken to refer to an awareness on Kurtz's part of what he believes himself to have become; or he could otherwise be recognizing the barbarity which lies at the 'heart' of the colonialist enterprise, and even his own complicity within that enterprise. Kurtz's words could mean all of these simultaneously, as well as meaning 'death'. His words figure the responsible response to that which is unreadable. Certainly, though, we can agree with Hillis Miller when he says that Kurtz's words are apocalyptic inasmuch as they figure for Kurtz a moment of unveiling (189).

But what is unveiled to us, to Marlow? Nothing, other than the moment of unveiling's unveiling, to paraphrase Miller (189). In the face of Kurtz's utterance, is it not the case to suggest that we cannot claim to know what either phrase means? I say 'either' advisedly because, given Derrida's insistence on the iterative nature of language, there is no reason not to suggest, however tentatively, in the face of the iterable structure (in the context of the book's various levels of undecidability and the parabolic impossibility of direct, or even indirect, access to meaning), that the first 'the horror' and the second 'the horror' are not the same part of an endlessly iterable system of unveiling/obscuring gestures, where meaning is inaccessible and truth forever differed in the play of the double phrase. To insist on 'death' as a meaning is to assert a 'metaphysical' meaning to a textual moment, and a meaning which is metaphysical, moreover, precisely because 'death' is nowhere as such in the text, unless of course we take death as 'a displaced name for a linguistic predicament', to quote Paul de Man (de Man cit. Bennington 1994, 150). Death is 'hidden', it is 'outside in the unseen', to use Conrad's words once more. It is perhaps for this reason that Conrad eliminated that phrase from the manuscript, tending as the phrase does to point too specifically, and thus illuminate, a potential or provisional 'meaning', however negative. At best we can speak of Kurtz's words and their performance indirectly.

We might, for example, recognize 'the horror, the horror' as a certain aphorism for what Derrida calls the *exemplary* secret of literature' (*ON* 29), which is 'a chance of saying everything without touching upon the secret' (*ON* 29). Drawing further from this commentary of Derrida's, we can say something else about Kurtz's phrase. Kurtz's comments make it impossible to make a decision about meaning. The potential for iterability and the undecidability installed in the reiterated phrase suggests that 'there is no longer even any sense in making decisions about some secret behind the surface of a textual manifestation (and it is this situation which I would call text or trace)' (*ON* 29). Thus 'the horror, the horror' not only repeats itself and promises to reiterate itself as never quite the same, but it also forestalls any possibility concerning decision-making. The singular example of the phrase exemplifies the work of literature because it makes its secret inaccessible, even while the words are in plain view. The phrase unveils its unreadability. The phrase remains as the trace and cannot be reduced to the simulacrum of some other. In being so elliptical and economical, to paraphrase a comment of Derrida's (on another equally inscrutable phrase), it maintains the other's alterity (*GD* 82–3). And, given that we can say nothing with regard to the meaning of the phrase, 'the horror, the horror', an aporia is opened between our experience and the impossible. We can even posit the possibility that, in its movement, the movement of *différance*, Conrad's phrase might be taken to figure the movement of deconstruction, if we can define that troublesome term as 'a certain aporetic experience of the impossible' (*P* 27; *A* 15). A certain border or limit is reached in this phrase. It expresses the very 'identity of language' which 'can only affirm itself as identity to itself by opening itself to the hospitality of a difference from itself or of a difference with itself' (*A* 10).

Of course, Miller is able to make his assertion concerning the truth which lies behind the last witness because he has just completed making a comparison between *Heart of Darkness* as parabolic, apocalyptic text, and the exemplary structure of relayed voices which compose the apocalyptic Book of Revelations, which he terms 'the paradigmatic example [of the genre of apocalypse] in our tradition' (1990, 188). And he is not wrong to do so. Miller's gesture towards death as the truth is a rhetorical gesture which names the aporetic otherwise, because the other cannot be named directly. His is a strong, well argued and presented discussion of the possibility of seeing how Conrad's novel works. He shows himself to be the good reader, acting with responsibility by limiting his incursions, bearing witness while acknowledging his being complicit in the gestures which the novel already performs. What I am seeking to suggest, though, is that Miller's gesture relies on a reading habit which favours the universal over the specific. As he puts it, 'no act of reading is direct experience' (1990, 190). Certainly not. On the other hand, if no act of reading is or can be direct experience, all we can experience indirectly through words is that torque within identity, the gesture of difference from or within itself. Miller knows this, and points to his own act of readerly violence in turning back on himself, allowing that he has attempted to fix the text by generic classification (193). He acknowledges that there is no 'last witness', not yet, by admitting, as we claimed earlier, that his place as 'demystifying commentator' is merely one more fold, one more unveiling of the veil (or the lack of unveiling) (193). If, as Miller concludes, the only enlightenment we gain from the text is that 'darkness can never be enlightened' (192), then we find ourselves where we have always been: reading interminably, in the dark, and seeking to decide on the undecidable.

Tracing the interminable

All of the following words appear in *Heart of Darkness*:

> interminable, immensity, imperceptible, unruffled, unceasing, untitled, unknown, immutability, immensity, inscrutable, unfold, imagine, imagine, incomprehensible, imagine, inconclusive, immense, immense, ungarnished, uneasy, indifferent, unconcerned, uncanny, introducing, unknown, immense, interesting, interrupted, uncomfortable, impostor, inviting, insipid, intense, immensity, incomprehensible, insanity, invaded, impotent, undersized, imagina-

tion, insoluble, insidious, impossible, inferno, uniform, uninterrupted, uncongenial, unfamiliar, inefficient, intolerable, unexpected, indissolubly, insensible, unbuttoned, indefinable, unconscious, intensified, inscrutable, uneasiness, uneasiness, impossible, interrupted, uneasy, interrupted, imbecile, incredible, uncongenial, unreal, inner, interrupted, indefatigable, incredible, impossible, impossible, impossible, uneasiness, inspired, impossibility, innumerable, inextricable, incredible, unpleasant, impudence, inducement, unequal, impenetrable, unrestful, implacable, inscrutable, intention, inspiration, inner, imagine, unpardonable, immense, imagined, unknown, inheritance, incomprehensible, inhuman, inhuman, intrepidity, improving, instructed, impromptu, interminable, illegible, imbecility, invariably, insight, unreasonably, immobility, unnatural, infinite, unexpectedness, intolerably, incontinently, unwholesome, inexorable, inborn, unfathomable, inexplicable, impossible, impenetrable, inconceivable, unexpected, irresistible, unrestrained, uninterrupted, unstable, understandable, inconceivably, immensely, impenetrable, impalpable, immense, inconceivable, initiation, impossible, untrammelled, unspeakable, immensity, unbounded, indisputable, inadmissible, improbable, inexplicable, insoluble, inconceivable, instantly, indestructible, uncalculating, impractical, unavoidably, unmoved, unapproachable, unexpectedly, intention, intolerable, uncomplicated, indistinctly, innumerable, immense, inscrutable, unanswering, unspeaking, intolerable, impenetrable, impossible, unnerved, unconnected, intolerable, unexpectedly, impending, unarmed, irretrievably, intimacy, immense, irresolutely, incantations, unlawful, invoke, intensity, unavoidable, inconceivable, interrupted, indefinable, inexorable, unsound, unforseen, unextinguishable, unearthly, invisible, impenetrable, infernal, intense, unexpressed, unextinguishable, unexciting, impalpable, inappreciable, invisible, innumerable, inconceivable, infamous, insignificant, imagination, intended, unexplored, unable, intended, impulse, unconscious, insatiable, impression, understand, intimacy, unsteadily, unearthly, impossible, infernal, inconceivable, unspeakable, indistinct, immense.

We see here over two hundred words (doubtless I have missed some in the text), in the order in which they appear in *Heart of Darkness*, their related prefixes threading themselves through the text, like that river down which Marlow travels. It seems appropriate that 'interminable' is the first of these words to appear. Many of the words are repeated and, together, this collection of words speaks to the idea of interminability, in the sense of that which is boundless or endless, that which is without end or limit. Most speak of that which cannot be known or experienced first-hand, or what cannot be expressed directly. They speak to the experience of an experience which cannot be communicated except *in*directly. These words bear witness to something which cannot be put into words. Each signifies or promises to signify the next, and all the others, in an *interminable* trace, a loop without beginning or end. None directs us towards a source, a location, a centre or origin: a *heart*. Yet they pulse through the story, like the beatings of some obscure heart, dimly perceived, barely heard, never encountered as such.

The words are not all Marlow's. Some belong to the first narrator, on board the *Nellie*. Others belong to the Harlequin-figure of the Russian. One or two belong to Kurtz's fiancé, his *intended* (even though he never reaches her), while a few others belong to the Manager. You see, don't you, what I am trying to show you is that it is not a question of Marlow, of his attempt to tell a story, to hold onto the thread of a narrative, and his repeated inability to make us see. For *in*communicability, *in*terminability, *un*decidability is *in*stalled, *in*scribed, within language, as the text refers all the while back to its own language, its own traces, its own relentless and *in*terminable movement into that *Heart of Darkness* and its own simultaneous retreat, as the *Heart of Darkness* retreats before the attempt to comprehend, to understand, to see. *Heart of Darkness* bears the mark of this retreat, the *trait* of the *retrait*, which is the very movement of writing, of text, of the contradictory impulse which signals the other within the same, the alterity within identity. Even the sentence within which that first *interminable* appears is troubled within its own logic: 'The sea-reach of the Thames stretched before us *like the beginning* of an interminable waterway' (*HD* 135; emphasis added). If you'll recall the definition of *interminable* – that which is boundless or endless – then the notion of a 'beginning' is troubled, contradicted even. What is more, within this sentence, the idea of the beginning belongs to the rhetorical gesture I've already mentioned: simile. The anonymous narrator's language, anticipating – or echoing in the wake of – Marlow's own discourse, breaks down as it 'begins', at the point when the *Nellie* has had to 'come to and wait for the turn of the tide' (*HD* 135). So, stasis, anticipation, awaiting the arrival of – what?

The prefixes with which I am concerning myself here – *in-*, *im-*, *un-*, *ir-*, *il-* – appear to comprise a family or to bear a family resemblance, sharing semantic values and etymological roots (while being 'related' to other prefixes such as *em-* , *en-*). The various forms, *im-*, *ir-*, *il-*, all are 'assimilated forms' of the prefix *in-*, the *OED* informs us. This might imply *in-* as a single origin, yet this prefix has a double or even triple sense within itself, having both positive and negative connotations which are determined only within a given semantic context (which context can always be broken through the iterability of the mark). However, whatever value the prefix might have, the ghost of its other values remains traced within its inscription. The prefix is itself derived, in both its negative and positive aspects, from the preposition *in*, the meaning of which is also doubled. It can be a preposition expressing 'the relation of inclusion, situation, position, existence or action, within the limits of space, time, condition, circumstances', or it can indicate a 'motion or direction' from a point outside to one within limits. Still, it is also a negative prefix expressing negation or privation. These definitions can be applied to all of the above prefixes, while the sense of negation or privation also applies to *un-*, which, while not immediately related to the other prefixes, nonetheless functions so as to bear apparently a family likeness. In the beginning, then, the multiple meaning: location, action, onwards motion, movement or change of state, continuance, negation, erasure, intensification.

Strictly speaking, such multiplicity leaves us with the possibility of reading only the unreadable, deciding on the undecidable. The iterability of the prefix, with its installation of a number of languages, troubles reading, while allowing us to bear witness to unreadability. When any of the voices in the narrative relay opts for similes or analogies, there is a sense that we're on shaky ground, and we know it. But then those limit-words appear, with their various prefixes leaving a mark between knowledge and non-knowledge. Effectively, the relay continues, with the movement or continuation of a certain motion, like the movement of the water beneath the various craft throughout *Heart of Darkness*. Yet what the relay also relays is precisely this erasure of decidability, of knowability. One of the definitions of the prefixes above is negation or privation. Alongside all those words I listed above are numerous terms for negation, privation, erasure, words such as: without, motionless, not, nothing, never, don't, nowhere; and phrases such as: nothing else to do, not extraordinary, not very clear, nobody seemed, not used, not quite right, I don't know why, nothing else, I can't explain, I did not see the real significance, I am not sure, you have no idea, I've never seen, he hadn't a word to say, nothing inside ... and so on, *interminably*.[6] All such phrases sound as though they are responses to a question (recall Ch. 1), coming before the question and anticipating its articulation.

The effect such figures and prefixes seem to have on the reader is one which performs the movement *and* frustration of Marlow's journey, so that narrative, the events being narrated *after the event*, and the act of reading come to resemble one another. Simultaneously, the constant mobility and negation all displace the location of meaning through constant deferral, denial, drifting, displacement and what Derrida in 'The *Retrait* of Metaphor' calls 'skidding' (*RM* 7). Thus, whether we choose to discuss form or content, we cannot choose but recognize, in Conrad's writing, the written mark as a certain expression of the limit – the limit of what may be known, what may be expressed – and also the undecidability which accompanies the 'differential splitting' (*RM* 28) which occurs as a result of the attempt to narrate, to bear witness. We may be in the *Heart of Darkness* but we're also on thin ice, and the cracks and fractures proliferate every time we skate across the textual surfaces.

The act of narration in *Heart of Darkness* is a constant performance of iterability, whether at the level of form or content, or at what we might call the *macrotextual* or *microtextual* levels, that is to say the level of the story, trope or prefix. The text is marked within itself by what Derrida terms a 'double gesture ... a double writing' (*LI* 21), one that effaces its own efforts in its very inscription and which also effects 'a general *displacement* of the system' (*LI* 21). In this case, that of Conrad's text, we might suggest that the system being displaced by the performance of this double writing is the idea of the system of narrative as coherent, decidable form and identity. As the frequency of prefixes, negations and erasures implies, there is always more to the relay, always an excess which remains to be read, and yet which can only be read as unreadable. The iterability installed by the family of prefixes (a family which have no common source or single origin, but which are, in themselves, always multiple) performs a spacing which inscribes 'a disruption of presence in a mark I call writing' (*LI* 19). Such a gesture in writing is performative also in that it produces a communication of the ways in which the text operates without relying on the generation of semantic content. (Indeed, as I've already said, we can read the text as highlighting the frustration of access to any semantic content.) Instead, the text seems constantly to cite itself without either referent to a meaning or value, an identity upon which we could decide, or to something outside-the-text (as though there were such a thing). Each encounter with the text reinforces the idea that there is no outside-the-text / *il n'y a pas de hors-texte*. Every time we read one of the limit-words with their articulating prefixes, one of the negations, we see at work what Derrida terms 'the structure of the mark' which frustrates the search for a centre or location outside (*LI* 10), and we recognize the 'chains of differential marks' (*LI* 10).

All of which is to figure the collapse of any binary distinctions we might care to make concerning our attempts to read the text and, by implication, all reading activity conventionally and institutionally understood. Principally, what my response to Conrad's writing leads me to understand is that the movement of the text dismantles the form/content binarism, for in this case each is traced by its other. *Heart of Darkness* is always already traced by its own doubleness, figuring as it does both the journey of a narrative and the narrative of a journey. The purpose of both parallel movements (recall those definitions for the family of prefixes) is to lead us back, as the narrative withdraws itself, to the point of supposed departure which is also a point of stasis: in an *'immense* darkness' (*HD* 252; emphasis added), on a boat or in the text, and figured, *performed*, by the reiteration of the 'waterway leading to the uttermost ends of the earth' (*HD* 137, 252). The text doubles itself and displaces itself (while displacing any limiting narrative system through iteration), directing us in two different directions at once, folding in on itself and seeming to unfold. Tracing the interminable leads us to where we began, but with a difference; we are left with the reading of undecidability through the iterable transition.

The figures of journey, of transport and movement are not merely, solely, figures for the literal event of Marlow's adventure, now retold second-hand as/in the motion of the narrative. They are also figures of narrative movement itself. Like the anchored *Nellie*, like the broken steamer in want of rivets, Marlow's narrative told to us by an anonymous narrator frequently finds itself stalled. It can only say repeatedly that it cannot say, it can only negate the possibility of assertion or definition, it can only open itself to the multiplication of indeterminacy. The desire for movement, the desire to move beyond Marlow's narrative for example, is therefore frustrated by the very performance of the narrative. If the figure of stalled, faulty or broken transport figures through the text, this is also a figure for broken, faulty and stalled communication. If Marlow desires to relay through narrative the attempt to keep an *appointment* with Kurtz, then his recounted narrative figures a *disappointment* for his audience, for himself, and for us, as all those phrases – such as 'I can't explain ...', 'you have no idea ...', 'I am not sure ...', 'don't you see ...', 'I did not see it any more ...', 'who could tell ...', 'who can tell ...', 'you can't understand. How could you?' – reinforce, with such intensity. The phrases all remain readable, yet they all speak to unreadability.

Where does this configuration – a configuration which is also a *disfiguring* – of undecidability and unreadability, reiteration and negation, lead? I mentioned earlier in this chapter that the reiterative mark may also be a wound for 'what remains unknown', in Cathy Caruth's words. This figurative wound is the expression of trauma, the expression of that which cannot be experienced. In the conclusion of this chapter, I want to turn to Caruth's work on trauma and literature, as a way of suggesting how *Heart of Darkness* may be understood to function.

Trauma and reiteration

Caruth's *Unreclaimed Experience: Trauma, Narrative, and History* offers the reader a rhetorical analysis of literature which works around the trope of trauma as a figure of repetition, of reiteration, and of supplementarity. Trauma calls those who hear, who attempt to read, to bear witness, not to the now irretrievable experience but to the constant return of suffering. In her introduction she maps out her understanding of the figural condition of trauma, beginning with Freud. Trauma, Caruth points out, originally means a wound on the body. Since Freud, the term has come to be understood figuratively as a mark or trace on the mind. She develops her comprehension through a brief reading of Freud's reading of Tasso's narrative of Tancred and Clorinda: Tancred kills Clorinda inadvertently, and does not find out that he has done so until, in an enchanted forest, he cuts at a tree with his sword. The wound made by his weapon speaks to him with Clorinda's voice, for her soul is imprisoned in the tree. Thus, when Tancred discovers what he has done, he does so on having wounded his lover *again*.

For Caruth it is this supplementary articulation which is important, for 'repetition [is] at the heart of catastrophe' (1996, 2):

> Just as Tancred does not hear the voice of Clorinda until the second wounding, so trauma is not locatable in the simple violent or original event in an individual's past, but rather in the way that its very unassimilated nature – the way it was precisely *not known* in the first instance – returns to haunt the survivor ... (1996, 4)

This return is what is figured by the relay of witnesses in *Heart of Darkness*, spoken of earlier by Hillis Miller. What Kurtz calls 'the horror, the horror' (*HD* 239) is so far removed to be completely inaccessible. Even Kurtz is not experiencing 'the horror' at the moment he utters this, but is in the process of being haunted by the return of traumatic experience, expressed otherwise and, now, assimilated, translated. This *now* is not the present moment of Kurtz's suffering; as the iterable movement of narrative makes clear, the *now* is the rhythm of trauma's return, its differential spacing, across the witnesses, Marlow, the narrator, ourselves. As Samuel Weber makes clear, iterability 'splits the mark into a past that can never be fully rendered present and a future which is always about to arrive ... *the future is what remains as the possibility of the past* (Weber 1996, 149). The constant movement and relay of narrative gestures in Conrad's text performs a past which has never been present while gesturing, through reiterative utterance, towards what Weber calls 'this *coming-to-pass of the future*' (1996, 149). As readers, we are not the final station in the relay but merely the latest in the series of witnesses to whom suffering, and the other, return. Reading trauma as the narrative transport in *Heart of Darkness* thus gives us to understand *différance* and the displacement of a present or presence which has never been *as such*. Kurtz's articulated response is merely part of a differential chain. It is a response to the other.

Our reading of the line is even further removed, for between us and the unknowable experience there is not only Kurtz, but also Marlow and the anonymous narrator (at the very least). All we can do is bear witness to this utterance, knowing that its undecidability is only multiplied through being reiterated across the relay of voices, and 'internally', within its own structural dissemination, of which I have already spoken.

Trauma is, then, (says Caruth)

> ... always the story of a wound that cries out, that addresses us in the attempt to tell us of a reality or truth that is not otherwise available.

> This truth, in its delayed appearance and its belated address, cannot be linked only to what is known, but also to what remains unknown in our very action and in our language. (1996, 4)

It is precisely because 'the horror' is what remains unknown that it comes to return as the traumatic articulation which spaces and disrupts, making access to full meaning, to presence, impossible. As such, 'the horror, the horror', already internally iterable as we have shown, stands, in my understanding of the text, as a singular example of writing in the Derridean sense, traced as it is by this 'differential fraying'. Kurtz's phrase is, I would suggest, comprehensible as an *apophatic aphorism*, the meaning of which is undecidable because of this internal difference which cannot be calmed. As such, it speaks to us, but away from the place of the other, projected from the other place within our own identities from which trauma comes to haunt us, from which it is projected. It is aphoristic because it is only readable as a figure for (dis)figuration, a figure of the work of writing across *Heart of Darkness*, traced in those iterable prefixes, and those negations.

All we can do, ethically, as good readers, is to listen, to bear witness, to what Caruth calls 'the address of another, an address that remains enigmatic, yet demands a listening and a response' (1996, 9). Conrad's text, like those of Duras and Renais analysed by Caruth, asks us indirectly to consider

> what it means to transmit and to theorize around a crisis that is marked, not by a simple knowledge, but by the ways it simultaneously defies and demands our witness ... [in] a language that defies, even as it claims, our understanding. (Caruth 1996, 5)

If we accept this as a provisional definition of the work of *Heart of Darkness*, we may suggest that the relay of witness, voices, writings and narratives, when understood as a constant self-displacing movement of traits, all figure the traumatic mark, cut or wound which constantly articulates the need to bear witness, despite or perhaps *because* of the double rhythm of defiance and demand. As Caruth suggests, 'literature ... is interested in the complex relation between knowing and not knowing' (1996, 3). It is this complex relation figured at every level of articulation and iteration, from one voice to another, across the various negations or among the words listed above, in

Heart of Darkness. The question of knowing and not knowing is crucial in this text, as it pertains intimately to our experience of the narrative, to the response we are obliged to give it in the face of its undecidability. The reiterative quality promised in 'the horror, the horror' points not to an experience which can be known, but to the need to understand the nature of Kurtz's cry: as iterable trace of trauma, and as the figure *par excellence* for narrative compulsion.

We may read the phrase as speaking indirectly to the condition of incompletion, of a certain to-come, a certain interminability. The work of Kurtz's phrase, the slippage of prefixes and negations, all are marks of deconstruction. I want to conclude by not concluding, but letting Jacques Derrida have the last word (about not having the last word). Here he is speaking, not about *Heart of Darkness* (he has never done so, to my knowledge), but about that ill-named thing, deconstruction. Without unpacking it at any length, I would merely like to suggest that you read this as a possible explanation for the ways in which writing in *Heart of Darkness* works: as the figure of itselves, interminable, iterable, undecidable, unreadable, and disjointing ahead of all encounters the question of identity:

> And yet, ... deconstruction *must* have the afterword that it *cannot* have. For, always incomplete, of an incompletion which is not the negativity of a lack, it is interminable, an 'interminable analysis'.... As it is never closed into a system, as it is the deconstruction *of* the systematic totality, it needs some supplementary afterword each time it runs the risk of stabilising or saturating into a formalised discourse.... It *must* be what it both is and is not in itself: an effect of after the event, a sort of afterword to 'all', this 'all' that cannot totalise itself; the 'all' of philosophy, the 'all' of western culture, or rather the infinite idea of totality, wherever and in whatever form it can *present* itself: *afterword to the presence or presentation of the present itself* (A 199)

(P.S. *Heart of Darkness*: the afterword to, and 'deconstruction' of, the idea of Western culture, the idea of the closed system, an interminable analysis perhaps?)

Part III

Some Supplementary Afterword(s)

Afterword(s): Contrary to the 'Logic of the Heading'

> For there *must* not be a last word – that's what I'd like to say finally; the *afterword* is not, that means *ought* not, ought never to be a last word.
>
> Jacques Derrida (A 197)

> ... it is no longer merely a question of deconstructing discourses and semantics, but also and primarily institutional and political structures.
>
> Jacques Derrida (A 202)

I cannot pretend in so short a space as an Afterword, or in afterwords, to sum things up, to present you with a neat conclusion or formula, which, after all I've said, lets you off the hook from thinking and responding to the unpredictable event of your own encounter with Derrida's work. This book will, therefore, not have been a guide book, much less a road map. I'm merely trying to point up a few headings, a few directions, without pretending to know the destination (if there is such a thing ...). At least we can conclude our introduction by borrowing Nicholas Royle's comment, from a collection of essays entitled *Afterwords*, that deconstruction (if such a thing exists) 'is never single, deconstruction is never itself but is always different' (1992, 1). This difference-from-itself is located above, in the title 'Afterword(s)', with that parenthetical plural, never single. We start to draw to an end which is not really one, as we began, by raising the ghost of an identity. This ghost may well be a certain Derrida, a certain image of deconstruction. But there is no sense that we have moved beyond Derrida. Samuel Weber sums up the problem for us: 'any attempt to move "beyond" deconstruction runs the risk of never getting to it and therefore winding up where one started, *before* deconstruction' (Weber 1996, 132). To restate Weber's remarks, if there is a sense that we are still before Derrida, then Derrida is still *before us*, yet to be read.

Let's begin to conclude, though, by examining a few statements pertaining to Derrida's texts. First, Drucilla Cornell:

> Derrida's text leaves us with the infinite responsibility undecidability imposes on us. Undecidability in no way alleviates responsibility. The opposite is the case. We cannot be excused from our own role in history because we could not know so as to be reassured that we were 'right' in advance. (Cornell 1992, 169)

This question of responsibility is something which has been stressed repeatedly throughout *Deconstruction* • *Derrida*, whether as an introductory comment, an acknowledgement of a principle of J. Hillis Miller's understanding of reading, or as a condition of responding to a specific literary work, such as Joseph Conrad's *Heart of Darkness*. Responsibility never ends, and undecidability means that we cannot abdicate our responsibility. Historically, as Cornell suggests, we have a role, involving a responsibility to respond, even while we cannot know the outcome of an event, of what takes place. Being 'good readers' means to read responsibly, to allow the text as other to dictate its reading to us. This is not merely a formalist concern. Cornell's highlighting of the 'historical role' we have to play points to the continuous assumption of a political and ethical activity, though not necessarily an activity dictated in advance by conventional systems, discourses, institutions which involve politics narrowly conceived.

The next comment comes from Peggy Kamuf:

> The fact that deconstruction can be positioned as at once too political and not political at all, as both PC and not PC, signals that the terms in which the political is posed in this debate are inadequate to account for all the effects being produced. (Kamuf 1997, 146)

Kamuf is suggesting nothing less than the fact that what is called 'deconstruction' has always exceeded the narrow conception of politics. As she points out, this is not a problem with deconstruction so much as with the conceptualization and theorization of politics, and the theoretical ideas behind political thought currently in place. So-called 'deconstruction' has been accused, as we have seen in Chapter 1, of being radical, apolitical, formalist, liberal (and, as in the appalling example of the so-called Paul de Man affair, fascist). To turn to Kamuf once more, all this means is that the terminology within which accusations are made concerning Derrida's work is generated from conceptual frameworks which do not have the wherewithal or the inclination to give Derrida a patient enough reading (or indeed, in some cases, to read him at all).

What disturbs those who judge deconstruction or Derrida as politically ineffective at least or problematic at worst is, once again, the problem of, if not identity, then certainly identification. For Derrida's practice never exactly appears to resemble any one system of thought. Instead, it seems to reshape itself, repeatedly. It always has the appearance of being in transition. And it is this activity, the refusal to coalesce, to solidify into a discernible identity, which most troubles all those thinkers for whom political thought is an exercise in mimesis, an exercise of making another's thought fit as closely as possible the ideal image one has in mind. It's a question, let's not pretend it's anything else, of turning Derrida's work into a copy, in other words, of a political discourse, reshaping it so as to improve the resemblance, while chipping away at that which is not-similar, that which is different, that which is other.

Yet, as Joan Brandt has recently contended, despite the critique of Derrida's supposed 'apolitical' stance, 'it is precisely [the] relation to otherness inscribed in the undecidable "logic" of *différance* and supplementarity that constitutes ... [and] contains distinctly political possibilities ... possibilities for assuming our political "responsibility to act" while rethinking the philosophical precepts upon which our concepts of political action are grounded' (Brandt 1997, 2). If we are to understand Derrida's practice as ethical/political at all, it is precisely over this matter of respect for and responsibility to the other, to that which has yet to arrive and which cannot be anticipated, as Gayatri Spivak also reminds us, in the next of our citations:

> For Derrida ... the responsibility of ethicopolitical practice comes from and is judged by an other who cannot be fully grasped. (Spivak 1995, 114)

Of course all of these remarks by Cornell, Kamuf, Brandt and Spivak are, in a sense, reformulations of Derrida's own words, commentaries as acts of responsibility, and as responses to Derrida as other. (We could cite many others in a similar, though singular, vein.) They come in the wake of Derrida's own comments concerning bearing witness, acting responsibly, responding to the other, while allowing the movement of the undecidable. As Derrida tells us in *Mémoires for Paul de Man*:

> *There is no* beyond-the-undecidable,... There remains to be thought an other undecidability, one no longer bound to the order of *calculation* between two poles of opposition, but to the incalculable order of the wholly other. It must be unpredictable, aleatory, beyond any calculation. (Acts 137)

Derrida's statement speaks to the very issue of an ethicopolitical decision, involved in deciding not to decide, to give oneself over to the aleatory, the undecidable, which a conventional politics cannot acknowledge, relying as it does on the dual action of mastery over the other, and the domestication of the other through its reformation into a family likeness. To assume a restricted economy[1] of likeness for deconstruction (so-called or otherwise) is to practice such a coercive politics of mimesis, whereby the differences between what Joan Brandt calls the 'various proponents of deconstruction' are made to vanish (1997, 10). It is implicitly against such a political activity that Derrida has sought to situate himself, through endless strategies of play, of give and take.

Whether writing on European identity, a line of a poem by Stéphane Mallarmé or Paul Celan, the topic of writing in the history of philosophy or a footnote in Martin Heidegger's texts, the writing of Jacques Derrida concerns itself with unveiling the folds of *différance* within a given identity, the self-same, homogeneity. All are unfolded at the limits of their economies, the limits at which their reliance on similarity, analogy, comparison, can be shown to operate only by the most violent suppression of the non-similar, difference, the other within. It is for such reasons that Derrida has, throughout his career, sought to engage with familiar terms and concepts, such as writing and text, in order to estrange their conventional meanings from some other location, if not from *the other of the location*. He does this, moreover, not through rejection; nor does he do this through assuming a static oppositional position against such terms, refusing to locate his own arguments within a binary hierarchy. Rather, he seeks to find ways into the very structures and values which inform and articulate the concepts in question, as well as numerous other subjects, topics, philosophemes.

But this is not his only process. Derrida also engages in a process throughout his writing of utilizing words (a number of which I have already mentioned) such as hymen, *parages, parergon,* jetty, and so on (recall the mechanical dredger with which we concluded our introduction as one singular example of what a Derridean reading practice might look like) which, strategically, provisionally, momentarily, are mobilized by Derrida as metaphors or figures of catechresis. Such tropes are employed, or, rather, *deployed* by Derrida – and deconstruction is, it should be remembered, merely one such trope, one more figure in Derrida's chain of nonsynonymous substitutions – as cantilevers which unbalance, feathers which tickle, prods and goads which disturb equilibrium, in the processes of delineating the structure of an argument, a thought, a concept. Derrida's pen may well be the thin end of a wedge, the width of which we've yet to comprehend. Each trope or figure serves a momentary purpose in the act of showing the reader how the economies of thought and logic work within the history of Western metaphysics. The trope employed by Derrida performs an estranging, defamiliarizing *amimetological* function by displacing not only the text or idea before us, but also by tripping up our understanding of what happens in acts of reading and writing, conventionally conceived.

A further act on Derrida's part is to play, in the most serious fashion, to put into play, homonymic and homophonic resemblances for the purpose not of re-enforcing similarity but, once again, to open up a gap in the experience of similarity, allowing the difference, the alterity, already installed in the structure to make itself known. Such an act is not itself a revelation of a certain presence for this, strictly speaking, is not possible. Instead, the self-same is prevented from asserting its identity through the unveiling of a contradiction within that identity, upon which presence and unity come to rely. Also, Derrida works strategically with neologisms, only to abandon them once they have served a particular purpose; or else, he resurrects very old words, such as deconstruction, *revenant*, and so on. In doing so, Derrida is not merely playing for the sake of the pun, a chance likeness or other comic or irrationalist effect. All of these concerns or interests are put to work by Derrida. They are part of the workings of Derrida's texts, after which we come and to which we respond. Yet in every, very *singular* instance, the singularity, though iterable, is never available for transformation into a general or universal principle. The condition of heterogeneity and non-resemblance forestalls and forbids such an activity. Deconstruction, if there is such a thing, is only one movement among many.

Trying to reach a momentary conclusion without making decisions for others, without trying to decide on a programme; (pretending to) try(ing) to come to a conclusion when we've yet to begin. The only conclusion we can make is that we must not yet come to a conclusion about Derrida. Responding to Derrida is, perhaps, understandable, understandable as a figure in our thought, of synecdoche. As Derrida himself suggests with regard to the ethical response to the other, 'one never acquits oneself of such a call' (Lacoue-Labarthe and Nancy 1997, 53). What does, what *might*, responding to Derrida mean, as synecdoche? Responding to the other. Awaiting the arrival of the other, without anticipating one's response, awaiting, in Derrida's words, the 'to-come [*l'à-venir*] of an event *and* a singularity, of an alterity that cannot be anticipated'.

> Awaiting without the horizon of the wait, awaiting what one does not expect yet or any longer, hospitality without reserve ... (*SM* 111)

This is to be responsible, in Derrida's understanding: responsibility involves a politics of hospitality. Yet what this means is that we have constantly to be on our guard against falling into those programmatic, conventional, institutionally approved modes of thought where everything is decided in advance, everything is planned and given some kind of anticipatory articulation, a strait-jacket with which to welcome the guest. Those who decide on the a/political status or condition of Derrida's thought usually have a model worked out, in mind, ahead of the event of the encounter with Derrida's text, as we have seen. Yet, to insist on this once more, if Derrida's text can teach us anything at all, it is that we should not, in all responsibility, out of an ethical sense, try to dictate the encounter or master the situation. Learning rules and protocols, even in the activity of reading literature, means to accede to systems and models, to give oneself to an authorized body of thought in a certain manner, to learn at the feet of a master, in order to gain mastery oneself.

Yet everything we *can* learn from Derrida (and we can learn quite a lot) suggests that giving up the desire for mastery is more important, ethically and politically speaking. As Derrida has patiently sought to demonstrate in every singular case, there is that which is undecidable, whether at the linguistic, grammatical, institutional or philosophical level; whether at the level of phoneme or philosopheme. There is always already the trace, the mark, the trait, *différance* within the structure, within identity, which disables mastery ahead of the encounter or event with the subject of enquiry. There is that within identity which disarms our attempts to pin identity down, whether that identity is that of a literary text, an author, a culture such as Europe, or whatever. Indeed, our only chance of identifying the subject is to accede to the movement of *différance*, the graphic, the spectral element.

In a discussion of the future of European identity, Derrida says:

> The expression 'The Other Heading' ... can mean to recall that there is another heading, the heading being not only ours ... but the other ... not only that which we identify, calculate, and decide upon, but the *heading of the other*, before which we must respond ... the heading of the other being perhaps the first condition of an identity or identification that is not an egocentrism destructive of oneself and the other.
>
> But beyond *our heading*, it is necessary to recall ourselves not only the *other heading*, and especially to the *heading of the other*, but also perhaps to the *other of the heading*, that is to say to a relation of identity with the other that no longer obeys the form, the sign, or the logic of the heading ... (*OH* 14–15)

The logic of the heading is that which chooses our route for us, defining our destination. Always remembering the multiple possibilities keeps our choices open, even as we must remain open to the heading of the other *and* the other of the heading: this is the question of a certain politics thought otherwise. To talk of a possible Derridean politics is to reproduce Derrida's reconfigurations with regard to the other heading, to open ourselves to consider not only an other politics, but also the politics of the other and the other of politics, where politics is no longer dictated by the attempt to force a family likeness at the cost of alterity. Derrida's strategic multiplication of possibilities keeps in play the undecidable which is already there but which the logic of the heading closes down. In opening the movement of the phrase, he alerts us to the necessity of remaining open to that play, between self and other for example. Yet as Derrida's unfolding makes clear, the play, the movement, *différance*, the freeing of time 'from its subordination to the present' (Levinas 1996, 60) is there, within identity, within ourselves. Making ourselves aware of this is to say 'yes' to the other, to respond ethically, to take the first step on that *other heading* towards becoming the good reader. It is also to ask the 'improper question', as I suggested earlier, as part of the good reader's response, uttered by Jacques Derrida in *Speech and Phenomena*, and reiterated by Emmanuel Levinas:

> – Is this certain? (*SP* 95; Levinas 1996, 58)

Notes

Introduction: 'Deconstruction, if such a thing exists ...'

1. This phrase is taken from a response by Jacques Derrida to a question from Colin MacCabe. The first epigraph of this introduction is taken from the same interview, 'Some questions and responses', in *The Linguistics of Writing: Arguments between Language and Literature*, ed. Nigel Fabb, Derek Attridge, Alan Durant and Colin MacCabe (1987), 252–64. All further references to this and other works by Derrida are given parenthetically in the text. Derrida's phrase is echoed elsewhere in this book, in the words of J. Hillis Miller, Peggy Kamuf, and in the title of Chapter 1, following this 'Introduction'. Together, and dispersed throughout the text, these phrases should disturb any certainty concerning received notions about the identity of deconstruction.

2. I am borrowing here from J. Hillis Miller, in *The Ethics of Reading: Kant, de Man, Eliot, Trollope, James, and Benjamin* (1987), 9, 43. Miller's work will be further discussed in Chapter 5, below. For more on Miller and his work as a critic in relation to narratology, see Mark Currie's volume in this series, *Postmodern Narrative Theory* (1998).

3. The title, its structure, function and operation, is discussed below in Chapter 1. The concept of the title is discussed in Chapter 3

4. I have chosen the French verb *entamer* for the multiple meanings which it puts into play. The verb can mean: to initiate, to enter into, to start (an activity or journey), to open, to undermine, to shake or to test, to eat into, to cut into, to take a bite. The senses of this verb defy a stable semantic identity because simultaneously the ideas of beginning, of introducing, and of already being underway, already being in the middle of something, of opening something out, are available to us. The verb performs its own 'deconstruction', the 'deconstruction' of any discrete, completely contained identity, as its meaning is dependent on what we call contexts. The verb's identity is not complete and self-present.

5. I am deliberately citing and echoing Bennington here as a performative

means of indicating or gesturing towards the impossibility of an absolute beginning.

6. I have avoided discussing de Man throughout this volume, as Mark Currie, in his volume in the Transitions series, *Postmodern Narrative Theory* (1998), deals so cogently with de Man's work in the context of narratology and theories of narrative.

7. For a fascinating discussion of Derrida's work, as well as that of Lacoue-Labarthe and Nancy in relation to questions of politics and mimesis (and the politics of mimesis), see Joan Brandt, *Geopoetics: The Politics of Mimesis in Poststructuralist French Poetry and Theory* (1997).

8. The title is, I think, typically Miller. Ostensibly 'Now and Then' has a temporal play about it. It suggests a present: whose present? Miller's when he wrote the essays, between 1965 and 1990, or that of the reader? Which reader? Miller as reader, when he came to assemble the collection or to write the preface? Which time of reading? When I first read these essays, when I re-read some? When any of you who read this note might read them? And what about then? Is not every now always destined to become a then, every then having been at one time – not the present time – a now? And should the phrase not be 'then and now', implying the comfort of a linear progression up to the so-called present moment? But aside from all these temporal complications and the differential, the differing and deferring which the terms of the phrase put into play, there is also another form of differentiation in that phrase, which suggests the rhythm of the occasion, the event of theory, and of Miller being more or less 'theoretical', occasionally theoretical: theoretical now, not theoretical (not) now. Being good readers will allow us to pursue the rhetoric of the phrase as its slippage is self-performing or, at the risk of using this word, 'deconstructive'. We are not reading deconstructively, unless we are the good readers of whom Miller speaks. We are, however, reading the 'deconstruction' of the stability of temporal and rhetorical identities which an initial glance at the phrase might well install. Reflecting upon that installation, the construction of a structure, gives us to re-read. Deconstruction, we might suggest following Miller, is nothing other than good re-reading, as such.

9. The lower case 'b' refers here to the layout of *Glas*, which is presented in two columns, left and right on the page. Both columns follow separate, yet interweaving readings, of Hegel on the left and Genet on the right. Both columns further disrupt the conventional linear reading process by having inserts within the columns. The lower case letter refers here to the right-hand column.

1 Another Introduction / *Entamer*

1. I have taken this phrase, 'ineluctable modality', from the Proteus episode of James Joyce's *Ulysses*, in which Stephen Dedalus, in considering the world as being composed of a series of signs there to be read by consciousness, forms the phrase, 'ineluctable modality of the visible' (3:1). My adoption of this phrase is deliberate, given Stephen's attempts to relate perception to interpretation, and to see the phenomena of the world translated into thought as a range of unstoppable, yet potential interpretable or translatable signifiers. Stephen's consideration of the structure of perception and its relation to vision as a primarily textual structure is available to us as an aphoristic figure for comprehending the nature of reading and writing. The visible, taken as a form of writing, is that which is not to be resisted.

2. The question of the question is raised and applied to in passing by Jean-Luc Nancy in his consideration of why there are several arts and not just one, and why our conception of the arts is governed by a singular plural: *the* arts (1996: 1–11). Nancy opens his discussion by pointing to the ways in which certain questions get asked about the arts, while others are avoided; the avoidance is such on occasions that even the question gets avoided, because, as he shows, there is an assumption that the answer is known ahead of the question (1–2).

3. By this, Derrida means the particular philosophical units or concepts which make up, construct or structure our ways of comprehending ourselves, our identity, our world; those ideas, for instance, which inform the *ways* in which a narrative is structured 'conceptually' or 'philosophically'. The philosopheme is the conceptual unit which signifies a supposedly stable value which in turn informs the operation of a system or structure. The philosopheme is itself structured or written, yet its structure remains concealed within Western thought, in order that it appear a unitary figure.

4. I have described this 'position' as a 'quasi-position' because of the difficulty which the concept of the position has, with regard to its mobilization of ideas of locatability and a mappable topography. The position is not really one at all, even though we assume its possible identification. We thus misunderstand the truth-value in a manner similar to the misunderstanding concerning the apparent locatability of the unconscious within certain strands of psychoanalytic discourse (see Andrew Roberts's forthcoming book in the Transitions series).

5. George Eliot writes in the epigraph to the first chapter of her last novel, *Daniel Deronda*, that '[m]en can do nothing without the make-believe of a beginning.... Science, too, reckons backwards as well as forwards,

divides his unit into billions, and with his clock-finger at Nought really sets off *in medias res*. No retrospect will take us to the true beginning ...' (1986, 35). Eliot's admission of the strategic, yet fictional necessity of assuming and inventing beginnings and origins offers an important 'deconstructive' lesson on the nature of narrative construction and teleological designs. Although the Latin tag in my title is a commonplace phrase, I have consciously borrowed it with reference to Eliot's epigraph, with its statement of intent concerning the *inter-ested* status of discursive, and other, 'introductions'.

6. Bennington's use of 'déjà' refers also to Derrida's own encoding of his own name through various French words and phrases in his texts in various ways, 'déjà' being one example of this, carrying in it Derrida's initials, transposed and sounding the phonetic beginning of each name.

7. Quotation and citation are just two among so many topics about which Derrida has asked improper questions, concerning the uses of discourse within the structures and politics of academic institutions and their various contexts.

8. See the discussion of a letter from the *Chronicle of Higher Education* in the note immediately below.

9. For a trenchant discussion of this politics, see Peggy Kamuf's significant intervention into the debate surrounding 'deconstruction' in her *The Division of Literature: or the University in Deconstruction* (1997). See particularly Chapter 5, 'The University in Deconstruction' (133–61).

   A vulgar example of the political and institutional assumptions concerning deconstruction and the need for it to exist as an institutionally recognized (albeit excoriated) literary methodology surfaces in a letter from the American academic weekly, the *Chronicle of Higher Education* (April 4, 1997; 43: 30), B13. In a letter which shows its ecological awareness by recycling what are already very worn-out arguments concerning obscurity of expression in writing by academics in the humanities, E.L. Pattullo points to a tripartite group of professional scholars defined as 'feminists, multiculturalists and deconstructionists' who are particularly guilty of obscurantism. You will notice that the three 'schools of thought' are clearly intended as both academic and political categories. Never mind that these groups might or might not exist as groups; never mind even that, supposing them to exist, said groups might have differences of opinion; what really scares this letter writer – what in fact motivates the author to put pen to paper – is that in her/his mind at least, the three groups have an alliance (the nature of which is beyond me to work out). This strange group are 'now so influential in the humanities'. And the bottom line (for the author of this missive) is that the public ought to have a hand in deciding on whether these influential, clearly politicized types get funding. A good tax-paying citizen, then, doesn't want to see his tax dollar wasted on diffi-cult words (such as 'deconstructionists') and complex sentences which might have some nefarious purpose, if only we could understand what they're saying! I cite this example not because it is in any way anom-alous, but because it is so wholly typical, even though the relative late-ness of its arrival is comparable with that of the LAPD at the scene of the 1992 Los Angeles riots.

10. See also Geoffrey Bennington's critique/review 'Genuine Gasché (Perhaps)' (1996b, 252–7).

11. See Mark Currie's comments on Derrida's reading of James Joyce in Chapter 3, 'Theoretical Fiction', of the Transitions volume, *Postmodern Narrative Theory* (1998).

12. It is not the purpose of this introduction to counter such charges; we would refer the reader to the collection of interviews with Derrida, *Points ... Interviews 1974–1994*, as one possible starting point, in which Derrida responds to questions in a number of interviews which concern such issues as are raised by Frank Lentricchia and Terry Eagleton.

13. In order to collapse the arbitrary distinction made between the ideas of 'theory' and 'practice', Immanuel Kant begins the essay, 'On the Common Saying: That may be correct in theory, but it is of no use in practice', by considering the concept of duty (Kant 1996, 280–1). As he argues, no idea or sense of duty can hold if the theory of duty is not borne out by the experience of duty, and, conversely, if the expression of duty is not informed by theoretical principles of what duty should be. Using the idea of duty as a strategic opening onto his subject, in which idea the 'theory' is always seen to be put into 'practice' and the practice to be an expression of that 'theory', Kant explores, amongst other issues, the idea that there can be no practice which is not informed by 'rational principles' (1996, 303). This self-informing, mutually recipro-cal structure may be said to be 'deconstructive', inasmuch as the opera-tion of Kant's thought, at both semantic and conceptual or 'philo-sophical' levels, demonstrates its own argumentative procedures, while affirming the resistance to separable, wholly discrete categories. Neither theory nor practice in Kant's argument can be said to maintain their supposedly autonomous truth-values, precisely because of the kind of questions that Kant raises with regard to such assumed auton-omy. In this, we may say that Kant anticipates Derrida, or that Derrida is influenced in part by the structures of Kantian thinking. This being the case, deconstruction is merely one word which acknowledges the activity of thinking which cannot be extracted into a theory which can

then be put into practice, for all the reasons Kant shows in the rigorous pursuit of his point in relation to his negotiation with the commonplace concepts which underpin both 'theory' and 'practice', as examples of philosophemes which are themselves internally disjointed and open to questioning from another place than the places from which they are conventionally articulated.

2 Preparatory to Anything Else

1. See Mark Currie's discussion of the narration or construction of identity in Chapter 1, 'The Manufacture of Identities', in *Postmodern Narrative Theory* (1998).
2. Again, refer to Currie's commentary on binary oppositions in the introduction to *Postmodern Narrative Theory* (see n.1, above).
3. Logocentrism was coined by Derrida to bring together two ideas: that of the logos, the Greek term for The Word or Truth (as an unquestionable and desired value, i.e. the Word of God); and centre, the concept of a central or originary point, a moment of absolute beginning or origin from which everything springs and around which all ideas circulate or to which they refer. Logocentrism thus suggests the conceptual movement in Western metaphysical thought where a philosophical system of thought orients itself around a key-concept term as the starting or originating point or centre as the truth or value of the particular system in question. In such a system the centre value remains outside the area of inquiry or field of investigation as an apparently stable identity or quality.
4. For an example of such reductive misinterpretation see Charles E. Bressler's *Literary Criticism: An Introduction to Theory and Practice* (1994, 71–87). Bressler, in an undergraduate, introductory textbook, puts forward the entire 'binary opposition reversal' theory as the methodology of 'deconstruction'.
5. Jeri Johnson, the editor of the Oxford edition of *Ulysses*, makes some comments on the nature of the opening phrase which are worth quoting here: '*Eumaeus*'s opening words are ... symptomatic of the pleasure the text takes in slyly drawing our attention to its ability constantly to revise itself. But these words also lie about their "preparatory" status, coming as they do, so late in *Ulysses*. Further, the seemingly empty phrase tempts us into impatience, for it appears to signify nothing but its own temporal position: the first words of a sentence are *always* "preparatory to anything else". So *Eumaeus* begins with words that are both false and true, significant and empty' (Joyce 1993, 944).

6. On the nature of citation and annotation, see Jacques Derrida, 'This is Not an Oral Footnote', trans. Stephen A. Barney and Michael Hanly, in *Annotation and its Texts*, ed. Stephen A. Barney (1991), 192–207. See also Claudette Sartiliot's Derrida-influenced *Citation and Modernity: Derrida, Joyce and Brecht* (1993).

7. This problem of meaning is troubled even further if we allow for the possibility that, as one more possible 'beginning', this is not a beginning at all but a rather 'imperfect' supplement or citation of the 'first' episode of *Ulysses*. 'Telemachus', the first episode, begins with Buck Mulligan, Stephen Dedalus's friend, mocking the mass with a shaving bowl and razor. The phrases in the opening sentence from 'Eumaeus' – 'shavings', 'bucked him up' – might be taken as references to that earlier scene. There is a possible ghost of a chance that we are dealing with some form of transcription or translation. We cannot tell with any certainty, however.

8. I offer an analysis of the relations between narration, text and identity in Gilman's text in Chapter 2 of my *The Rhetoric of Affirmative Resistance: Dissonant Identities from Carroll to Derrida* (1997).

9. Richard Jefferies, 'Snowed Up: A Mistletoe Story', in *Literary Theories: A Case Study in Critical Performance*, ed. Julian Wolfreys and William Baker (1996), 19–30. See also my essay in *Literary Theories*, 'An "Economics" of Snow and the Blank Page, or, "Writing" at the "Margins": "Deconstructing" "Richard Jefferies"?' (179–244), which pursues a number of the themes pertinent to this book as a whole. Fragments of this essay appear throughout *Deconstruction • Derrida*, particularly in this present chapter.

10. On the gift, see also Derrida's essay, 'At This Very Moment in This Work Here I Am', trans. Ruben Berezdivin, in *Re-Reading Levinas*, ed. Robert Bernasconi and Simon Critchley (1991), 11–48.

11. I have coined the term 'aneconomic' with various etymological sources for the prefix 'an-' in mind, and as a term with which to counter the economic discourse of the text. According to the *OED* 'an-' can mean, depending on the context of its use, possibly 'against', 'towards', 'in return for'. It can also imply 'not', 'without', or 'about'. Thus the possible sense of the term 'aneconomic' may be 'against economics', 'towards economics', 'in return for economics', 'not economics', 'without economics', 'about economics'. It is such possible meanings that I am playing with in relation to the figure of snow in the text; also this is the homonymic play in the title of the essay referred to above (p.199, n.9): 'An 'economics' of Snow', which also sounds like 'An "Economics" of Snow'. The point here is that I am reading snow 'against', 'without' economics. There is not an economics of snow,

snow cannot be an economic figure, so what we find is that instead of a false binarism, say economics/snow, what we have is snow as the overflow, the excess or supplement which cannot be economized in the text.

12. 'Theological' in the sense of a reading or interpretive process which attempts to reveal – is endowed with the desire to reveal – absolute knowledge. As Derrida suggests in 'Circumfession', there is always the unpredictable which can derail the theological enterprise (C 1993, [3–315] 26–31).

13. See Bennington (Db, 104 ff.) on the proper name.

14. See also Bennington (Db, 148–66) on the related subject of the signature.

15. The date is, of course, Independence Day, and may have a certain contextual irony for our comprehension of the narrator, who lacks any independence.

16. On the nature and the law of the title, see Jacques Derrida, 'Before the Law' (AL 181–221).

17. For a fascinating reading of the operation of parables as narrative forms, see J. Hillis Miller's 'Parable and Performative in the Gospels and in Modern Literature' (1990, 135–50).

18. Jacques Derrida, 'Le Facteur de la vérité' (PC 411–97). A shorter version of the text, under the title 'The Purveyor of Truth' (trans. Alan Bass), is to be found, along with Poe's and Lacan's texts, in *The Purloined Poe: Lacan, Derrida, and Psychoanalytic Reading*, ed. John P. Muller and William J. Richardson (1988, 173–213), a useful source of essays on the issue of psychoanalytic literary criticism. Extracts from the text are provided by Peggy Kamuf in her *A Derrida Reader* (DR 466–84), which version retains the French title with its play on the French word 'facteur', which can mean postman/factor/element. Also there is the sense of 'purveyor' as used in the Muller/Richardson version. There is also the possible translation in some contexts of 'facteur' as 'risk'. Derrida's essay is a rigorous, lengthy analysis of the strategies of Lacan's reading of Poe's text, whilst also unveiling the blindspots in the Lacanian text and providing an alternative reading of 'The Purloined Letter'. In their preface, Muller and Richardson summarize Derrida's critique in the following words: 'In his critique Derrida argues that Lacan has ignored the story's literary context and idealizes the notion of the letter as signifier' (xiii). Kamuf expands this point in her introduction to the text, commenting on how Derrida's essay constitutes a resistance to those who wish to assimilate 'deconstruction' to Lacanian psychoanalytic theory (DR 464–5). As Kamuf suggests in conclusion, 'Le Facteur' marks a connection between the earlier Derridean analyses of

logocentrism and phonocentrism begun in *Speech and Phenomena* and *Of Grammatology*, and the type of analysis found in 'Envois' and 'To Speculate on Freud', both of which are in *The Post Card*. Any further references to 'Le Facteur' will be taken from the full text in *The Post Card*.

3 Writing (of) Identities

1. In these questions I have replaced Mallarmé's name with that of Derrida. I understand the essay, with its self-problematizing position of Mallarmé in relation to *French* Literature (the very idea of such a possibility), to have an importance for understanding and exploring Derrida's own, often self-conscious positioning, in relation to *French* culture, *French* literature, *French* philosophy, *French* traditions in thinking and a certain *French* institutional location of a variety of poetic and non-poetic discourses. Derrida's thinking on Mallarmé, and his essays in various places on Valéry, offer interesting, if sometimes tangential, insights into the relationships I address in the opening paragraphs of this essay.

2. There are a number of 'untranslatables' in this passage, not least that opening word, which I have given as 'Within the subject's consciousness' in order to provide the context of the passage from which this extract is taken. There is an elegance in the French, wherein what is being stated collapses into a performance of its propositions, which ties in with remarks made further on in this essay on the collapse between constative and performative utterance (along with other remarks concering this collapse in previous chapters). As Valéry's passage makes clear, the voice, far from producing one's identity as a self-evident presence (to itself), instead is always already marked by a written difference in its self-dividing dissemination. This is strikingly marked in the doubling of identity and difference given by Valéry as *one* of the essential secrets.

3. I wish to stress at this point that this is the case with all Derrida's encounters with other writers, even though each encounter or transaction remains necessarily idiomatic, as Derrida is of course responding and being responsible to the other text.

4. On the ethical question of awaiting the other's arrival, see Derek Attridge, 'Expecting the Unexpected in Coetzee's *The Master of Petersburg* and Derrida's Recent Writings', in *Applying: to Derrida*, ed. Brannigan, Robbins, Wolfreys (1996, 21–40).

5. The pagination of 'Psyche' referred to is taken from the first English

language translation of the text by Catherine Porter, published in the collection of essays, *Reading de Man Reading* (1989, 25–65).

6. Valéry, cit. Philippe Lacoue-Labarthe, 'The Echo of the Subject', in Lacoue-Labarthe, *Typography: Mimesis, Philosophy, Politics*, introd. Jacques Derrida, trans. and ed. Christopher Fynsk (1989, 139).

7. The reader is referred to *Of Spirit* (*OS* 61, 122–4 n. 2), in which Derrida offers a brief discussion of Valéry's thinking on spirit, European spiritual identity in particular, during the interwar years, as a comparison in passing between Valéry's writing and that of both Heidegger and Husserl. In a number of ways other headings are being pointed out in this note and on the page to which the note refers, with the references in Valéry's writing to 'Psyche', to ashes and to the revenant, to spectrality in general. Valéry's own references to Hamlet (which Derrida paraphrases and quotes) are themselves clearly anticipatory of *Specters of Marx*. As with the notes in *The Other Heading* (of which more in the body of the essay), in this note commentary gives way before more extensive citation, Derrida once again allowing Valéry to return as the other to his own text, as Derrida becomes the shadowy ghost behind Valéry and in his wake.

8. We should recall, every time that Derrida writes this word, the inversion of his own initials – JD, *DéJà* – by which device he encrypts his name, as mentioned in the first chapter, above.

9. In talking of Valéry and Paris, the capital, Derrida is also speaking of and putting into play the idea of capital and economic exchange, as well as invoking the head, and with that once more, the face (of the other) seen from the place of the other.

10. Derrida discusses the contradictory ambiguities of the *pharmakon*, a classical Greek term, in *Dissemination*, in the section entitled 'Plato's Pharmacy'. The term refers to a drug whch can either kill or cure, depending on the amount ingested. The term thus carries in itself two contradictory meanings at the same time, rendering an absolute meaning undecidable. This ambiguity raises for Derrida the problematic nature of translation. As Derrida is at pains to demonstrate:

> When a word inscribes itself as the citation of another sense of the same word, when the textual center-stage of the word *pharmakon*, even while it means *remedy*, cites, recites, and makes legible that which *in the same word* signifies, in another spot and on a different level of the stage, *poison* ... the choice of only one of these renditions by the translator has as its first effect the neutralization of the citational play, ... and, in the end, quite simply, *the very textuality of the translated text*.... Textuality being constituted by differences,

it is by nature absolutely heterogeneous and is constantly composing with the forces that tend to annihilate it. (*DR* 127)

4 The Hauntological Example

1. Earlier versions of this chapter were presented at research seminars at the Universities of Dundee and Stirling. I would like to thank Nicholas Royle for inviting me to Stirling to give the paper at his 'Phantom fx' research seminar. I would also like to thank Jane Stabler and Martin McQuillan for their ingenious questions which, in different ways, allowed me to reshape this essay, which bears their indelible spectral traces.

2. Sinclair's works are as follows: *Flesh Eggs and Scalp Metal: Selected Poems 1970–1987* (1989); *Radon Daughters* (1994); Lud Heat *and* Suicide Bridge (1995a); *White Chappell Scarlet Tracings* (1995b); *Downriver (Or, the Vessel of Wrath) A Narrative in Twelve Tales,* (1995c); *Lights Out for the Territory: 9 Excursions in the Secret History of London* (1997); Iain Sinclair and Dave McKean, 'The Griffin's Egg' (1996, 43–52).

3. Some of these spectral figures are less familiar than others. For those not familiar with either the Krays or Jack McVitie, the former were gang bosses in London's East End during the 1960s, and whose extortion, vice and club interests extended into London's Soho, once the home of William Blake. McVitie was one of the Kray's foot-soldiers, who was murdered by the brothers, and whose murder was to bring about their eventual arrest and life imprisonment. Ronnie Kray's funeral is written about by Sinclair in *Lights Out,* and is discussed below. Reggie Kray is still living, and imprisoned in Broadmoor, a high security prison for those who are termed the 'criminally insane'.

4. On the relation between the city's architecture and the ineffability of London, see my 'Dickensian Architextures or, the City and the Ineffable', in *Victorian Identities: Social and Cultural Formations in Nineteenth-Century Literature,* ed. Ruth Robbins and Julian Wolfreys (1995, 199–214).

5. Jacques Derrida invents this comment, describing himself as a ghost in McMullen's film. In this film the visual and aural recordings of Derrida's improvisations haunt the film, thereby performing as well as suggesting the condition of being ghostly in the age of technology. Derrida suggests that technology such as film and telecommunication proliferates the possibility of spectres.

6. Like McVitie, Lambrianou was a member of the Kray gang.

7. Like Jeffrey Archer, Tebbit was a member of Thatcher's cabinet, and often portrayed in cartoons as a violent, crazed skinhead.
8. Another member of Britain's criminal 'sub-culture', who, like the Krays, was given a degree of celebrity status by the media. A student of mine, who grew up with Fraser, suggested that Frankie might not be too pleased with the comparison with Margaret Thatcher, for which, Frankie, I apologize.

5 *Heart? of Darkness?*

1. See J. Hillis Miller's essay, 'Anastomosis', in his *Ariadne's Thread: Story Lines* (1992, 144–222).
2. See also Mark Currie's outline of, and response to, Miller's reading of *Heart of Darkness*, in his Transitions volume, *Postmodern Narrative Theory* (1998).
3. Stephen thinks, a moment later: 'Limit of the diaphane in. Why in? Diaphane, adiaphane' (1993, 37). Joyce is quoting indirectly from the French translation. The moment at which Stephen pauses, on the preposition, is one of those wonderfully performative gestures on Joyce's part which installs the paradoxical. Instead of making things diaphanous, Stephen's rhetorical turn obscures, and he further enacts this simultaneous illumination/obscurity by articulating 'diaphane, adiaphane', noting the movement between transparency and non-transparency.
4. The line from *Ulysses* quoted in the essay and above, in n.3, is taken from a passage in which Stephen Dedalus concerns himself with what Miller calls the 'two senses of seeing'. For Stephen, physical seeing does not allow us to see through. What Stephen on the same page describes as the 'ineluctable modality of the visible' obscures our ability to see through to the heart of things because the visible is so inescapable. Paradoxically, Stephen can only 'see through' or apprehend the world by closing his eyes in order to see through hearing as he moves through the world.
5. Miller's phrase seems to beg the question: which enterprise? That of telling the story, or of finding and bringing back Kurtz?
6. Such words and phrases are very frequent throughout *Heart of Darkness*. There are far too many to reproduce here, given the lack of space. There are, however, well over four hundred.

Afterword(s)

1. See Derrida's essay, 'From Restricted to General Economy: Hegelianism without Reserve', in *Writing and Difference* (1967), trans. Alan Bass (London: Routledge and Kegan Paul, 1978), 251–77. 'Restricted economy' here indicates a mode of intellectual production which aims at reproduction or re-presentation for the purposes of affirming a family resemblance, affirming the same at the expense of the other. Georges Bataille, whose work influenced Derrida and who is considered in the essay just named, defines 'general economy' as the production of excess which overflows strictly useful material or intellectual production. For further discussion of this, and Derrida's work, see Arkady Plotnitsky, *In the Shadow of Hegel: Complementarity, History, and the Unconscious* (1993), 10–30.

Annotated Bibliography

This annotated bibliography is necessarily highly selective, since Jacques Derrida alone has authored or co-authored approximately 70 books in French, and has published, in a number of languages, well over 200 articles (not including interviews). In addition, he has contributed over 200 chapters to books edited by others, so what is presented here is merely the tip of an immense iceberg. In selecting from this vast range of material for the Annotated Bibliography, I have had to make some brutally unfair decisions as to what should be included and what should be excluded.

This bibliography is divided into two sections, those which are by Jacques Derrida, and those which either draw on Derrida's work or which are more explicitly about Derrida.

I • Books by Jacques Derrida

(dates in parenthesis following title refer to French publication)

Of Grammatology (1967), trans. Gayatri Chakravorty Spivak. Baltimore: The Johns Hopkins University Press, 1975.

One of three books to appear in 1967. Divided into two parts, 'Writing Before the Letter' and 'Nature, Culture, Writing'. The first part provides a philosophical consideration of the nature of writing in relation to the concept of Being; it proposes through its own writing practice a critical reading – called by Derrida 'grammatology' – which looks at the gaps in the logic of Western metaphysical thinking; in this section Derrida puts forward the idea that metaphysics relies on the suspension of logical movement and the hierarchical manipulation of binary oppositions which support such thinking. Derrida takes the binary opposition of voice/writing and its corollary, presence/

absence, and through a series of closely argued analyses, shows how, while such oppositions privilege the former term over the latter in Western philosophical thought, the meaning of the former depends on the latter, so that, for example, the latter term really incorporates and articulates the former: so that 'voice' or 'speech' is in fact a form of writing. Writing is particularly important to Derrida as a form which philosophy has ignored as necessary to the expression of philosophical concepts throughout its history. In this text, Derrida works with many terms which have subsequently been deemed part of the lexicon of deconstruction: trace, inscription, reserve, gramme, *différance*, supplement, logocentrism. Derrida also offers a critique of the structuralist linguistics of Ferdinand de Saussure which concentrate on phonetic speech and ignore written forms of language. The second half offers a reading of structural anthropologist Claude Lévi-Strauss and, subsequently, Jean-Jacques Rousseau's *The Essay on the Origin of Languages*, developing what he calls 'the logic of the supplement'.

Speech and Phenomena and Other Essays on Husserl's Theory of Signs (1967), trans. David Allison. Evanston: Northwestern University Press, 1973.

The essay 'Speech and Phenomena' positions Derrida's interest in the question of voice and phonetic writing in relationship to the history of philosophical thinking in the West from Plato to Edmund Husserl. Derrida's focus is on the relationship between language and Being, and he explores that relationship as it emerges out of his critique of Husserl's theory of signs. Once again, there is interest in the notion of the supplement, the relation between speech and the illusion of presence created by speech in human utterance, along with the issues of meaning and representation. Also in this volume is the essay 'Différance', which through an explication of Derrida's substitution of 'a' for 'e' in the French 'différence' (which, when spoken sounds the same), shows how speech is itself a form of writing.

Writing and Difference (1967), trans. Alan Bass. Chicago: University of Chicago Press, 1978; London: Routledge and Kegan Paul, 1978.

A collection of essays written between 1959 and 1967, in which Derrida provides a range of readings of literary and philosophical texts, along with one of his earliest engagements with the thought of

Sigmund Freud. Also features readings of Michel Foucault and the history of madness, Edmund Jabès (a consideration of the problem of being Jewish and writing poetry), Emmanuel Levinas, the concepts of genesis and structure in Husserl, Antonin Artaud's Theatre of Cruelty, G.W.F. Hegel; the essays 'Force and Signification' and 'Structure, Sign, and Play in the Discourse of the Human Sciences' continue Derrida's critique of structuralist modes of thought, while extending his own considerations of signifying practices and the play of differences which help our comprehension of how binary oppositions such as nature/culture function within discourse.

Dissemination (1972), trans. Barbara Johnson. Chicago: University of Chicago Press, 1981; London: Athlone Press, 1981.

One of three books published in 1972. There are four main sections: 'Outwork, Prefacing', 'Plato's Pharmacy', 'Double Session', 'Dissemination'. 'Plato's Pharmacy' considers the '*pharmakon*' in relation to writing with its double or supplementary logic (in Plato's text, the *pharmakon* has the double value of providing a cure while also being capable of poisoning); Derrida's purpose is to analyse the dual powers of textuality. 'The Double Session' offers a reading of Stéphane Mallarmé through further thinking on the supplement. 'Dissemination', originally published in 1969, takes the logic of supplementarity further, considering the borders of texts, displacement and difference.

Margins of Philosophy (1972), trans. Alan Bass. Chicago: University of Chicago Press, 1982; Brighton: Harvester Press, 1982.

This collection contains a number of essays which had a marked influence on literary interpretation, particularly in the United States in the development of the institutionalized form of 'deconstruction' as a critical practice and methodology distinct from Derrida's own acts of reading. The essays here cover Derrida's wide-ranging interests, including readings of and between literature and philosophy. As the title suggests, Derrida explores marginal elements of philosophical texts for the ways in which those margins disrupt the logic of the philosophical text. Derrida looks at philosophical writing for its literary and rhetorical elements, for which philosophy, as an institutional form of thought, cannot account. Derrida explores the relationship between philosophy and other discourses and disciplines.

'Différance' is the starting point for such discussions in this collection. 'Ousia and Gramme' provides a forty-page note to a note in Martin Heidegger's *Being and Time*. 'The Pit and the Pyramid' considers signification through an exemplary reading of Hegel. 'The Ends of Man' provides a critique of existentialist-humanist thought in French intellectual circles. Other essays such as 'White Myth' and 'Signature Event Context' consider the work of metaphors and context, and their importance to the fundamental structures of Western metaphysical thought. Also contains the essay 'Qual Quelle: Valéry's Sources', a reading of French poet Paul Valéry, which is discussed in this volume, above.

Positions (1972), trans. Alan Bass. Chicago: University of Chicago Press, 1982; London: Athlone Press, 1982.

This collection of three interviews which, in very different contexts, sees Derrida discussing with his interlocutors, the work of his thought, and the notion of *différance*, in the context of philosophical thought, semiology and metaphysics, and the possible relationship – or antagonism – between Derrida's thought and Marxism. A number of readers find interviews with Derrida more immediately accessible than his written texts. *Points ...* is another collection of interviews.

Limited Inc. (1977), trans. Samuel Weber and Jeffrey Mehlman. Baltimore: The Johns Hopkins University Press, 1977. Reprinted: ed. Gerald Graff. Evanston: Northwestern University Press, 1988.

Contains the 1971 essay, 'Signature Event Context', in which Derrida sets out notions of iterability. Following this essay's initial reception, Speech Act Theorist John R. Searle issued a critique of Derrida's essay. *Limited Inc.* contains Derrida's response to Searle (Searle's own piece is not included as he chose to decline giving permission for the reprinting of his article). The Afterword of the volume contains a discussion of related matters between Derrida and Gerald Graff.

The Truth in Painting (1978), trans. Geoff Bennington and Ian McLeod. Chicago: University of Chicago Press, 1987.

Comprising four main sections, *The Truth in Painting* sees Derrida examine the major theories and philosophies of art through a consideration of supplementary and marginal features in painting. In

'Parergon', he examines the notion of the *parergon*, that which is neither of the work, nor, properly speaking, outside it. The next two sections deal with the *trait*, the graphic mark, and so on. The final, lengthy essay considers two major articles by Martin Heidegger and Meyer Schapiro on a painting of shoes by Vincent Van Gogh, offering an analysis of his own in response to the painting which relies in part on what has already gone before in this volume. In considering the supplement in art, Derrida considers issues of spectrality and the trace as an effect of haunting, while suggesting that, detached from specific contexts, Van Gogh's painting of shoes always, and in a certain manner, refers back to the act of painting itself.

The Post Card: From Socrates to Freud and Beyond (1980), trans. Alan Bass. Chicago: University of Chicago Press, 1987.

In this work, Derrida raises the question of posting, of transmission, of the problematic of delivery between an addresser and addressee, of the possible failures of communication which are already installed in the system. There is always the chance that, even if the transmission is delivered to the person for whom it was intended, the said transmission will not be properly received. Thus Derrida concerns himself with the movement of thought throughout history. The question becomes one of the destination (and non-arrival) of the future of a thought, a body of thought. Particularly, in this consideration of postal- and tele-communications, Derrida chooses the post card as a figure which is open to reading by anyone, not merely the person to whom it is destined. The post card is a message which can be taken out of its context. What then can happen to a word, a phrase, a statement, which has drifted down countless years? This movement for Derrida means that not only is it possible that a message may not arrive at its destination but that, in fact, it cannot. Also included in this collection are essays on Freud and Derrida's critique of Lacan's reading of Edgar Allan Poe's 'The Purloined Letter', entitled 'Le facteur de la vérité'.

The Ear of the Other: Otobiography, Transference, Translation: Texts and Discussion with Jacques Derrida (1984), trans. Peggy Kamuf. New York: Schocken Books, 1985.

This collection features a roundtable discussion on autobiography, and the essay 'Otobiographies: The Teaching of Nietzsche and the Politics of the Proper Name', which follows a close reading of Nietzsche, beginning with the trace of the proper name. Oto- (the Greek for ear) is substituted by Derrida for the prefix auto- in the title. This refiguration gives us to understand the difference already installed in narrating oneself; we always hear the other within our selves, even as any autobiographical writing (or any writing for that matter) will have within it the voice of the other, while the writing will become other through its future reception.

Ulysse gramophone: Deux mots pour Joyce. Paris: Galilée, 1987. 'Two Words for Joyce', trans Geoff Bennington, in Derek Attridge and Daniel Ferrer, eds, *Post-Structuralist Joyce: Essays from the French.* Cambridge: Cambridge University Press, 1984. 145–59. 'Ulysses Gramophone: Hear Say Yes in Joyce', trans. Tina Kendall and Shari Benstock, in Derek Attridge, ed., *Acts of Literature.* London: Routledge, 1992. 256–309.

These two essays on James Joyce, published as a monograph in France, were originally two separate lectures, given first in 1982 and 1984. 'Two Words for Joyce' is a reading of two words from Joyce's *Finnegans Wake*, the two words being 'HE WAR'. Derrida spins out a fascinating analysis of the grammatical possibilities within English of the words, as well as looking at the words' play between English and German. From this Derrida opens his reading to the passage in which the words are found, and from there to the entirety of the text, arguing that Joyce's text anticipates all critical discussions, all readings, all discourses. The second essay, 'Ulysses Gramophone', begins with a reading of the word 'yes', from which Derrida examines the various telecommunicative figures of *Ulysses*, all the while showing how these figures are connected to the affirmative response 'yes', whether in English, in other languages, installed within other words – Derri*da*, Eli*jah* – or as anagrams. The exhaustive, and exhausting, installation of 'yes' in Joyce's text leads Derrida to consider whether it is possible to be an 'expert' on Joyce. What Derrida finds, in finding 'yes' by chance throughout Joyce's text, is that the random, the chance, the aleatory, is always already at work in Joyce's writing, and it is this which forestalls any kind of critical programme or model from being imposed.

Mémoires for Paul de Man (1988), trans. Cecile Lindsay, Jonathan Culler, Eduardo Cadava and Peggy Kamuf. The Wellek Library Lectures at the University of California, Irvine, 1986. Revised edition, New York: Columbia University Press, 1989.

The essays collected together here were originally lectures given in honour of Paul de Man. Derrida discusses de Man's theories of memory, allegory, autobiography, and his comprehension of the ways in which language operates, as part of Derrida's broader comprehension of de Man's contribution to literary study in general and to deconstruction in particular. The final piece in the collection, 'Like the Sound of the Sea Deep Within a Shell: Paul de Man's War', was added to the revised edition, and is Derrida's passionate, moving defence of de Man, in the face of accusations made shortly after de Man's death that, because de Man had written a small number of articles for a Belgian collaborationist newspaper during the Second World War, this automatically (in some people's eyes) tainted all of de Man's work subsequently.

Of Spirit: Heidegger and the Question (1987), trans. Geoffrey Bennington and Rachel Bowlby. Chicago: University of Chicago Press, 1989.

Derrida examines the relative absence of the term *spirit* from Heidegger's writing, asking why Heidegger used the term within the context of National Socialism during his Rectorship Address at the University of Freiburg in 1933, only subsequently to abandon or avoid all apparent reference to the question of spirit, an avoidance, suggests Derrida, perpetuated by many readers of Heidegger. In addressing this 'absent' subject, Derrida gives consideration to Heidegger's ideas concerning philosophy and culture.

The Other Heading: Reflections on Today's Europe (1991), trans. Pascale-Anne Brault and Michael B. Naas, introd. Michael B. Naas. Bloomington: Indiana University Press, 1992.

The two essays in this volume address the politics of European identity. Derrida asks how European identity is to be reconfigured, understood, after the fall of the Berlin Wall. Drawing on Heidegger and Valéry (see Chapter 3, above), Derrida concerns himself with the possibility of imagining viewing European identity from some other place, the place of the other, while positing the possibility, the hope of other headings for Europe.

Points ... Interviews, 1974–1994 (1992), ed. Elisabeth Weber, trans. Peggy Kamuf et al. Stanford: Stanford University Press, 1995.

A significant and wide-ranging collection of interviews, gathered from a twenty-year period, which cover diverse topics such as national identity, the question of autobiography, politics, poetics, Derrida's responses to the transformation of his work, AIDS, sexuality, translation, and the teaching of philosophy. This collection, which is highly accessible because of the interview format, is one possible 'entry' point into Derrida's thought. Particularly interesting are Derrida's thoughts on the issue of the honorary degree awarded him by Oxford University. One interview, 'The Work of Intellectuals and the Press (The Bad Example: How the *New York Review of Books* and Company Do Business)', was commissioned specially for the volume, and is an accurate picture of the willingness and bad faith on the part of some to misrepresent Derrida. Sixteen of the twenty-three interviews appear in English for the first time.

Aporias (1993), trans. Thomas Dutoit. Stanford: Stanford University Press, 1993.

Two essays comprise this book, 'Finis' and 'Awaiting (at) the Arrival'. In the two essays Derrida addresses the aporia between singularity and the general, while examining various modes of specificity of experience. Also considered is the aporetic obligation involved in playing host to the foreign while respecting its foreignness. Derrida articulates these concerns around a critique of various cultural histories and theorizations of death.

Specters of Marx: The State of the Debt, the Work of Mourning, and the New International (1993), trans. Peggy Kamuf, introd. Bernd Magnus and Stephen Cullenberg. New York and London: Routledge, 1994.

Derrida's first book-length engagement with Marx, eagerly expected by many Derrida commentators since, perhaps, his earliest publications and, certainly, since his comments on the possible relationship between Marxism and deconstruction in *Positions*. This work engages Marxist discourse through various analyses of figures of ghosts, spirits and other tropes of haunting which appear and reappear in Marx's writing, and which are termed by Derrida 'spectropoetics'. Derrida's argument is that we have a responsibility to Marx today, despite the triumphalist efforts of some to exorcise his ghost, and that the most responsible way of acknowledging that responsibility is to be attendant on the various spirits or specters of Marx.

On the Name (1993), ed. Thomas Dutoit, trans. David Wood, John P. Leavey, Jr. and Ian McLeod. Stanford: Stanford University Press, 1995.

The three essays in this collection were published originally in France as three separate, though related works. The three pieces see Derrida turning once again to consider the issue of the name, and what occurs when one gives or is given a name, how the name functions, how the name is singular. The first essay, *Passions*, considers the necessity and obligation of response, of responding, of the ethical and political dimensions involved in the responsibility of responding. *Sauf le nom* involves considerations of naming developed from close readings of Angelus Silesius. The final essay, *Khōra*, examines issues of spacing and place through a reading of Plato's *Timaeus*.

Archive Fever: A Freudian Impression (1995), trans. Eric Prenowitz. Chicago: University of Chicago Press, 1996.

In this book, first given as a lecture, Derrida considers the genealogy and nature of the archive and the cultural practice of archiving, as that relates to issues of memory and technology. As Derrida shows in his study, the archive is at once both public and private: it is the civic and collective storage place, the official 'memory' of the community, and yet it is composed of, constructed from records and documents which are often the most private, intimate expressions. Examining Freudian discourse, Marxism and Judaic traditions, Derrida considers possible relationships between various technologies of inscription and psychic processes, while paying attention to electronic forms of communication, such as e-mail, and the possible effect electronic media may have on conceptions of public and private.

II • Books by other authors

Beardsworth, Richard, *Derrida and the Political*. London: Routledge, 1996.

Beardsworth's book looks at the challenges Derrida's thought can issue to conventional political thought and philosophy, and its institutional manifestations. In doing so, he criticizes those who have read Derrida's work as being apolitical, liberal or anti-democratic. Beardsworth's understanding of the political import of Derrida's work is arrived at through considerations of the trace, singularity, the Law, modernity, violence, temporality, the ethical and aporia, and through critiques of Kant, Hegel, Heidegger and Levinas. Beardsworth unfolds the question of a Derridean politics through an examination of Derrida's own engagements with these philosophers.

Bennington, Geoffrey, *Legislations: The Politics of Deconstruction*. London: Verso, 1994.

A collection of mostly previously published essays and reviews which, together, aim to broaden the reader's understanding of deconstruction and the work of Jacques Derrida as having a political thrust. Bennington achieves this through a number of readings of a wide range of philosophers and other authors, including Rousseau, Kant, Hegel, Freud, de Man, and Jean-François Lyotard. In so doing, Bennington also offers criticism of those, such as Rodolphe Gasché and Irene Harvey, for example, whose purpose it is, Bennington suggests, to appropriate Derrida for a narrowly conceived philosophical project. Bennington argues that deconstruction is a form of political thought because it always entails an ethical opening onto the other which, on its arrival, announces the possible taking place of 'legislation' between positions.

Brunette, Peter, and Wills, David, *Screen/Play: Derrida and Film Theory*. Princeton: Princeton University Press, 1989.

An interesting attempt to explore the possible relation between Derrida's work and film theory. In doing so, the authors seek to suggest how current film theory might benefit from an engagement with Derrida's thought, while also considering where such an interaction might lead in the future. The volume offers summaries of both a number of key Derridean texts and the work of major film theorists.

Butler, Christopher, *Interpretation, Deconstruction, and Ideology: An Introduction to Some Current Issues in Literary Theory*. Oxford: Clarendon Press, 1984.

Butler's work focuses on three principal aspects of Derrida's work of particular interest in the early days of Derrida's reception in the Anglophone world, particularly amongst literary commentators and philosophers. The relationship between scepticism and deconstruction is considered, as is the notion of free play, while attention is paid to the metaphoricity of philosophical discourse.

Caputo, John D., *The Prayers and Tears of Jacques Derrida: Religion without Religion*. Bloomington: Indiana University Press, 1997.

Caputo focuses on religious motifs which have emerged increasingly in Derrida's more recent writings, especially those, such as 'Circumfession', which appear markedly autobiographical. Caputo argues, from his readings, for an understanding of Derrida as a man of faith in the most rigorous manner, while not assimilable within conventional religious or theological frameworks. Caputo's readings focus on the prophetic, messianic and apocalyptic tones of a number of Derrida's books and essays.

Carroll, David, *Parasthetics: Foucault, Lyotard, Derrida*. London: Methuen, 1987.

An extended consideration of Derrida's work, particularly in the context of the literary and the aesthetic as they inform Derrida's writing. Carroll also usefully offers a sustained analysis of the relationships and tensions between Derrida's work and that of Michel Foucault and Jean-François Lyotard.

Corlett, William, *Community without Unity: A Politics of Derridian Extravagance*. Durham: Duke University Press, 1989.

Corlett seeks to develop the political implications of Derrida's writing by focusing on the possible deconstruction of the binary pairing of individual/collective and by employing Derrida's work in order to reformulate notions of community, as part of the expression of what

Corlett calls 'affirmative politics'. Corlett's political project moves through both a reassessment and analysis of Derrida's texts and also extended commentary on those places in Derrida's writing where he engages critically with more explicitly political thinkers such as Bataille and Foucault.

Critchley, Simon, *The Ethics of Deconstruction: Derrida and Levinas.* Oxford: Blackwell, 1992.

Critchley challenges the notion that deconstruction and the work of Jacques Derrida are nihilistic and irresponsible. He does so through understanding Derrida's work as issuing an ethical demand, the formulation of which is the result of the influence of Emmanuel Levinas on Derrida. Critchley pursues the textual dialogue between the two men in their published works, providing not only a re-reading of Derrida but also a valuable introduction to Levinas. Critchley also raises the issue of the ethical in Hillis Miller, Heidegger, Lacoue-Labarthe, Nancy and Husserl.

Culler, Jonathan, *On Deconstruction: Theory and Criticism after Structuralism.* London: RKP, 1982.

Culler, one of the most influential of Derrida's commentators in the early 1980s, examines the concerns of what he terms 'deconstructive criticism', seeing its function as the interpretation and analysis of textual logic within literary texts. His writing is formally oriented in this volume, without any sustained historicization or politicization of the development of 'deconstructive criticism' in universities in the United States.

de Man, Paul, *Allegories of Reading: Figural Language in Rousseau, Nietzsche, Rilke and Proust.* New Haven: Yale University Press, 1979.

This collection of essays demonstrates de Man's fascination with European Romanticism and its legacy, the rhetoric of identity, and the relationship between figural language and reality. Language is taken as a form of reflection, which, for de Man, is a highly problematic process. De Man works through a number of close readings in order to show how the relationship between word and thing is conventional, not phenomenal. Amongst many issues, de Man demonstrates how, while as humans we may intend to mean something in language, meaning is subject to arbitrary linguistic properties which are not in our control.

Gasché, Rodolphe, *The Tain of the Mirror: Derrida and the Philosophy of Reflection*. Cambridge, Mass.: Harvard University Press, 1986.

Gasché attempts to rescue Derrida from literary critics in the name of philosophy, seeing Derrida's project as amounting to a philosophy of/as reflection. For a sustained critique of this work and others like it, see Geoffrey Bennington's *Legislations* (Ch. 1).

Hartman, Geoffrey, *Saving the Text: Literature, Derrida, Philosophy*. Baltimore: The Johns Hopkins University Press, 1981.

Hartman's *Saving the Text* is the first work which gives extended attention to the question of Derrida's styles through a lengthy consideration of *Glas*, one of Derrida's most forbidding texts. Hartman approaches the text primarily with literary interests in mind, and develops his reading of *Glas* throughout the first three chapters. The fourth chapter examines the reception and transformation of psychoanalysis, particularly Freudian discourse, in the work of Jacques Derrida and Jacques Lacan.

Johnson, Christopher, *System and Writing in the Philosophy of Jacques Derrida*. Cambridge: Cambridge University Press, 1993.

From his critique of structuralism to his engagement with Freud, Derrida's comprehension of the condition of writing is placed within a range of contexts by Christopher Johnson. Specifically, Johnson draws on a range of 'philosophical re-evaluations' of Derrida's work, in order to connect Derrida's considerations of writing to natural science and systems theory, thereby situating the emergence of Derrida's texts within the paradigmatic shifts occurring in the French intellectual scene and in contemporary scientific thought of the 1950s and 1960s.

Kamuf, Peggy, *The Division of Literature or the University in Deconstruction*. Chicago: University of Chicago Press, 1997.

One of Derrida's principal translators, Kamuf here offers a sustained historicization of the development of literary studies within the modern university, whilst also looking critically at the political aspect of debates surrounding the perception of so-called 'deconstruction' and its supposed or assumed relationship to the question of 'political correctness' amongst academics and within institutions. *The Division of Literature* develops its critique of the North American academic institution through a series of close readings of, principally, Gustave Lanson, Charles Péguy, G.W.F. Hegel and Herman Melville.

Lacoue-Labarthe, Philippe, *Typography: Mimesis, Philosophy, Politics*, trans. and ed. Christopher Fynsk. Cambridge, Mass.: Harvard University Press, 1989.

The collection of essays by Lacoue-Labarthe is an edited version of the longer French edition, and features a lengthy introduction to Lacoue-Labarthe through a consideration of mimesis by Derrida. Lacoue-Labarthe, like his colleague and co-author Jean-Luc Nancy, is a prominent French philosopher whose work is attuned to Derrida's and who shares a number of Derrida's interests and concerns. Compare, for example, both men's understanding of mimesis and its politics, or Lacoue-Labarthe's thinking on the supplement, which is indebted to Derrida's own work on this topic. The volume, which is highly significant in its own right, demonstrates Derrida's influence, albeit indirectly, on certain aspects of philosophical thought.

Miller, J. Hillis, *Topographies*. Stanford: Stanford University Press, 1995.

As its title suggests, Miller's collection of essays concerns itself with the related topics and concepts of place, site, location, and mapping, as figures and tropes appearing in literary and philosophical works. The essays do so through a series of rhetorical analyses of the work of Martin Heidegger, Thomas Hardy, Charles Dickens, Kleist, Plato, Tennyson, Hopkins, Nietzsche, William Faulkner, Wallace Stevens, Jacques Derrida, and the Book of Ruth from the Old Testament. Miller concerns himself in the readings gathered in this volume with issues of ethics and responsibility, the possibility (or otherwise) of the 'translation' of theory from one location to another, the function of speech acts, and the relation of personification to landscape. Miller provides the reader with the consideration of terms which are used to name topographical locations as figures which alter conceptual and narrative mapping in the reading of poetry and novels.

Royle, Nicholas, *After Derrida.* Manchester: Manchester University Press, 1995.

A collection of essays which engage in a wide range of analyses covering a number of authors, from Shakespeare and William Wordsworth to Salman Rushdie and Toni Morrison, and a number of topics, such as ghosts, telepathy, laughter and love. The essays are both explorations of their subjects informed by Derrida's work, whilst also offering the reader performative extrapolations of Derridean thinking. Playful and witty, Royle's work comprehends the profundity of Derrida's thinking and the challenges it poses to the conventional conceptual frameworks which inform interpretation and thought.

Ryan, Michael, *Marxism and Deconstruction: A Critical Articulation.* Baltimore: The Johns Hopkins University Press, 1982.

Ryan's is one of the earliest sustained works which attempts to place Derrida's thought within the context of radical political discourse. He compares the Derridean and Marxist critique of metaphysics, and draws on Derrida's work to point up the limits within Marxist thought, as a way of moving Marxism forward. While Ryan is aware that deconstruction is not explicitly political (at least in a conventional sense) it does provide the potential for a radical epistemological re-think.

Bibliography

This bibliography is in two sections: a selection of books and articles by Jacques Derrida, most translated into English; and works which either discuss Derrida, draw on his work, or to which I have referred in *Deconstruction • Derrida*. Through lack of space I have omitted most French texts by Derrida, but have included their original date of publication in parentheses. Where there are French titles, these have been included either (i) because the collection as a collection has not yet appeared in English, even though some essays may have been translated; or (ii) I have referred to the French text in *Deconstruction • Derrida*. I have given lists of contents for the two edited collections of Derrida's essays, Peggy Kamuf's *A Derrida Reader: Between the Blinds* (1991) and Derek Attridge's *Acts of Literature* (1992).

For bibliographies which refer extensively to Derrida's publications in French and other translations (and which also include comprehensive lists of works on, or influenced by, Derrida), the reader is referred to the bibliographies provided by Geoffrey Bennington in *Jacques Derrida* (1993), Peggy Kamuf in *A Derrida Reader: Between the Blinds* (1991),William B. Schultz and Lewis L.B. Fried, *Jacques Derrida: An Annotated Primary and Secondary Bibliography* (1992), and Albert Leventure, 'A Jacques Derrida Bibliography 1962–90', *Textual Practice*, 5:1 (Spring 1991).

Books and articles by Jacques Derrida

Derrida, Jacques. *Speech and Phenomena and Other Essays on Husserl's Theory of Signs.* (1967) Trans. David B. Allison. Evanston: Northwestern University Press, 1973.

——. *Of Grammatology.* (1967) Trans. Gayatri Chakravorty Spivak. Baltimore: The Johns Hopkins University Press, 1974.

——. *Edmund Husserl's 'Origin of Geometry': An Introduction.* (1962) Ed. David B. Allison. Trans. and Preface, John P. Leavey, Jr. Stony Brook: Nicholas Hays, 1978. Rpt. Lincoln: University of Nebraska Press, 1989.

——. *Writing and Difference.* (1967) Trans. Alan Bass. London: RKP, 1978.

——. 'Me – Psychoanalysis: An Introduction to the Translation of "The Shell and the Kernel" by Nicholas Abraham'. (1982) Trans. Richard Klein. *Diacritics.* 9:2 (1979): 4–12.

——. 'Scribble (writing-power)'. (1977) Trans. Cary Plotkin. *Yale French Studies.* 58 (1979): 116–47.

——. *Spurs: Nietzsche's Styles.* (1976) Trans. Barbara Harlow. Chicago: University of Chicago Press, 1979.

——. *The Archeology of the Frivolous: Reading Condillac.* (1973) Trans. John P. Leavey, Jr. Pittsburgh: Duquesne University Press, 1980.

——. 'La Loi du genre/The Law of Genre'. Trans. Avital Ronell. *Glyph* 7 (1980): 176–232.

——. *Dissemination.* (1972) Trans. Barbara Johnson. Chicago: University of Chicago Press, 1981.

——. 'Economimesis'. (1975) Trans. Richard Klein. *Diacritics* 11:2 (1981): 3–25.

——. *Margins of Philosophy.* (1972) Trans. Alan Bass. Chicago: University of Chicago Press, 1982.

——. *Positions.* (1972) Trans. Alan Bass. Chicago: University of Chicago Press, 1982.

——. 'The Principle of Reason: The University in the Eyes of its Pupils'. Trans. Catherine Porter and Edward P. Morris. *Diacritics* 13:3 (1983): 3–20.

——. 'The Time of a Thesis: Punctuations'. Trans. Kathleen McLaughlin. *Philosophy in France Today.* Ed. Alan Montefiore. Cambridge: Cambridge University Press, 1983. 34–51.

——. 'Deconstruction and the Other'. *Dialogues with Contemporary Continental Thinkers: The Phenomenological Heritage.* Ed. Richard Kearney. Manchester: Manchester University Press, 1984. 107–26.

——. 'My Chances/*Mes Chances*: A Rendez-Vous with Some Epicurean Stereophonies'. Trans. Irene E. Harvey and Avital Ronell. *Taking Chances: Derrida, Psychoanalysis, and Literature.* Ed. Joseph H. Smith and William Kerrigan. Baltimore: The Johns Hopkins University Press, 1984. 1–32.

——. 'No Apocalypse, Not Now (full speed ahead, seven missiles, seven missives)'. Trans. Catherine Porter and Phillip Lewis. *Diacritics* 14:2 (1984): 20–31.

——. *Signéponge/Signsponge*. (1984) Trans. Richard Rand. New York: Columbia University Press, 1984.

——. 'Two Words for Joyce'. Trans. Geoff Bennington. *Post-Structuralist Joyce: Essays from the French*. Ed. Derek Attridge and Daniel Ferrer. Cambridge: Cambridge University Press, 1984. 145–61.

——. 'Choreographies'. Trans. Christie McDonald. *The Ear of the Other: Otobiography, Transference, Translation*. Trans. Peggy Kamuf et al. Ed. Claude Levesque and Christie McDonald. Lincoln: University of Nebraska Press, 1985.

——. *The Ear of the Other: Otobiography, Transference, Translation*. (1982) Trans. Peggy Kamuf et al. Ed. Claude Levesque and Christie Mc Donald. Lincoln: University of Nebraska Press, 1985.

——. 'Letter to a Japanese Friend'. Trans. David Wood and Andrew Benjamin. *Derrida and Différance*. Ed. David Wood and Robert Bernasconi. Coventry: Parousia Press, 1985. 1–6.

——. 'Des Tours de Babel'. Trans. Joseph F. Graham. *Difference in Translation*. Ed. Joseph F. Graham. Ithaca: Cornell University Press, 1985. 165–248.

——. 'The Age of Hegel'. Trans. Susan Winnett. *Glyph* 1 (1986): 3–44.

——. 'Fors: The Anglish Words of Nicholas Abraham and Maria Torok'. (1976) Trans. Barbara Johnson. *The Wolf Man's Magic Word: A Cryptonomy*. Nicholas Abraham and Maria Torok. Minneapolis: University of Minnesota Press, 1986. xi–xlviii.

——. *Glas*. (1974) Trans. John P. Leavey, Jr. and Richard Rand. Lincoln: University of Nebraska Press, 1986.

—— *Parages*. Paris: Galilée, 1986.

——. 'Shibboleth (on Paul Celan)'. (1986) Trans. Joshua Wilner. *Midrash and Literature*. Ed. Geoffrey Hartman and Sanford Budick. New Haven: Yale University Press, 1986. 307–47.

——. '*Geschlect* II: Heidegger's Hand'. (1985) Trans. John P. Leavey, Jr. *Deconstruction and Philosophy: The Texts of Jacques Derrida*. Ed. John Sallis. Chicago: University of Chicago Press, 1987. 161–96.

——. 'The Laws of Reflection: Nelson Mandela, in Admiration'. Trans. Mary Ann Caws and Isabelle Lorenz. *For Nelson Mandela*. Ed. Jacques Derrida and Mustapha Tlili. New York: Henry Holt and Company, 1987. 13–42.

———. 'Living On • Borderlines'. Trans. James Hulbert. *Deconstruction and Criticism*. Harold Bloom, Paul de Man, Jacques Derrida, Geoffrey Hartman and J. Hillis Miller. New York: Continuum Books, 1987.

———. *The Post Card: From Socrates to Freud and Beyond*. (1980) Trans. Alan Bass. Chicago: Chicago University Press, 1987.

———. 'The *Retrait* of Metaphor'. (1987) Trans. F. Gasdner et al. *Enclitic* 2:2 (1987): 5–33.

———. 'Some Questions and Responses'. *The Linguistics of Writing: Arguments between Language and Literature*. Ed. Nigel Fabb, Derek Attridge, Alan Durant and Colin MacCabe. Manchester: Manchester University Press, 1987.

———. *The Truth in Painting*. (1978) Trans. Geoff Bennington and Ian McLeod. Chicago: University of Chicago Press, 1987.

———. 'Ulysses Gramophone: Hear Say Yes in Joyce'. (1987) Trans. Tina Kendall and Shari Benstock. *James Joyce: The Augmented Ninth*. Ed. Bernard Benstock. Syracuse: Syracuse University Press, 1988. 27–75.

———. *Limited Inc*. Trans. Samuel Weber and Jeffrey Mehlman. Evanston: Northwestern University Press, 1988.

———. 'Acts'. *Mémoires for Paul de Man*. Revised Edition. Trans. Cecile Lindsay, Jonathan Culler, Eduardo Cadava and Peggy Kamuf. New York: Columbia University Press, 1989. 89–153.

———. 'The Art of *Mémoires*'. *Mémoires for Paul de Man*. Revised Edition. Trans. Cecile Lindsay, Jonathan Culler, Eduardo Cadava and Peggy Kamuf. New York: Columbia University Press, 1989. 45–88.

———. 'Biodegradables: Seven Diary Fragments'. Trans. Peggy Kamuf. *Critical Inquiry* 15:4 (1989): 812–73.

———. 'How to Avoid Speaking: Denials'. (1987) Trans. Ken Frieden. *Languages of the Unsayable*. Ed. Sanford Budick and Wolfgang Iser. New York: Columbia University Press, 1989. 3–70.

———. 'Introduction: Desistance'. (1986) Trans. Christopher Fynsk. *Typography: Mimesis, Philosophy, Politics*. Philippe Lacoue-Labarthe. Trans. Christopher Fynsk et al. Cambridge, Mass.: Harvard University Press, 1989. 1–42.

———. *Of Spirit: Heidegger and the Question*. (1987) Trans. Geoffrey Bennington and Rachel Bowlby. Chicago: University of Chicago Press, 1989.

——. 'Psyche: Inventions of the Other'. (1987) Trans. Catherine Porter. *Reading de Man Reading*. Ed. Wlad Godzich and Lindsay Waters. Minneapolis: University of Minnesota Press, 1989. 25–65.

——. *Du droit à la philosophie*. Paris: Galilée, 1990.

——. 'Some Statements and Truisms about Neologisms, Newisms, Postisms, Parasitisms, and Other Small Seismisms'. Trans. Anne Tomiche. *The States of 'Theory'*. Ed. David Carroll. New York: Columbia University Press, 1990. 63–94.

——. 'At This Very Moment in This Work Here I Am'. Trans. Ruben Berezdivin. *Re-Reading Levinas*. Ed. Robert Bernasconi and Simon Critchley. Bloomington: Indiana University Press, 1991. 11–50.

——. *l'autre cap*. Paris: Les Éditions de Minuit, 1991.

——. 'Che cos'è la poesia'. (1988) Trans. Peggy Kamuf. *A Derrida Reader: Between the Blinds*. Ed. Peggy Kamuf. New York: Columbia University Press, 1991. 221–40.

——. *Cinders*. (1987). Trans., ed. and introd. Ned Lukacher. Lincoln: University of Nebraska Press, 1991.

——. '"Eating Well," or the Calculation of the Subject: An Interview with Jacques Derrida'. Trans. Peter Connor and Avital Ronell. London: Routledge, 1991. 96–120.

——. *Given Time. I. Counterfeit Money*. (1991) Trans. Peggy Kamuf. Chicago : University of Chicago Press, 1991.

——. 'This is Not an Oral Footnote'. Trans. Stephen A. Barney and Michael Hanly. *Annotation and its Texts*. Ed. Stephen A. Barney. New York: Oxford, 1991. 192–205.

——. *Acts of Literature*. Ed. Derek Attridge. New York: Routledge, 1992. Contents: '"This Strange Institution Called Literature": An Interview with Jacques Derrida'; '... That Dangerous Supplement ...'; 'Mallarmé'; 'The First Session'; 'Before the Law'; 'The Law of Genre'; 'Ulysses Gramophone: Hear Say Yes in Joyce'; *From* 'Psyche: Invention of the Other'; *From* 'Signsponge'; *From* 'Shibboleth: For Paul Celan'; 'Aphorism Countertime'.

——. 'Afterw.rds or, at Least, Less Than a Letter About a Letter Less'. Trans. Geoffrey Bennington. *Afterwords*. Ed. Nicholas Royle. Tampere: Outside Books, 1992. 197–217.

——. 'Force of Law: The "Mystical Foundation of Authority"'. (1989) Trans. Mary Quaintance. *Deconstruction and the Possibility of Justice*. Ed. Drucilla Cornell, Michael Rosenfeld and David Gray Carlson. New York: Routledge, 1992. 3–67.

——. 'Mochlos: or, The Conflict of the Faculties'. (1984) Trans. Richard Rand and Ann Wygant. Lincoln: University of Nebraska, 1992. 3–34.

——. 'Onto-Theology of National-Humanism'. *Oxford Literary Review.* 14:1–2 (1992): 3–24.

——. *The Other Heading: Reflections on Today's Europe.* (1991) Trans. Pascale-Anne Brault and Michael B. Naas. Introd. Michael B. Naas. Bloomington: Indiana University Press, 1992.

——. 'Passions: "An Oblique Offering"'. Trans. David Wood. *Derrida: A Critical Reader.* Ed. David Wood. Oxford: Blackwell, 1992. 5–35.

——. 'Post-Scriptum: Aporias, Ways and Voices'. Trans. John P. Leavey, Jr. *Derrida and Negative Theology.* Ed. Harold Coward and Toby Foshay. Albany: SUNY Press, 1992. 283–324.

——. *Aporias.* (1993) Trans. Thomas Dutoit. Stanford: Stanford University Press, 1993.

——. 'Back from Moscow, in the USSR'. Trans. Mary Quaintaire. *Politics, Theory, and Contemporary Culture.* Ed. Mark Poster. New York: Columbia University Press, 1993. 197–236.

——. 'Circumfession: Fifty-nine periods and periphrases *written in a sort of internal margin, between Geoffrey Bennington's book and work in preparation (January 1989–April 1990)*'. *Jacques Derrida.* (1991) Geoffrey Bennington and Jacques Derrida. Trans. Geoffrey Bennington. Chicago: University of Chicago Press, 1993. 3–315.

——. 'Heidegger's Ear: Philopolemology (*Geschlect* IV)'. Trans. John P. Leavey, Jr. *Reading Heidegger: Commemorations.* Ed. John Sallis. Bloomington: Indiana University Press, 1993. 163–218.

——. *Memoirs of the Blind.* (1990) Trans. Pascale-Anne Brault and Michael Naas. Chicago: University of Chicago Press, 1993.

——. 'On a Newly Arisen Apocalyptic Tone in Philosophy'. (1983) Rev. version. Trans. John P. Leavey, Jr. *Raising the Tone of Philosophy: Late Essays by Immanuel Kant, Transformative Critique by Jacques Derrida.* Ed. Peter Fenves. Baltimore: The Johns Hopkins University Press, 1993. 117–73.

——. 'Maddening the Subjectile'. (1988) Trans. Mary Ann Caws. *Yale French Studies* 84 (1994): 154–71.

——. *Force de loi.* Paris: Galilée, 1994.

——. 'The Spatial Arts: An Interview with Jacques Derrida'. *Deconstruction and the Visual Arts: Art, Media, Architecture.* Ed. Peter Brunette and David Wills. Cambridge: Cambridge University Press, 1994. 9–33.

——. *Specters of Marx: The State of the Debt, the Work of Mourning, and the New International.* (1993) Trans. Peggy Kamuf. Introd. Bernd Magnus and Stephen Cullenberg. New York and London: Routledge, 1994.

——. 'Geopsychoanalysis: ... and the Rest of the World'. (1981) Trans. Donald Nicholson-Smith. *New Formations* 26 (1995): 141–62.

——. *The Gift of Death.* (1992) Trans. David Wills. Chicago: University of Chicago Press, 1995.

——. *On the Name.* (1993) Ed. Thomas Dutoit. Trans. David Wood, John P. Leavey, Jr. and Ian McLeod. Stanford: Stanford University Press, 1995.

——. *Points ... Interviews 1974–1994.* (1992) Ed. Elisabeth Weber. Trans. Peggy Kamuf et al. Stanford: Stanford University Press, 1995.

——. 'The Time is Out of Joint'. Trans. Peggy Kamuf. *Deconstruction is/in America: A New Sense of the Political.* Ed. Anselm Haverkamp. New York: New York University Press, 1995. 14–41.

——. *Archive Fever: A Freudian Impression.* (1995) Trans. Eric Prenowitz. Chicago: University of Chicago Press, 1996.

——. '"As if I were Dead": An Interview with Jacques Derrida'. *Applying: to Derrida.* Ed. John Brannigan, Ruth Robbins and Julian Wolfreys. London: Macmillan, 1996. 212–27.

——. 'Foi et savoir: Les deux sources de la «religion» aux limites de la simple raison'. *La Religion: Séminaire de Capri sous la direction de Jacques Derrida et Gianni Vattimo.* Paris: Seuil, 1996.

——. 'Remarks on Deconstruction and Pragmatism'. Trans. Simon Critchley. *Deconstruction and Pragmatism.* Simon Critchley, Jacques Derrida, Ernesto Laclau and Richard Rorty. Ed. Chantal Mouffe. London: Routledge, 1996. 77–88.

——. *Politiques de l'amitié.* Paris: Galilée, 1996.

——. 'Spectrographies'. *Échographies: de la télévision. Entretiens filmés.* Jacques Derrida and Bernard Stiegler. Paris: Galilée–INA, 1996.

Other works

Adamson, Joseph. 'Deconstruction'. *Encyclopedia of Contemporary Literary Theory: Approaches, Scholars, Terms.* Ed. Irena R. Makaryk. Toronto: University of Toronto Press, 1993. 25–31.

Arac, Jonathan, Wlad Godzich and W. Martin, eds. *The Yale Critics: Deconstruction in America*. Minneapolis: University of Minnesota Press, 1983.

Arata, Stephen. *Fictions of Loss in the Victorian Fin de Siècle*. Cambridge: Cambridge University Press, 1996.

Attridge, Derek. 'Expecting the Unexpected in Coetzee's *The Master of Petersburg* and Derrida's Recent Writings'. *Applying: to Derrida*. Ed. John Brannigan, Ruth Robbins and Julian Wolfreys. London: Macmillan, 1996.

Beardsworth, Richard. *Derrida and the Political*. London: Routledge, 1996.

Behler, Ernst. *Confrontations: Derrida, Heidegger, Nietzsche*. (1988) Trans. Steven Taubeneck. Stanford: Stanford University Press, 1991.

Bennington, Geoffrey. 'Derridabase'. (1991) *Jacques Derrida*. Geoffrey Bennington and Jacques Derrida. Trans. Geoffrey Bennington. Chicago: University of Chicago Press, 1993. 3–316.

——. *Legislations: The Politics of Deconstruction*. London: Verso, 1994.

——. 'X'. *Applying: to Derrida*. Ed. John Brannigan, Ruth Robbins and Julian Wolfreys. London: Macmillan, 1996a. 1–21.

——. 'Genuine Gasché (Perhaps)'. *Imprimatur* 1:2/3 (Spring 1996b): 252–7.

Boyne, Roy. *Foucault and Derrida: The Other Side of Reason*. London: Unwin Hyman, 1990.

Brandt, Joan. *Geopoetics: The Politics of Mimesis in Poststructuralist French Poetry and Theory*. Stanford: Stanford University Press, 1997.

Bressler, Charles E. *Literary Criticism: An Introduction to Theory and Practice*. Englewood Cliffs: Prentice Hall, 1994.

Brunette, Peter, and David Wills, eds. *Screen/Play: Derrida and Film Theory*. Princeton: Princeton University Press, 1989.

——, eds. *Deconstruction and the Visual Arts: Art, Media, Architecture*. Cambridge: Cambridge University Press, 1994.

Butler, Christopher. *Interpretation, Deconstruction, and Ideology: An Introduction to Some Current Issues in Literary Theory*. Oxford: Clarendon Press, 1984.

Butler, Judith. *Bodies that Matter: On the Discursive Limits of 'Sex'*. New York: Routledge, 1993.

Caputo, John D. *Radical Hermeneutics: Deconstruction and the Hermeneutic Project*. Bloomington: Indiana University Press, 1987.

——. *The Prayers and Tears of Jacques Derrida: Religion without Religion*. Bloomington: Indiana University Press, 1997.

Carroll, David. *Parasthetics: Foucault, Lyotard, Derrida.* London: Methuen, 1987.

Caruth, Cathy. *Unreclaimed Experience: Trauma, Narrative, and History.* Baltimore: The Johns Hopkins University Press, 1996.

Caruth, Cathy, and Deborah Esch, eds. *Critical Encounters: Reference and Responsibility in Deconstructive Writing.* New Brunswick: Rutgers University Press, 1995.

Clark, Timothy. *Derrida, Heidegger, Blanchot: Sources of Derrida's Notion and Practice of Literature.* Cambridge: Cambridge University Press, 1992.

Corlett, William. *Community without Unity: A Politics of Derridian Extravagance.* Durham: Duke University Press, 1989.

Cornell, Drucilla. *The Philosophy of the Limit.* New York: Routledge, 1992.

Coward, Harold. *Derrida and Indian Philosophy.* Albany: SUNY Press, 1990.

Critchley, Simon. *The Ethics of Deconstruction: Derrida and Levinas.* London: Blackwell, 1992.

Culler, Jonathan. *On Deconstruction: Theory and Criticism after Structuralism.* London: RKP, 1982.

Currie, Mark. *Postmodern Narrative Theory.* London: Macmillan, 1998.

de Man, Paul. *Allegories of Reading: Figural Language in Rousseau, Nietzsche, Rilke and Proust.* New Haven: Yale University Press, 1979.

Dickens, Charles. 'The Haunted Man'. (1848) *The Christmas Books: Volume 2.* Ed. Michael Slater. London: Penguin, 1985a.

——. *David Copperfield.* (1850) Introd. Trevor Blount. London: Penguin, 1985b.

——. *Our Mutual Friend.* (1865) Ed. Stephen Gill. London: Penguin, 1986.

——. *Our Mutual Friend.* (1865) Ed. Michael Cotsell. Oxford: Oxford University Press, 1991.

——. *Bleak House.* (1853) Ed. Nicola Bradbury. London: Penguin, 1996.

Eagleton, Terry. *Literary Theory: An Introduction.* Oxford: Blackwell, 1983.

Elam, Diane. *Feminism and Deconstruction: Ms. en Abyme.* London: Routledge, 1994.

Eliot, George. *Daniel Deronda.* (1876). Ed. Barbara Hardy. London: Penguin, 1986.

Finkielkraut, Alain. *The Wisdom of Love*. (1984) Trans. Kevin O'Neill and David Suchoff. Lincoln: University of Nebraska Press, 1997.

Forrester, John. *The Seductions of Psychoanalysis: Freud, Lacan and Derrida*. Cambridge: Cambridge University Press, 1990.

Gasché, Rodolphe. *The Tain of the Mirror: Derrida and the Philosophy of Reflection*. Cambridge, Mass.: Harvard University Press, 1986.

——. *Inventions of Difference: On Jacques Derrida*. Cambridge, Mass.: Harvard University Press, 1994.

Gilman, Charlotte Perkins. *The Yellow Wall-Paper and Other Stories*. Ed. Robert Shulman. Oxford: Oxford University Press, 1995.

Hart, Kevin. *The Trespass of the Sign: Deconstruction, Theology and Philosophy*. Cambridge: Cambridge University Press, 1989.

Hartman, Geoffrey. *Saving the Text: Literature/Derrida/Philosophy*. Baltimore: The Johns Hopkins University Press, 1981.

——. 'Preface'. *Deconstruction and Criticism*. Harold Bloom, Paul de Man, Jacques Derrida, Geoffrey Hartman and J. Hillis Miller. New York: Continuum, 1987. vii–ix.

Harvey, Irene E. *Derrida and the Economy of Difference*. Bloomington: Indiana University Press, 1986.

Jabès, Edmond. *The Book of Margins*. (1975, 1984) Trans. Rosemarie Waldrop. Introd. Mark C. Taylor. Chicago: University of Chicago Press, 1993.

Jefferies, Richard. 'Snowed Up: A Mistletoe Story'. *Literary Theories: A Case Study in Critical Performance*. Ed. Julian Wolfreys and William Baker. London: Macmillan, 1996.

Johnson, Barbara. *The Critical Difference: Essays in the Contemporary Rhetoric of Reading*. Baltimore: The Johns Hopkins University Press, 1980.

Johnson, Christopher. *System and Writing in the Philosophy of Jacques Derrida*. Cambridge: Cambridge University Press, 1993.

Joyce, James. *Ulysses*. (1922) Ed. and introd. Jeri Johnson. Oxford: Oxford University Press, 1993.

——. *A Portrait of the Artist as a Young Man*. (1914–15) Ed. Seamus Deane. London: Penguin, 1992.

Kamuf, Peggy, ed. *A Derrida Reader: Between the Blinds*. New York: Columbia University Press, 1991.
Contents: Part One: Differance at the Origin: 1. From *Speech and Phenomena*; 2. From *Of Grammatology*; 3. From 'Différance'; 4. 'Signature Event Context'; 5. 'Plato's Pharmacy'; Part Two: Beside Philosophy – 'Literature': 6. 'Tympan'; 7. From 'The Double

Session'; 8. From 'Psyche: Inventions of the Other'; 9. 'Che cos'è la poesia?'; Part Three: More Than One Language: 10. From 'Des Tours de Babel'; 11. From 'Living On: Border Lines'; 12. 'Letter to a Japanese Friend'; 13. From 'Restitutions of the Truth in Pointing'; Part Four: Sexual Difference in Philosophy: 14. From *Glas*; 15. From *Spurs: Nietzsche's Styles*; 16. *'Geschlect:* Sexual Difference, Ontological Difference'; 17. From 'At This Very Moment in This Work Here I Am'; 18. From 'Choreographies'; Part Five: Tele-Types (Yes, Yes): 19. From 'Le Facteur de la vérité'; 20. From 'Envois'; 21. From 'To Speculate – on "Freud"'; 22. From 'Ulysses Gramophone: Hear Say Yes in Joyce'.

——. *The Division of Literature or the University in Deconstruction.* Chicago: University of Chicago Press, 1997.

Kant, Immanuel. 'On the Common Saying: That may be correct in theory, but it is of no use in practice'. (1793) *Practical Philosophy.* Trans. and ed. Mary J. Gregor. Cambridge: Cambridge University Press, 1996. 273–311.

Krupnick, Mark, ed. *Displacement: Derrida and After.* Bloomington: Indiana University Press, 1983.

Lacoue-Labarthe, Philippe. *Typography: Mimesis, Philosophy, Politics.* Introd. Jacques Derrida. Trans. and ed. Christopher Fynsk. Cambridge, Mass.: Harvard University Press, 1989.

Lacoue-Labarthe, Philippe, and Jean-Luc Nancy. *Retreating the Political.* (1979, 1981, 1983) Ed. Simon Sparks. London: Routledge, 1997

Lechte, John. *Fifty Key Contemporary Thinkers: From Structuralism to Postmodernity.* London: Routledge, 1994.

Leitch, Vincent B. *Deconstructive Criticism: An Advanced Introduction.* New York: Columbia University Press, 1983.

Lentricchia, Frank. *After the New Criticism.* London: Athlone Press, 1980.

Levinas, Emmanuel. *Proper Names.* (1975 and 1976) Trans. Michael B. Smith. Stanford: Stanford University Press, 1996.

Llewelyn, John. *Derrida on the Threshold of Sense.* London: Macmillan, 1986.

McCance, Dawne. *Posts: Re Addressing the Ethical.* Albany: SUNY Press, 1996.

Melville, Stephen W. *Philosophy Beside Itself: On Deconstruction and Modernism.* Minneapolis: University of Minnesota Press, 1986.

Michelfelder, Diane P., and Richard E. Palmer, eds. *Dialogue and Deconstruction: The Gadamer–Derrida Encounter*. Albany: SUNY Press, 1989.

Miller, J. Hillis. *Fiction and Repetition: Seven English Novels*. Oxford: Blackwell, 1982.

———. *The Ethics of Reading: Kant, de Man, Eliot, Trollope, James, and Benjamin*. New York: Columbia University Press, 1987.

———. *Tropes, Parables, Performatives: Essays on Twentieth-Century Literature*. Hemel Hempstead: Harvester Wheatsheaf, 1990.

———. *Theory Now and Then*. Hemel Hempstead: Harvester Wheatsheaf, 1991.

———. *Ariadne's Thread: Story Lines*. New Haven: Yale University Press, 1992a.

———. 'Deconstruction Now? The States of Deconstruction or Thinking without Synecdoche'. *Afterwords*. Ed. Nicholas Royle. Tampere: Outside Books, 1992b. 7–19.

———. 'The Disputed Ground: Deconstruction and Literary Studies'. *Deconstruction is/in America: A New Sense of the Political*. Ed. Anselm Haverkamp. New York: New York University Press, 1995a. 79–86.

———. *Topographies*. Stanford: Stanford University Press, 1995b.

———. '*Heart of Darkness* Revisited'. *Tropes, Parables, Performatives: Essays on Twentieth-Century Literature*. Hemel Hempstead: Harvester Wheatsheaf, 1990. 181–94. Rpt. in *Heart of Darkness*. Joseph Conrad. Case Studies in Contemporary Criticism. 2nd edn. Ed. Ross C. Murfin. Boston: St Martin's Press, 1996. 206–20.

Muller, John P., and William J. Richardson, eds. *The Purloined Poe: Lacan, Derrida, and Psychoanalytic Reading*. Baltimore: The Johns Hopkins University Press, 1988.

Naas, Michael B. 'Introduction: For Example'. In *The Other Heading*. Jacques Derrida. Bloomington: Indiana University Press, 1992. vii–lix.

Nancy, Jean-Luc. *The Muses*. (1994) Trans. Peggy Kamuf. Stanford: Stanford University Press, 1996.

Niranjana, Tejaswini. *Siting Translation: History, Post-Structuralism, and the Colonial Context*. Berkeley: University of California Press, 1992.

Norris, Christopher. *Deconstruction: Theory and Practice*. London: Methuen, 1982.

———. *Derrida*. London: Fontana Press, 1987.

——. 'Deconstruction, Post-Modernism and the Visual Arts'. *What is Deconstruction?* Christopher Norris and Andrew Benjamin. London: Academy Editions/St Martin's Press, 1988. 7–33.

Pepper, Thomas. *Singularities: Extremes of Theory in the Twentieth Century.* Cambridge: Cambridge University Press, 1997.

Plotnitsky, Arkady. *In the Shadow of Hegel: Complementarity, History, and the Unconscious.* Gainesville: University Press of Florida, 1993.

——. *Complementarity: Anti-Epistemology After Bohr and Derrida.* Durham: Duke University Press, 1994.

Robbins, Ruth, and Julian Wolfreys, eds. *Victorian Identities: Social and Cultural Formations in Nineteenth-Century Literature.* London: Macmillan, 1995.

Ronell, Avital. *The Telephone Book: Technology, Schizophrenia, Electric Speech.* Lincoln: University of Nebraska Press, 1989.

——. *Crack Wars: Literature, Addiction, Mania.* Lincoln: University of Nebraska Press, 1992.

——. *Finitude's Score: Essays for the End of the Millennium.* Lincoln: University of Nebraska Press, 1994.

Rorty, Richard. 'Deconstruction'. *The Cambridge History of Literary Criticism: Volume 8 From Formalism to Poststructuralism.* Ed. Raman Selden. Cambridge: Cambridge University Press, 1995. 166–97.

Royle, Nicholas, ed. *Afterwords.* Tampere: Outside Books, 1992.

——. *After Derrida.* Manchester: Manchester University Press, 1995.

Ryan, Michael. *Marxism and Deconstruction: A Critical Articulation.* Baltimore: The Johns Hopkins University Press, 1982.

Sartiliot, Claudette. *Citation and Modernity: Derrida, Joyce, and Brecht.* Norman: University of Oklahoma Press, 1993.

Shumway, David R. 'The Star System in Literary Studies'. *PMLA* 112:1 (January 1997): 85–100.

Sinclair, Iain. *Flesh Eggs and Scalp Metal: Selected Poems 1970–1987.* London: Paladin, 1989.

——. *Radon Daughters.* London: Jonathan Cape, 1994.

——. *Lud Heat and Suicide Bridge.* Introd. Michael Moorcock. London: Vintage, 1995a.

——. *White Chappell Scarlet Tracings.* (1987) London: Vintage, 1995b.

——. *Downriver (Or, the Vessel of Wrath) A Narrative in Twelve Tales.* (1991) London: Vintage, 1995c.

——. *Lights Out for the Territory: 9 Excursions in the Secret History of London.* London: Granta, 1997.

Sinclair, Iain, and Dave McKean. 'The Griffin's Egg'. *It's Dark in London*. Ed. Oscar Zarate. London: Mask Noir/Serpent's Tail, 1996. 43–52.

Smith, Robert. *Derrida and Autobiography*. Cambridge: Cambridge University Press, 1995.

Spivak, Gayatry Chakravorty. 'Translator's Preface'. *Of Grammatology*. Jacques Derrida. Baltimore: The Johns Hopkins University Press, 1974. ix–lxxxix.

——. 'At the *Planchette* of Deconstruction is/in America'. *Deconstruction is/in America: A New Sense of the Political*. Ed. Anselm Haverkamp. New York: New York University Press, 1995. 237–49.

Stevenson, Robert Louis. *The Strange Case of Dr Jekyll and Mr Hyde*. (1886) *Dr Jekyll and Mr Hyde and Weir of Hermiston*. Ed. and introd. Emma Letley. Oxford: Oxford University Press, 1990. 1–76.

Subotnik, Rose Rosengard. *Deconstructive Variations: Music and Reason in Western Society*. Minneapolis: University of Minnesota Press, 1996.

Taylor, Mark C., ed. *Deconstruction in Context: Literature and Philosophy*. Chicago: University of Chicago Press, 1986.

Tschumi, Bernard. *Architecture and Disjunction*. Cambridge, Mass.: MIT Press, 1994

Weber, Samuel. *Mass Mediauras: Form Technics Media*. Stanford: Stanford University Press, 1996.

Weedon, Chris. *Feminist Practice and Poststructuralist Theory*. Oxford: Blackwell, 1987.

Wheeler, Kathleen M. *Romanticism, Pragmatism and Deconstruction*. Oxford: Blackwell, 1993.

Wigley, Mark. *The Architecture of Deconstruction: Derrida's Haunt*. Cambridge, Mass.: MIT Press, 1993.

Wihl, Gary. *The Contingency of Theory: Pragmatism, Expressivism, and Deconstruction*. New Haven: Yale University Press, 1994.

Wills, David. *Prosthetics*. Stanford: Stanford University Press, 1995.

Wolfreys, Julian. *The Rhetoric of Affirmative Resistance: Dissonant Identities from Carroll to Derrida*. London: Macmillan, 1997.

Wolfreys, Julian, and William Baker, eds. *Literary Theories: A Case Study in Critical Performance*. London: Macmillan, 1996.

Wood, David, ed. *Derrida: A Critical Reader*. Oxford: Blackwell, 1992.

——, ed. *Of Derrida, Heidegger, and Spirit*. Evanston: Northwestern University Press, 1993.

Woolf, Virginia. 'Street Haunting: A London Adventure'. *The Death of the Moth and Other Essays*. (1942) Harmondsworth: Penguin, 1965. 23–36.

Index of Proper Names and Titles